FAMILY GROUP CONFERENCES

PERSPECTIVES ON POLICY & PRACTICE

EDITORS:

Joe Hudson, Allison Morris, Gabrielle Maxwell
and Burt Galaway

The Federation Press
Criminal Justice Press
1996

PUBLISHED IN AUSTRALIA BY

The Federation Press,
P.O. Box 45, Annandale, NSW, 2038,
3/56-72 John St, Leichhardt, NSW, 2040,
AUSTRALIA
Ph (02) 552 2200. Fax (02) 552 1681.

PUBLISHED IN THE UNITED STATES BY

Willow Tree Press, Inc.,
P.O. Box 249,
Monsey, NY 10952,
U.S.A.
Ph (914) 354 9139. Fax (914) 362 8376.

National Library of Australia
Cataloguing-in-Publication entry

Family group conferences : perspectives on policy and practice.

Bibliography
Includes index.
ISBN 1 86287 201 5 (pbk.)
ISBN 1 86287 208 2.

1. Family counselling. I. Hudson, Joe.

362.8286

Typeset by The Federation Press, Leichhardt, NSW, Australia.
Printed by Ligare Pty Ltd, Riverwood, NSW, Australia.

AUSTRALASIAN STUDIES IN CRIMINOLOGY

Published under the auspices of the Crime Research Centre, University of Western Australia; the Institute of Criminology, University of Sydney; the Institute of Criminology, Victoria University of Wellington; and the Federation Press.

GENERAL EDITORS

Mark Findlay
> Director, Institute of Criminology, University of Sydney

Richard Harding
> Director, Crime Research Centre, University of Western Australia

Christopher Holt
> Publisher, The Federation Press

Allison Morris
> Director, Institute of Criminology, Victoria University of Wellington

EDITORIAL BOARD

David Biles
> Formerly Deputy Director, Australian Institute of Criminology

Professor John Braithwaite
> Research School of Social Sciences, Australian National University

Dr Janet Chan
> Acting Director, Institute of Criminology, University of Sydney

Dr Sandra Egger
> Faculty of Law, University of New South Wales

Arie Frieberg
> Professor of Criminology, University of Melbourne

Dr Peter Grabosky
> Principal Criminologist, Australian Institute of Criminology

Gordon Hawkins
> Formerly Director, Institute of Criminology, University of Sydney

Dr Joy Wundersitz
> Director, South Australian Office of Crime Statistics

Warren Young
> Deputy Vice-Chancellor (Research), Victoria University of Wellington

TITLES IN THIS SERIES:

Violent Property Crime, David Indermaur

Foreword

I have always seen family group conferences as an invaluable tool for involving families and children in decisions about them. Not as some magical panacea to stop juvenile offending or for changing abusive and neglectful families into caring and safe ones but rather as providing the great benefits which can flow from the process itself. First and foremost, family group conferences provide unique opportunities for families and, in the youth justice context, for victims to become truly involved in the consequent proceedings rather than being passive bystanders.

Many youth justice systems have failed to recognise the needs of victims and have disregarded the contribution that families can make to the resolution and healing of the damage cause by crime, in both a material and an emotional sense. Many welfare systems have ignored families in deciding about the care and safety of their children; this is to deny them to their children. But change is occurring.

Since November 1989 when the Children, Young Persons and Their Families legislation came into force in New Zealand, a large number of family group conferences have been convened. In the youth justice area, a remarkably high proportion of conferences have achieved successful outcomes if success is equated with young offenders and their families having to physically confront their victims; the opportunity to personalise crime by being exposed to the hurt and loss occasioned by criminal behaviour; and realistic arrangements about reparation. On the other hand, some flaws in practice have been exposed. This book presents the research that validates these successes and describes the conditions for achieving good practice.

To those of us of a 'restorative' bent, one of the primary objectives of a criminal justice system must include healing the breaches in social harmony and social relationships, putting right the wrong and making reparation, rather than concentrating on punishment. On the basis of our experience to date, I and many of my colleagues have been amazed by the generosity of spirit of many victims and the absence of retributive demands and vindictiveness. This response from victims is in direct contrast to the hysterical, media-generated responses to which we are often exposed. It puts in question the stance so often taken by the enforcement authorities that they 'represent the interests of victims'. As with so many aspects of life, the reality is far more complex.

If the process is a valid one which may have an even larger role in criminal jurisdictions, then the public who ultimately pay are entitled to have that process rigorously scrutinised. Indeed, for mad enthusiasts such as myself who see a wider role for the conference in dispute resolution in other sectors, we need desperately to employ strict auditing. First to establish the credibility of the method and, of equal importance if it passes the first test, to constantly look towards refinement of the procedure.

I have less direct knowledge of family group conferences in the care and protection system in New Zealand. Some have suggested that they are less effective in this domain in providing for effective participation of families and in ensuring positive outcomes for children. The reality is that we do not know this because of the lack of research. Some of the chapters in this book open up these questions and debate the effective use of family group conferences to protect children and provide for their care. I hope that the discussion of these matters will provoke further research on the way in which family group conferences can serve families and children's interests in a variety of arenas.

This excellent collection of papers represent a significant and valuable step towards answering the important questions about how family group conferences can achieve the objectives that have been hoped for from them.

M.J.A. Brown
Principal Youth Court Judge
New Zealand

Contents

List of Contributors

Ban, Paul. Consultant Social Worker, West Melbourne, Australia.

Barkwell, Lawrence. Manitoba Children and Youth Secretariat, Winnipeg, Manitoba, Canada.

Burford, Gale. Associate Professor, School of Social Work, Memorial University of Newfoundland, St. John's, Newfoundland, Canada.

Crow, Gillian. Senior Researcher, Family Partners Project, Department of Sociological Studies, University of Sheffield, Sheffield, U.K.

Fraser, Sarah. Care and Protection Coordinator, New Zealand Children and Young Persons Service, Nelson, New Zealand.

Galaway, Burt. Professor, Faculty of Social Work, University of Manitoba, Winnipeg, Manitoba, Canada.

Graber, Larry. Retired Program Manager for Family Based Services, State Office for Services to Children and Families, Salem, Oregon, U.S.A.

Hassall, Ian. Independent Children's Advocate, Auckland, New Zealand.

Hetzel, Sue. Senior Youth Justice Coordinator, Family Conference Team, Courts Administration Authority, South Australia.

Hudson, Joe. Professor, Faculty of Social Work, The University of Calgary, Calgary, Alberta, Canada.

Immarigeon, Russ. Child Welfare and Criminal Justice Consultant, New York, U.S.A.

Keys, Ted. Program Coordinator for Family Based Services, State Office for Services to Children and Families, Salem, Oregon, U.S.A.

Longclaws, Lyle. Manager of Native Services, Health Sciences Center, Winnipeg, Manitoba, Canada.

Marsh, Peter. Senior Lecturer, Department of Sociological Studies, University of Sheffield, Sheffield, U.K.

Maxwell, Gabrielle. Senior Researcher, Office of the Commissioner for Children, Wellington, New Zealand.

Morris, Allison. Director, Institute of Criminology, Victoria University of Wellington, Wellington, New Zealand.

Norton, Jenni. Area Manager, Upper South, New Zealand Children and Young Persons Service, Nelson, New Zealand.

Pennell, Joan. Associate Professor, School of Social Work, Memorial University of Newfoundland, St. John's, Newfoundland, Canada.

Robertson, Jeremy. Researcher, Office of the Commissioner for Children, Wellington, New Zealand.

Stewart, Trish. Youth Justice Coordinator, New Zealand Children and Young Persons Service, New Plymouth, New Zealand.

White, Jim. Research Analyst, State Office for Services to Children and Families, Salem, Oregon, U.S.A.

Wundersitz, Joy. Director, South Australian Office of Crime Statistics, Attorney General's Department, Adelaide, South Australia.

1

Introduction

Joe Hudson, Burt Galaway, Allison Morris
and Gabrielle Maxwell

This book presents a set of chapters which assess the principles and practices of family group conferences in the juvenile justice and child protection systems. Examples of family group conferences (sometimes referred to as FGCs) in diverse settings are described and current research is reported from New Zealand, Australia, England, Canada and the United States. All the chapters emphasise a set of values and assumptions that underlie family group conferences: respecting the integrity of the family unit, including the extended family, by focussing on strengthening families and community supports; sharing power and creating opportunities for parents to feel responsible for their children and themselves; and showing sensitivity and respect for families' cultures. For those family group conferences which deal with young offenders, another key value is providing opportunities for victims of crime to be involved in settling the offences committed against them and in receiving redress.

The United Nations Convention on the Rights of the Child recognises the importance of children's rights and imposes obligations on the state to ensure the well-being of children. At the same time, the limitations of state intervention in the lives of families, the costly and often perverse effects of caring for young persons in institutional settings and the negative effects that often result from removing young persons from their culture of origin have all been increasingly recognised. Too often, child welfare professionals focus on family weaknesses rather than strengths and services are provided to families rather than in partnership with them. Too often also, service professionals act as if they alone know what is in the best interests of the family, even though they know little about what family members want or the community supports that could be mobilised and available to them.

These pressures provided the impetus in many countries to seek new decision-making forums, new responses to the abuse and neglect of children and offending by young people and new solutions to the problems confronting and challenging young persons and their families. The development of family group conferences reflects this desire to make dramatic changes and represents a conscious attempt to collaborate with families when the state becomes involved in the lives of their children.

Focussing On Families As Decision-Makers

Central to the practice of family group conferences is the idea that children and families have a fundamental right and responsibility to participate in decisions that affect them. This principle is explicitly stated in the United Nations Convention on the Rights of the Child and the chapters that follow demonstrate how family decision-making is practised. The notion that young persons and their families should be consulted and involved in decisions affecting them, regardless of whether the issue is abuse, neglect or offending, stems from a belief that all people should be treated with respect, even though their behaviour may not always have been adequate. Providing choice communicates respect and at the same time recognises that families are essential to children's sense of identity and belonging in the world, despite the fact that the parents may have been abusive or neglectful of their children. Family group conferences offer an opportunity for families to contribute substantially to their children and to address what are, in a most fundamental sense, both private family problems and public issues. Balancing the public and private dimensions of family group conferences, then, becomes a critical practice issue.

While the right of family members to participate in decisions affecting them is an important value in family group conferences, it also has practical dimensions. It is within the family that the child develops and forms an identity and basic competency and it is the family that has the potential to provide resources throughout the child's life cycle. It makes sense, therefore, for the family to be used as both the context and means for addressing problems. For professionals, this means that the family should be a central unit of attention and viewed as an integral resource that can contribute substantially to the process of change.

When parents perceive themselves as unable to adapt to the demands of parenthood, they are likely to fail at fostering social competence in their children. In turn, children may respond adversely, confirming their parent's low self-esteem and generating rejection, withdrawal or aggression. By participating in family group conferences and in decisions that affect them, family members can, however, be empowered. This empowering of families creates the conditions in which children can recover from adverse circumstances, allows and encourages families to grow and thrive and can lead to improvements in self-esteem by involving families in making decisions about their children and themselves. In this way, family group conferences can build on families' resources and operate in ways which are responsive to the questions and concerns of family members.

The key assumptions underlying family group conferences – that families are competent to make decisions rather than the more traditional view that they are 'pathological', 'dysfunctional' or 'deficient' in some way – are identified by Hassall in his chapter: if family members are recruited, involved and provided with sufficient information, they will develop appropriate plans to care for their young people and deal with family problems. Family group conferences are aimed at promoting effective functioning in families by focussing on their unique strengths and by enlisting them in a problem-solving process.

Family group conferences can also be seen as an educational tool, a forum for teaching and practising problem-solving skills. Family members can learn and practice these skills and can learn about the strengths of family members and the resources available to them; young offenders can learn that their actions have real consequences for victims and that they are able to make amends. For victims, family group conferences provide a concrete expression of the value placed on them by society. For the community, family group conferences help to illustrate the responsibility of citizens to participate in community affairs. The reciprocity evident in the family group conference process helps emphasise the point that people can benefit from the challenge and opportunity of helping others. Receiving help can actually weaken one's self-esteem, but giving help as well as receiving it can empower people and strengthen their sense of self worth.

Cultural Sensitivity

Sensitivity and practical recognition of culture and cultural identity is another principle of family group conferences that is clearly recognised in the United Nations Convention on the Rights of the Child. Affirming the values of indigenous peoples and enabling these values to be reflected in decision-making contexts is emphasised. Without an appreciation of the cultural context in which young people grow and develop, individual differences cannot be respected. Appreciation of culture is a key element in family group conferences simply because of the fact that, if practitioners do not recognise and accommodate the cultural significance of communication styles, family and community boundaries, and child rearing practices, then the services provided are likely to seem foreign and relatively unhelpful. Furthermore, failure to recognise cultural diversity may well result in overlooking potential solutions to problems confronting child welfare and juvenile justice practitioners. Family group conferences are based to a great extent on the cultural priorities of Maori families in New Zealand and illustrate the value of building on cultural strengths. Appreciating the differences between people on the basis of their culture does not equate to assuming a deficiency: difference is not the measure of absurdity.

Opportunities For Victims of Crime

The use of family group conferences within the juvenile justice system is an example of the emerging attention being given to a restorative as distinct from a retributive or treatment approach. While both retributive and treatment approaches largely deny victims' participation and require only passive participation by offenders, restorative justice is concerned with the broader relationships between offenders, victims and communities. All parties are involved in the process of settling the offence and reconciliation. Crime is seen as more than simply the violation of the criminal law. Instead, the key focus is on the damage and injury done to victims and communities and each is seen as having a role to play in responding to the criminal act. As a result of meeting with victims in family group conferences, offenders are expected to gain an understanding of the consequences of their behaviour and to develop feelings of remorse.

Family Group Conferences

To help elaborate the nature of family group conferences, the notion of a programme model is used and related to the chapters that follow. As is evident from Figure 1.1, programme models depict the structure and logic of programmes and answer questions about the resources used, activities carried out and chain of results intended. Programme outcomes, effects or results are ordered in the model from 'immediate' to 'ultimate'. In this way, a programme model amounts to a description of the causal chain of resources used to carry out activities to achieve specific results, outputs, or outcomes. The model described here provides an introduction to key participants in family group conferences, their work and the expected results. Using the model as a focus for this introductory chapter can also provide a better appreciation of the practice of family group conferences and research on them.

Figure 1.1: Model of Programme Structure and Logic

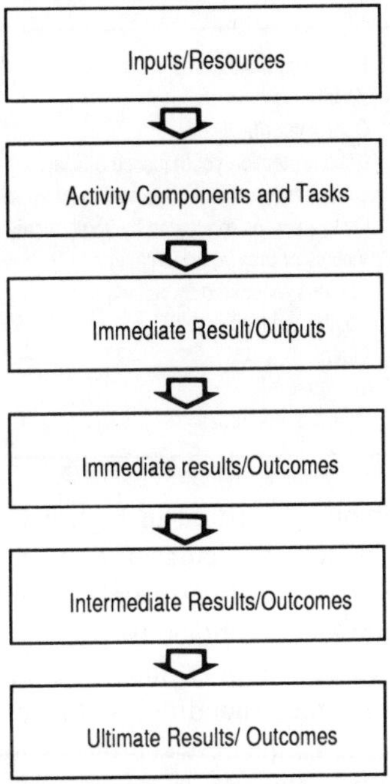

The projects and programmes covered in this book have many features in common and these are illustrated in the model presented. This should not be read as minimising the differences in the ways in which family group conferences operate. Family group conferences have been implemented in different settings – for example, in both the child protection and juvenile justice systems. Some family group conferences are mandated by state authority while others operate on the basis of administrative discretion. Programmes differ in their referral procedures and criteria, as well as in the philosophies supporting their use, particularly with respect to juvenile justice. Some of the major practice differences are discussed in the chapters that follow. In this chapter, the main headings within the model are described in brief.

Inputs or Resources

Types of inputs or resources used in family group conference are identified in Figure 1.2.

Figure 1.2: Key inputs or resources in family group conferences

> - Family/kin/tribal group
> - Youth
> - Coordinator/facilitator
> - Child protection/youth justice official
> - Other persons/officials providing information
> - Other persons requested by youth/family
> - Victims or their representatives
> - Persons requested by victims
> - Youth's legal counsel
> - Elders
> - Interpreters
> - Financial resources

Besides the key persons identified in Figure 1.2, others persons may play a significant role in any particular family group conference. Also missing from Figure 1.2 are the different types of material resources used. While these include equipment, supplies, travel, and so on, the fact is that family group conferences are largely labour intensive; they involve a substantial number of people spending a lot of time collaborating. Establishing working relationships between the various parties involved in a family group conference is the key to its success. The different parties are seen as sharing common concerns about the children and their families, as having common goals for the process and as making joint contributions of time, people and other resources. Family group conferences amount to people with different strengths working together to achieve mutual ends.

Children and their families are the most important resources for family group conferences. To what extent are they, including extended families, actually participating in family group conferences? Are families taking the time, enduring the inconvenience, and spending their money to attend? Many of the chapters address this question and provide strong evidence that both immediate and extended family members attend. For example, based on his review of research on care and protection family group conferences in New Zealand, Robertson concludes that family members do attend and take part. He reports research showing that an average of six family members, other than the child, attended family group conferences. Ban reports similar findings from the pilot project held in Victoria: an average of six family members attended the first 19 conferences held there. And, from Manitoba, Longclaws, Galaway & Barkwell report that 23 family members attended the six conferences in their pilot project and that over one-quarter of them travelled long distances at their own expense.

Crime victims are another key resource in family group conferences. To what extent are victims attending and participating in conferences? The evidence reported by Maxwell & Morris in their review of New Zealand juvenile justice family group conferences is that victims attended less than half the conferences they might have attended. However, they also report that only a very small proportion of victims said they failed to attend because they did not want to meet the offenders. Maxwell & Morris suggest that the low attendance rate by victims was due to poor preparation of victims by social workers: they did not give victims adequate notice of the scheduled conference or set meetings at times inconvenient for victims. However, somewhat different findings are reported by Wundersitz & Hetzel in their review of the South Australian experience. They report preliminary findings that 75 to 80 percent of conferences held for offences in which there was a victim had at least one victim present. These different results suggest that the more consideration Coordinators give to recruiting victims, by giving them adequate advance notice and scheduling conferences at convenient times and places, the higher the rate of victims' participation is likely to be.

All of the chapters bring out the critical importance of the coordinator's role. Marsh & Crow probably capture this best when they describe the coordinator as the 'linch pin' of family group conferences. The complexity of this role is described by Fraser &

Norton in terms of the delicate balance that must be struck by coordinators between the power of the state and the power of the family to make decisions. This fundamental tension between the state's and the family's responsibilities in family group conferences is nested, first and foremost, in the role of the coordinator. The chapters by Ban and Marsh & Crow emphasise another aspect of this tension with respect to the necessary characteristics of the coordinator. They argue that the coordinator must be seen as independent, but must also have good knowledge about child protection or juvenile justice matters and possess sound practice skills. As Marsh & Crow note, however, these characteristics of perceived independence and knowledge and skills often conflict. Sound knowledge of child protection or juvenile justice is often associated with experience of working in the systems. The question then arises of the extent to which this affects the way family participants view coordinators as independent of the state.

Also helping determine the extent to which coordinators are perceived as independent is the organisational context in which they are located. If coordinators report to officials having responsibility for managing the social work staff who refer young people to family group conferences, they may not be seen as independent, at least to the extent that they might if they were located in another Department. Wundersitz & Hetzel illustrate this point in their chapter. They note that family group conferences for young offenders were deliberately located in the South Australia, Courts Administrative Authority rather than with the police or social welfare departments. The reason for this was that it was believed that the Courts Authority would be perceived as more independent and neutral. Furthermore, Wundersitz & Hetzel make the point that if coordinators were located with either the police or social welfare, their roles as key referral sources might place too much power in one set of officials and have the effect of the police and social workers taking over and bureaucratising the family group conference process.

A related issue is the relative advantages and disadvantages of mandating family group conferences in policy or legislation as compared to their operating on the basis of administrative discretion. For example, in their chapter on family group conferences in Oregon, Graber, Keys & White describe the benefits which they see from Oregon not mandating the use of family group conferences. In contrast, Immarigeon and Marsh & Crow identify in their chapters some of the difficulties that have been experienced elsewhere when trying to implement family group conferences in jurisdictions where their use is not officially required.

Those jurisdictions that have mandated family group conferences provide funds to defray families' travel costs to attend conferences and carry out their plans. However, although the chapters on New Zealand report that financial assistance is available for family group conferences, the amounts budgeted are presented as inadequate. Maxwell & Morris, for example, note that the resources available for arranging and financing the plans of family group conferences has substantially decreased since the passage of the legislation in 1989 and that some youth justice coordinators have an average of one hundred dollars to resource conferences.

Immediate Results and Outputs

A number of the chapters describe the sequence of events that take place in planning and holding family group conferences. While different names are used, the key events and activities are remarkably similar, regardless of geographic context or whether the conference operates in the juvenile justice or child welfare systems. Common activities and the main outputs of the three phases of a family group conference are presented in Figure 1.3.

Preparing for the Family Group Conference

Three key sets of activities are involved in preparing for a conference. An initial set of activities carried out by the coordinator is receiving and reviewing referrals from child protection workers, the police or other officials. Robertson makes the point that the crucial issue here is the degree of discretion exercised by referring officials in setting thresholds. Setting the threshold too high may restrict the use of family group conferences. Ban refers to this issue in his chapter. He describes the practice of officials referring for conferences only families seen as having decision-making skills. Setting eligibility criteria too low, on the other hand, may result in spreading the net of social control widely by admitting young people who would otherwise have been handled in less costly and intrusive ways. One solution to this is to structure and confine the discretionary authority of officials in referring children or young people to family group conferences. This can be done by specifying the admission criteria for the target

Figure 1.3: FGC Program Activities and Outputs

Activity Components and Tasks	Preparing for FGCs:	Holding the FGC:	Post-FGC:
	• Receive/Review referral reports, consult with police, court, child protection officials.	• Arrange seating; provide refreshments/prayers; introduce participants; make opening statement about purpose and process.	• Prepare record of plan/distribute to participants.
	• Identify, locate, and discuss the FGC with family, victims, youth, and other persons to be invited:	• Information provides/referring officials/victims describe concerns; young offender explains circumstances of the offence, expresses remorse, admits guilt; family asks questions and discusses.	• Locate needed resources for youth/family.
	⇒ discuss the purpose and process to be followed;	• Family meets privately to discuss and reach decisions; reports back to the full group.	• Monitor plan implementation/remind and warn as necessary.
	⇒ assess youth's attitude to the offence, acceptance of responsibility and willingness to participate.	• Group discusses family decisions; negotiates changes; arrive at consensus on:	• Notify youth/family/victims that the matter has been completed/file closed, or return matter for further action.
	• Invited parties discuss and agree on time, date, place of meeting and protocol to be followed.	⇒ decisions;	
	• Identify and arrange for handling necessary travel expenses; arrange venue.	⇒ procedures to be followed to carry out decisions;	
		⇒ resources needed and time for plan completion;	
		⇒ monitoring/review procedures and time lines.	
		• Final comments and closing statements.	
Immediate Results/ Outputs		• Adequate and sustainable FGC plan, containing:	• Monitoring and review reports covering plan completion and actions taken.
		⇒ decisions reached/sanctions imposed/reparations ordered;	
		⇒ tasks to be carried out, timing and responsibilities;	
		⇒ monitoring/review procedures/timing.	
		• Participants satisfied with FGC meeting process and outcome.	

population through either policy or legislation. The more detailed and precise the admission criteria, the more likely it is that the appropriate target population will be served.

Figure 1.3 shows that a second key set of activities carried out by coordinators in preparing for family group conferences is recruiting conference participants. Many chapter writers note that this is the most difficult and time consuming part of the coordinator's job. This task amounts to identifying family and locating and informing them about the planned family group conference and encouraging them to participate. The larger the number of persons to be invited to the family group conference, the more time will be involved in preparation.

A number of the chapters address difficulties in securing agreement from immediate family to invite extended family members to the family group conference. Fraser & Norton, Stewart, Robertson and Marsh & Crow all discuss this and list some reasons given by immediate family members for not wanting to invite other kin, including:

- not wanting family members to know about their problems;
- fear of being scapegoated;
- not being in contact with other kin;
- not knowing how to locate kin;
- desiring privacy;
- not wanting to place demands on others.

The trade-off for coordinators is striking a balance between the timeliness of the conference and securing wider participation by the family. The more time and effort coordinators put into recruiting participants, the less timely the conference meeting is likely to be.

Information on the timeliness of family group conferences is reported in several chapters. For example, in his review of care and protection family group conference in New Zealand, Robertson reports that two-thirds of conferences were convened within five weeks of referral, one-sixth took more than two months, and the average was 36 days. Maxwell & Morris report that 85 percent of youth justice family group conferences in New Zealand were resolved within six weeks and that 95 percent were resolved within nine weeks. These times do not seem excessive, especially when coupled with quite high levels of participation by family members.

Besides the reluctance of families to invite kin, several chapters give another set of reasons why much time and effort needs to be spent recruiting participants. These have to do with the inconvenience for kin and others to participate because conferences tend to be scheduled to fit with the work day of professionals. Robertson reports, for example, that 89 percent of family group conferences were held on a weekday, that less than 20 percent of these started after late afternoon, and that most were held in social welfare offices. Longclaws, Galaway & Barkwell report similar findings from their project. They explain that social workers would only attend conferences if they were held during normal work hours. This may help explain why coordinators report that recruiting participants is time consuming and difficult. While the times scheduled are convenient for the professionals who attend, they may not be convenient for others who may have to take time from work or travel considerable distance. Coordinators may have to spend a lot of time trying to overcome these constraints.

The Conference Phase

As with the pre-conference preparation phase, the chapters generally describe the same range of practices carried out during a family group conference: making introductions and statements of purpose, giving and receiving information, deliberating and preparing a plan, and ending the meeting. Chapters by Fraser & Norton, Ban, Longclaws, Galaway & Barkwell, Pennell & Burford, Stewart and Wundersitz & Hetzel emphasise the importance of the opening statement, manner of introductions and language in which the conference is conducted; all convey strong messages to children and parents. These authors note that opening statements should clearly define the purpose of the conference and the processes to be followed and should emphasise the family's responsibility for decision-making.

The amount of time taken to hold a family group conference is approximately the same across different programmes and countries. Robertson, for example, notes that care and protection family group conferences in New Zealand are almost always completed in a single meeting, taking from one to eleven hours with an average of 3.5 hours. Ban and Longclaws, Galaway & Barkwell report similar experiences in Australia and Canada. This stands in contrast with the time taken in preparing for conferences. Ban and Marsh & Crow note that preparing for conferences takes approximately four times as long as actually holding them.

A key theme that runs through almost all the chapters is the attention given to adapting conference practices to the cultural background of the participants. This sensitivity to culture is reflected in seating arrangements, opening prayers, welcoming statements and introductions, participation by tribal elders, and closing ceremonies. Maxwell & Morris, however, report research from youth justice family group conferences in New Zealand which showed that they often failed to operate according to Maori protocol. The fact that coordinators are not always (and in some jurisdictions not usually) members of the same culture as the family may pose problems for each of the parties in understanding the subtleties of communications at the conference. This can be exacerbated if the coordinator is seen as an official in the child welfare or juvenile justice systems which are managed by the dominant culture. This may well pose barriers to conducting conferences in culturally appropriate ways. Also, if the coordinator is not a member of an indigenous group, this can create difficulties in identifying, locating, and recruiting cultural figures to attend the conferences.

The evidence is clear from the chapters that participants are able to reach decisions (the agreement rate can be as high as 95 percent) and are able to prepare plans. However, some chapters raise questions about the extent to which the decisions at the family group conference are dictated by the officials who participate. Do families simply defer to state officials? Is the conference process taken over by professionals? The chapters on New Zealand in particular question the extent to which the conferences truly reflect families making decisions rather than professionals dictating outcomes. As examples of professionals taking over conferences, authors note the use of professional jargon which is little understood by families and officials presenting clear views or 'bottom lines' about the decisions to be made. At the other extreme is the experience from Manitoba reported by Longclaws, Galaway & Barkwell in which judges largely ignored the decisions reached by the family group conference. If state officials take over family group conferences they will quickly be seen by family members as fraudulent and family members will express considerable dissatisfaction with them. In fact, however, the evidence reported in these chapters does not support the claim that families are dissatisfied. Families are reported to have felt involved in the process and in the outcomes of the conferences. The chapters also report that other participants are satisfied with conferences, including victims, referring officials and information-providers such as police and child protection workers and the coordinators.

After the Family Group Conference

The main tasks to be carried out following a conference are monitoring and reviewing follow-through by participants with respect to the decisions reached. Chapters highlight the importance of this and note some mixed research findings about the extent to which good follow-up work is carried out. Poor follow-up may reflect the difficulties that some workers have balancing the state's and families' responsibilities. Moving too far either way can lead to family autonomy or state dominance. To protect against these extreme positions, the parties to a family group conference should have clearly defined responsibilities that have been clearly communicated when planning and holding the family group conference.

Results and Outcomes

Figure 1.4 presents a listing of the major goals, objectives, outcomes and effects that are identified in the chapters. These have been sequenced from the more immediate to longer term.

The chapters' authors identify a variety of outcomes that family group conferences are expected to achieve with respect to family members, young persons, victims and the state. However, relatively little research is available on these presumed outcomes. Robertson, writes that, in New Zealand, out-of-home placements have decreased and that kinship placements have increased. Preliminary results from Ban indicate a similar trend in Victoria. Maxwell & Morris, referring to young offenders in New Zealand, show that custodial sentences are much less frequently imposed now than before the *Children, Young Persons and Their Families Act* 1989 and that approximately 40 percent of young offenders had not been re-convicted four years after 'their' family group conference.

A Look Ahead

The chapters that follow demonstrate that family group conferences represent an exciting new practice development. Since their introduction in 1989 in New Zealand, family group conferences have received considerable attention in the professional literature and have

Figure 1.4: Results and Outcomes

Immediate Results/Outcomes ↓	**Family:**	
		• Culture recognized and respected
		• Feel sense of support in dealing with problems; mobilised network and resources to care for youth
		• Feel empowered/sense of responsibility
		• Sense of hope
		• Learn about the nature of abuse and offending
	Youth:	
		• Experience of family support/strengthened relationships
		• Acceptance of responsibilty for behavior
		• Be recognised as part of the decision
		• Realisation of nature and magnitude of offense and its impact on victims
	Victims:	
		• Feel involved in decisions
		• Receive compensation and other reparations
	Community Agencies:	
		• Increased inter-agency collaboration
		• Responsibility shared/partnership for youth justice or child protection decisions
Intermediate Results ↓	**Family:**	
		• Strengthened ability to ensure child's safety
		• Motivated to seek lasting solutions to problems
		• Improved functioning
		• Diverted from further juvenile justice processing
		• Retained within extended family network
		• Returned to family from state care
Ultimate Results ↓	**Youth:**	
		• Chilfren protected form abuse and neglect
		• Youth less likely to re-offend
		• Communal sense of responsibility for children and families

been implemented in parts of Australia, England, and Wales, Canada and the United States. As reported by Immarigeon, one can confidently expect that in the next few years at least as many more States in the United States and provinces in Canada will require family group conferences to play a central role in carrying out the work of the child protection and juvenile justice systems. To a large extent, this will come about because of a growing emphasis on the key principles of family group conferences – the right of children and families to participate in making decisions affecting them, the importance of family for young people and respect for culture. The chapters that follow explore issues about implementing family group conferences, report on current research, describe a range of ways of involving the family in making decisions and critically assess the potential of family group conferences.

2

Origin and Development of Family Group Conferences

Ian Hassall

The Antiquity of Family Decision-making

There is a long history to the development of family group conferences. Families, however defined, existed long before lawyers and social workers, courts and counsellors. They have been subject to the forces of evolution and are as much a part of our human identity as the shape and function of our bodies. Our behaviour within families and as families is integrated into our overall strategy for survival as a species.

Families are de facto decision-making bodies. It is inherent in the idea of family that members will act jointly rather than as individuals in some matters. Mutual responsibility of individuals toward one another is a usual feature and the absence of or weaknesses in that responsibility are a signal of malfunction. It is characteristic of families that some individuals take more responsibility than others for decisions of various kinds affecting one member or the family as a whole. Just as there is a range of family forms so too is there a range of family decision-making styles: from autocratic to democratic. Cultural tradition, individual style and the circumstances of the moment each have a bearing on which model is in operation at any one time.

We are the inheritors, then, of the family functions of the care, protection, education and social integration of children and the means of deciding how these functions are best fulfilled. This may appear obvious but an alternative view is commonly presented of child rearing as a task which can be learned only with difficulty and with the assistance of professionally qualified experts, and which, once learned in this way, equips us to handle whatever difficulties arise. What may be closer to the truth is that our personal and socially proximate resources equip us well to deal with most contingencies but they may need to be supplemented by expertise from elsewhere from time to time. It is possible to respect our social heritage, its complexity and its utility, without lapsing into primitivism. With such respect we are defended against naively adopting simple mechanical models for crucial and integrated human functions such as the rearing of children.

Communities, too, are an ancient human social form. An attendant part of child rearing seen from a community perspective over time has, inevitably, been the making of decisions as to where children who have lost a part of their family or whose family are otherwise unable to care for them are to be placed and who is to take responsibility for them.

The Introduction of Family Group Conferences into New Zealand Law

Like other countries, New Zealand has, for a century or so, had laws to deal with children and young people who come to official notice because they are alleged to have offended against the law, are without adequate care, are notified as having been abused or neglected, or are under threat of abuse or neglect. Until 1989, as in many other countries, these laws placed primary responsibility with the courts, assisted by the police and child protection service, for deciding where these children were to live and what else was needed.

In 1989, New Zealand passed an Act, the *Children, Young Persons and Their Families Act*, which departed radically from previous law. It placed primary responsibility with extended families for making decisions about what was to be done with their children and young people who had come to official notice. Families were to have the assistance of the police, in the case of young offenders, the child protection service, in the case of children in need of care or protection, and any others the family wished to be present at the meeting. Family decisions were to be made using a process not previously encountered in statute called the family group conference. It was to be the key process under the new Act. If a case proceeded beyond the stages of investigation and disposition by the police or child protection service the family group conference was to be a mandatory part of its resolution, except in very limited circumstances. If there were to be court proceedings they could not, in general, take place unless there had been a family group conference. Entitlement to participate, convenorship, and the means of implementing family decisions were set out. Venue and process were to be determined by the family in consultation with the official convenor. The aim was to ensure as far as possible that the proceedings were meaningful to the family and productive of an outcome that satisfied the objectives of the Act.

Why did New Zealand adopt this new approach? The Minister of Social Welfare in the Labour Government which enacted the law spoke to the Bill then before Parliament:

> I shall summarise the main strands of the philosophy underlying the Bill. First, the Bill reflects a belief that greater emphasis is needed upon the responsibility of families for the care, protection and control of children and young persons. Secondly, it reflects a belief that more attention should be paid to the rights of children and young persons – the right to safety, the right to protection from abuse and neglect, the right to a say in decisions that affect them, and the right to a fair hearing and to appropriate sanctions when they have offended against the law. Thirdly, the Bill reflects a widely held conviction that ways must be sought of assisting and supporting children and young persons and their families in a manner that recognises New Zealand's cultural diversity. Fourthly, the Bill represents a commitment by the Government, and the Department of Social Welfare in particular, to encouraging a partnership between the communities and the State in providing services to children and young persons and their families (Parliamentary Debates, 1989).

These four 'philosophical strands' – family responsibility, children's rights (including the right to due process), cultural acknowledgment and partnership between the state and the community – are found in discussions of child welfare legislation worldwide. The *Children Act* 1989 in England, for example, uses them as reference points. The full meaning attached to them differs from person to person. In the minds of some, 'family responsibility' is undoubtedly a code for 'reduced cost to the state'.

These ideas are eddies in the larger sociopolitical currents of our civilisation: consumerism, the market economy, minimal state intervention, the decline of organised religion, the rise of interest groups and their empowerment through rights. These and some local forces that shaped the new law can be traced in the history of its development.

Contributing Factors in the Development of the Children, Young Persons and Their Families Act 1989

The law relating to care and protection and youth justice is bound to be controversial. Many people have strong opinions about what should be done with children and the families of children who are ill-treated, are not looked after properly or make nuisances of themselves. While the public does not want children to live in misery or to be subjected to abuse, it resents and fears intrusion into family affairs by agents of the state. It is probably generally understood that if children are to be protected, some intrusion is necessary, but how much and in what form becomes the subject of fierce public debate when celebrated cases arise.

Politicians are acutely aware of the dilemma in which this places them as lawmakers. The chairperson of the Social Services Committee of Parliament on reporting to Parliament on her committee's work on the 1989 redraft of the Children and Young Persons Bill said:

> I am reporting back the Bill at a time of heightened public concern about child abuse, particularly the sexual abuse of children. People are anxious that the law to protect children from abuse should be as strong as possible. Balanced with that concern is increased concern that families should not be wrongly accused of abusing their children and should not have their children taken away from them without the chance to have a say (Parliamentary Debates, 1989).

The major methods applied by the state in recent times for making decisions that aim to achieve an appropriate balance of interests have been court proceedings, case conferences of experts, intervention by social workers and other agents of state services and no action. One way of looking at these processes is to place them on a gradient according to the degree of state intervention they represent.

At one end is no intervention or laissez faire, which was virtually the situation before Kempe and others (Kempe, Silverman, Steele, Droegemuller & Silver, 1962) set in motion the exposure of child abuse as we now understand it. At the other is the large scale removal of children from families on the orders of a court and their placement with strangers in foster residences. When public frustration rises over a case of abuse, or anguish is expressed over seemingly excessive state intervention, it should be remembered that neither of the models at the extreme ends of this continuum guarantees that the child will be protected from further abuse, let alone do well.

An intervention to non-intervention axis does not describe the spectrum of possibilities very well. Intervention in terms of agency activity can be at a high or low level, independently of whether the child remains in the family or is placed elsewhere. In terms of its impact on the stability of the child's world, the intervention level is low in the first case and high in the second. Furthermore, the relevance of intervention by the state has to be considered in relation to the level and kind of community and family processes that can be brought to bear. Bearing in mind these qualifications of the meaning of the terms, the 1989 Act saw a shift away from state intervention and toward family autonomy.

The New Zealand law it replaced, the *Children and Young Persons Act* 1974, was unremarkable for its time. It provided for members of the police and social workers of the Department of Social Welfare to take complaints to a Children and Young Persons Court that children or young people were in need of care, protection or control. The court was to hear and determine all complaints and had a range of orders available, including discharge, warning, counselling, various penalties and placement under the guardianship of the Director-General of Social Welfare.

Following the passage of the 1974 Act, ideas on how child abuse and neglect should be handled evolved rapidly. The influence of the Denver model of multi-disciplinary evaluation and decision-making (Schmitt, 1978, pp. 1-4) was gaining ascendancy and the inadequacy of the 1974 Act soon became apparent. In 1979, as one of the International Year of the Child events, a seminar was held on what was to be done about child abuse and neglect. The report of the seminar (Geddis, 1979) listed as 'current inadequacies': lack of recognition of the problem of abuse; lack of co-ordination, with an inadequate administrative framework; inadequate preparation of professionals; and lack of services for parents and children. As a sequel to the seminar, a National Advisory Committee on the Prevention of Child Abuse was set up by the Minister of Social Welfare in 1981. It drew on the expertise then available in New Zealand and overseas to formulate plans for dealing with the abuse and neglect of children. Central to these plans as they evolved was the multi-disciplinary approach.

During the 1980s, with the encouragement of the National Advisory Committee, ad hoc multi-disciplinary groups known as 'child protection teams' established themselves in many parts of the country. Some became government funded. Most continued to operate largely on a voluntary basis while receiving varying degrees of financial support from their local office of the Department of Social Welfare and from other sources. They considered cases that had been brought to the attention of agencies represented on the team and made plans to deal with them. The relationship of the teams to the local office of the Department of Social Welfare was obviously a crucial factor in determining their effectiveness. From the standpoint of the Department the teams could be legitimately considered to be consultative bodies or individuals assisting them in their statutory duties. In practice they aimed to follow a more co-operative and participatory model.

There was considerable variation in the makeup of these groups and the ways in which they worked. Families were involved to varying degrees and it was not uncommon for them to be a part of a decision-making meeting or case conference, usually as a sequel to a case conference at which the facts of the case were shared among the regular team members. Toward the end of the 1980s, two of the groups (Department of Social Welfare, Lower Hutt office, 1988; Department of Social Welfare, Panmure office, 1988) began regularly to invite families and their supporters to meetings and to involve them increasingly in the decision-making.

The National Advisory Committee pressed for replacement of the 1974 Act with legislation which would, among other reforms, recognise the place of the child protection teams. They recommended that teams should consist of people with expertise in various aspects of child protection work and represent professions, community bodies and other interested groups which dealt with child abuse cases. Meanwhile, many Maori New Zealanders were voicing their dissent in relation to existing law and practice. They felt that the processes by which decisions were made about their children were alien to their values and traditions and damaged the fabric of Maori society. Children were being removed from their families in large numbers; this was seen as particularly disturbing because in Maori tradition children were an integral part of the descent line and the wider kinship structure which together formed a seamless and sacred entity. Children belonged with their kin. Too little was being done to help strengthen *whanau*, *hapu* and *iwi*, the Maori kinship groupings which can be translated very loosely as extended families, clans and tribes. One of a number of processes of discussion and consultation was particularly influential in defining grievances among Maori and led in 1988 to the publication of the booklet, *Puao-te-Atatu* (Ministerial Advisory Committee, 1986).

At the same time, in New Zealand and worldwide, there was a growing recognition that out-of-family placement of children was sometimes unstable and harmful. It could, of course, work splendidly for the child and the success of many foster families and residential caregivers who looked after children with love and care and established lasting relationships with them should be recognised. Even in these situations, though, many children as they grew up felt a sense of displacement and loss. For these and other reasons, efforts to maintain links between the child and his or her family of origin, although not always successful, have gradually become standard practice (Millham, Bullock, Hosie & Haak, 1986). There is also now a wariness about placing children with strangers and a growing movement to have them looked after by kin and others with whom they can identify when their parents and immediate family are unavailable. There is an increasing recognition of the human need of a sense of belonging.

During the 1980s, the treatment of young offenders who had been placed in residences, particularly those placed in secure care, became a public issue in New Zealand. There were accusations of brutality and racism. There was certainly disillusionment with such placement as an instrument of reform. It became apparent in some cases that young people were being subjected to prolonged incarceration in the name of 'welfare'.

The Process of Development of the Children, Young Persons and Their Families Act 1989

There was, then, clamour for reform of the law from various quarters. It tended in the direction of less state intrusion and more in-family placement consistent with children's safety or, in the case of young offenders, community safety. The development of the family group conference and its placement at the centre of the care and protection and youth justice processes in the *Children, Young Persons and Their Families Act* 1989 can be traced using published reports, Bills and speeches as signposts.

In the foreword to a public discussion paper ordered by her after the 1984 general election (Department of Social Welfare, 1984) the incoming Minister of Social Welfare set out the principles that she believed should be applied in a new law. Among them were:

- a presumption in favour of leaving or placing a child in a family group and recognising his/her need to establish and maintain stable relationships with at least one psychological parent (note that the Minister says and means *a* family group, not *the* family group);

- recognition and support for the independence and integrity of the family, with intervention being kept to the minimum that is consistent with the safety, well-being and proper development of the child;

- help or assistance being provided on a voluntary basis whenever possible rather than through coercive court measures;

- the provision of services which recognise the cultural diversity of New Zealand and are delivered in a culturally appropriate and sensitive manner;

- so far as practical, the child and his/her family being consulted about the child's needs and invited to participate in all significant decisions concerning the child;

23

- all intervention should be based on time-limited, goal-directed plans which have been discussed with the child and family and are subject to independent review; and

- the right of the child and the child's family to access to services and their right to challenge official intervention.

The multi-disciplinary model for dealing with cases of alleged child abuse or neglect was incorporated into the 1984 discussion paper's proposals. It was proposed that the child protection team should have a central place in the child protection process. It would become a statutory body, its structure, role and function being defined in the law; and it would investigate reports in parallel with the statutory social worker, convene case conferences, which were to have status in the law, and make plans. A youth assessment panel with a somewhat similar structure and role was to be incorporated into the youth justice process. Plans proposed by child protection teams and youth assessment panels were to be considered, if necessary, by a court which could endorse them if it saw fit. Four hundred written submissions were received in relation to this paper, an indication of the wide public interest in the issue.

In 1986, a *Children and Young Persons Bill* was introduced into Parliament. It incorporated many of the features recommended in the 1984 discussion paper including the key role of the child protection teams in the child protection process. Reports to the Department of Social Welfare of abuse and neglect were to be referred mandatorily to a child protection team, which was to include in its membership a representative of the Department. Cases were to be carried forward by the team rather than by the Department. The multi-disciplinary model was not to be applied to the youth justice process which was to be largely in the hands of a youth court to be established under the Act.

The Bill was referred to a select committee of Parliament to be considered in detail. It remained before the select committee through the next general election. The Government was returned but a new Minister of Social Welfare was appointed. He asked for another review of the Bill by a working party of officials from his Department. Their terms of reference made clear that the Bill was unacceptable in its present form. Two of the principles guiding their work which differed significantly from those propounded by the previous Minister were (Department of Social Welfare, 1987):

- The Bill must have a cultural perspective which can be demonstrated by its maintenance of the status and cultural identity of the *tangata whenua* (the people indigenous to or belonging in an area), its sensitivity to and support of culturally appropriate procedures, and its emphasis away from intrusive and disempowering interventions.

- The Bill must involve parents, family groups, *whanau*, *hapu* and *iwi* in developing solutions to problem situations.

The concerns expressed in some of the 148 submissions made in response to the 1986 Bill were listed in the review report as: its monocultural nature; the lack of emphasis on prevention and family support; its length and complexity; the role and composition of child protection teams; mandatory reporting; a lack of diversionary procedures; the split jurisdiction for offending and care and protection; its review mechanisms; and procedures for redress. The report said that although there was wide support for the concept of child protection teams, there was some opposition to their being given executive power. Child protection teams, it said, should be advisory to the authorities. There was also criticism of the child protection teams' 'top heaviness' with 'professionals'. In short, the report expressed concern at decision-making power in relation to the protection of children being placed in the hands of experts who were able to act independently of the statutory authorities.

The working party proposed that in all care and protection cases where there was sufficient concern, there should be a 'case conference/*whanau* meeting' in which there would always be 'family involvement'. The meeting's purpose would be to prepare plans and arrange for their review. This model was not proposed for the youth justice component of the report.

A greatly modified Bill was subsequently reintroduced to Parliament in 1989. In it the idea of the case conference/ *whanau* meeting had been further developed into the family group conference which in effect took the place that had been occupied by the child protection team in the original Bill. Family group conferences were included as the major decision-making body in both care and protection and youth justice proceedings. Community advisory groups to be known as "care and protection resource panels" were introduced as successors to the child protection teams. While consultation with them by Department of Social Welfare social workers was to be mandatory, they were to have no executive power. In reintroducing the Bill to Parliament, the chairperson of the select committee summarised the objections to the original Bill as:

> setting up a complex and costly structure to detect problems rather than provide the means by which to deal with them or to prevent them. Many submissions asked for more involvement for families in decision making and more flexibility in the process available to assist them. The

> monocultural nature of the Bill was criticised in several submissions . . .
> the Bill did not take sufficient account of the place of the child as a
> member of a family, whanau, hapu or iwi, and . . . undermined the role of
> tribal authorities and the responsibilities of families, whanau, hapu and iwi
> (Parliamentary Debates, 1989).

Despite these criticisms and its new appearance, the 1989 version of
the Bill was not based on a complete rejection of the 1986 original; many
features were retained. In particular, the basic design of the 'flow chart'
for the care and protection process remained and was also applied in
adapted form to the youth justice process.

Family group conferences did not arise simply because of the
ascendancy of one viewpoint over another. To a considerable extent the
process that eventually resulted in them having a central role in New
Zealand's care and protection and youth justice systems occurred
progressively. Recommendations in successive reports increased, or
claimed to have increased, the role of the family in decision-making. The
central position of family group conferences in the law and the level of
autonomy and decision-making power given them is in some measure the
result of reaction against the proposals in the 1986 Bill: families were
preferable to professionals in making decisions. It is possible to take a
cynical view and say that this was because families were viewed by some
as likely to be more malleable and cheaper, that children were not in a
position to protest and that the power of community leaders and others
who were likely to be a part of the new process would be enhanced.
However, many of those who championed the family group conference did
so because they believed it was more likely to be effective, was more just
and was simply right. The final place of the family group conference
under the Act also owes a great deal to the fact that it had been the place
occupied by the child protection team in the carefully designed child
protection process of the 1986 Bill. The substitution was easily made.

Family Group Conferences – Purpose and Principle under the Children, Young Persons and Their Families Act 1989

Critical analyses of the concept of family group conferences (Atkin, 1991;
Brown & MacElrea, 1993; Durie-Hall & Metge, 1992; Geddis, 1993;
Maxwell & Morris, 1993; Tapp, 1990), detailed descriptions of the family
group conference process (Hassall & Maxwell, 1991; Paterson & Harvey,
1991), information on outcomes (Maxwell & Morris, 1993), and case law
(Trapski, 1995) are available. The central question is 'Do they work?' To
answer this question it is necessary first to answer the question 'What do
they set out to do?'

The fundamental reason for the existence of the law is to protect children from abuse and neglect and ensure that they are adequately looked after and, in the case of young offenders, that they are held to account and do not reoffend. Other objectives have been added to indicate how this is to be achieved. The most important of these is the objective of strengthening families. It is incorporated into the law not only as a means of meeting the primary purpose but because it is considered to be in itself of value.

In the decade that preceded the enactment of the *Children, Young Persons and Their Families Act* 1989 the arguments were largely about matters of principle. The architects of the Act having heard and contributed to those arguments saw merit in setting out as clearly as they could in the Act the principles that were to govern its operation. Sections 5, 13 and 208 of the Act consist of carefully balanced sets of principles by which people exercising powers under the Act, including participants in family group conferences, are to be guided. They state:[1]

> S.5 [Applying to all proceedings under the Act, and subject to s.6. which affirms the primacy of the best interests of the child]
>
> (a) . . . wherever possible, a child's or young person's family, whanau, hapu, iwi, and family group should participate in the making of decisions affecting that child, and accordingly, . . . wherever possible, regard should be had to the views of that family:
>
> (b) . . . wherever possible, the relationship between a child and his or her family should be maintained and strengthened:
>
> (c) . . . consideration must always be given to how a decision affecting a child will affect-
>
>   (i)   The welfare of that child; and
>
>   (ii) The stability of that child's family:
>
> (d) . . . consideration should be given to the wishes of the child, so far as those wishes can reasonably be ascertained, and . . . those wishes should be given such weight as is appropriate in the circumstances, having regard to the age, maturity, and culture of the child:
>
> (e) . . . endeavours should be made to obtain the support of-
>
>   (i)   The parents or guardians or other persons having the care of the child; and
>
>   (ii) The child himself or herself-
>
> to the exercise or proposed exercise, in relation to that child, of any power conferred by or under [the] Act:

---

1   Except for the first time they appear, in order to avoid repetition the word 'child' is used where the phrase 'child and young person' appears in the Act and the word 'family' is used where the words 'family, whanau, hapu, iwi, and family group' appear in the Act.

(f) . . . decisions affecting a child should, wherever practicable, be made and implemented within a time-frame appropriate to the child's sense of time.

S.13 [Applying to care and protection proceedings and subject to ss. 5 & 6.]

(a) . . . children must be protected from harm, their rights upheld, and their welfare promoted:

(b) . . . the primary role in caring for and protecting a child lies with the child's family, and . . . accordingly-

   (i) A child's family should be supported, assisted and protected as much as possible; and

   (ii) Intervention into family life should be the minimum necessary to ensure a child's safety and protection:

(c) . . . it is desirable that a child live in association with his or her family, and that his or her education, training, or employment be allowed to continue without interruption or disturbance:

(d) Where a child is considered to be in need of care or protection . . . wherever practicable, the necessary assistance and support should be provided to enable the child to be cared for and protected within his or her own family:

(e) . . . a child should be removed from his or her family only if there is a serious risk of harm to the child:

(f) Where a child is removed from his or her family . . . -

   (i) Wherever practicable, the child should be returned to, and protected from harm within, that family; and

   (ii) Where the child cannot immediately be returned to, and protected from harm within, his or her family, until the child can be so returned and protected, he or she should, wherever practicable, live in an appropriate family-like setting-

      (A) That, where appropriate, is in the same locality as that in which the child was living; and

      (B) In which the child's links with his family are maintained and strengthened; and

   (iii) Where the child cannot be returned to, and protected from harm within, his or her family, the child should live in a new family group, or (in the case of a young person) in an appropriate family-like setting, in which he or she can develop a sense of belonging, and in which his or her sense of continuity and . . . personal and cultural identity are maintained:

(g) Where a child cannot remain with or be returned to his or her family, . . . in determining the person in whose care the child should be placed, priority should, where practicable, be given to a person-

   (i) Who is a member of the child's hapu or iwi (with preference being given to hapu members), or, if that is not possible, who has the same tribal, racial, ethnic, or cultural background as the child; and

   (ii) Who lives in the same locality as the child:

(h) Where a child cannot remain with, or be returned to, his or her family, . . . the child should be given an opportunity to develop a significant psychological attachment to the person in whose care the child is placed:

(i) Where a child [under 14 years of age] is considered to be in need of care or protection on the ground specified in 14(1)(e), i.e., offending causing serious concern for the child's wellbeing [due regard should be had to the interests of any victims of the offending].

S.208 [Applying to youth justice proceedings and subject to s.5]

(a) . . . unless the public interest requires otherwise, criminal proceedings should not be instituted against a child if there is an alternative means of dealing with the matter:

(b) . . . criminal proceedings should not instituted against a child solely in order to provide any assistance or services needed to advance the welfare of the child or his or her family:

(c) . . . any measures for dealing with offending by children should be designed-
  (i) To strengthen the family of the child concerned; and
  (ii) To foster the ability of families to develop their own means of dealing with offending by their children:

(d) . . . a child who commits an offence should be kept in the community so far as that is practicable and consonant with the need to ensure the safety of the public:

(e) . . . a child's age is a mitigating factor in determining-
  (i) Whether or not to impose sanctions in respect of offending by a child; and
  (ii) The nature of any such sanctions:

(f) . . . any sanctions imposed on a child who commits an offence should-
  (i) Take the form most likely to maintain and promote the development of the child within his or her family; and
  (ii) Take the least restrictive form that is appropriate in the circumstances:

(g) . . . any measures for dealing with offending by children should have due regard to the interests of any victims of that offending:

(h) . . . the vulnerability of children entitles a child to special protection during any investigation relating to the commission or possible commission of an offence by that child.

The lawmakers foresaw that the aim of protecting and enhancing the well-being of the child could on occasion conflict with the aim of family integrity and other matters. They included a provision, s. 6 in the Act, which applies to care and protection but not to youth justice proceedings, to the effect that where such conflict existed the best interests of the child would be the deciding factor. This was later interpreted by the courts as being the equivalent of the provision which it replaced in the 1974 Act and which is standard in laws of this kind; that is, a requirement that in all care and protection proceedings under the Act, the best interests of the child are to be the paramount consideration. To make this clearer, and because of concern that the clause was operative only in the case of identified conflict, an amendment to the 1989 Act was passed in 1994 to make the child's best interests paramount in all proceedings under the care and protection sections of the Act.

Family Group Conferences – Purposes and Outcomes

The purposes of family group conferences are set out in ss. 28 and 258 of the Act. In care and protection conferences the task is to consider matters relating to the care or protection of the child or young person referred to it, make such decisions, recommendations or plans, in relation to that child or young person, as it considers necessary or desirable and to review these from time-to-time. In youth justice, the focus is different. The conference has to consider whether the young person should be prosecuted or dealt with in some other way, make decisions where appropriate about the custody of the young person and make such decisions, recommendations or plans as it considers necessary to deal with the offending. The hope and expectation of those who established the family group conference model was that, given a wide enough recruitment of family members, sufficient information and recognition of the authority of the family as a whole, plans and recommendations would be formulated that would accord with the principles of the Act and meet its objectives.

The crucial question 'Do they work?' is not likely to have a simple answer. In asking the question it should be borne in mind that the family group conference was not established simply as a functional expedient. It is founded not only on the expectation that it would work better, but on a belief in the right of family members, particularly senior family members, and the family as a whole to have the opportunity as far as possible to determine family matters. The question 'Do family group conferences work?' in terms of the Act's objectives is nevertheless worth asking and worth attempting to answer through appropriate research. In the case of care and protection family group conferences, regrettably, this research has yet to be done. In the case of youth justice, Maxwell and Morris (1993) conducted research which shows that the objectives of the Act can be achieved in many cases and there is reason to believe from the data they present that the chances of this happening are greater than with the previous system. More research needs to be done in this area, however.

Although information on outcomes is in short supply, it is possible, nevertheless, to have some understanding of anticipated outcomes by considering the likely advantages and risks of the model. In considering advantages, it is always as well to keep in mind the question 'Compared with what?' The following list of advantages of the family group conference model is in comparison with decision-making by a more remote tribunal such as a court or case conference of experts. This list relates to the primary objectives of the Act rather than to the secondary objective of strengthening families although, of course, bringing families together to make important decisions about their kin can strengthen them. Some anticipated advantages of family group conferences are:

- *Continuity*. Severance or attenuation of familiar associations and relationships should be less likely. There must, of course, be change, principally that the abuse of or offending by the child stops, but many children suffer if they are separated from their family, from others they know and from familiar surroundings. A family group conference may have a greater chance of avoiding this by finding a way of maintaining continuity in the child's life while still bringing the abuse or offending to an end.

- *Pride*. A sense of identity, belonging and pride in one's family and self confidence may be more likely to be maintained in the child if it is perceived that the family has responded to his or her needs, dealt with them and kept the child with them.

- *Ownership*. The family, through assuming responsibility for the problem, may be better motivated to seek lasting solutions.

- *Extension*. Solutions may operate not just for the child in question but for others in the family, some yet unborn.

- *Meaningfulness*. The family group conference, through taking place in familiar territory, in familiar language and style and with familiar people may be more meaningful to all the participants. Plans and decisions may then be better understood and more likely to be followed.

- *Learning*. The family group conference presents an opportunity for participants to hear and to understand. The family should learn something of the nature of the abuse and offending from the officials and others present and, in particular, the likely effectiveness of various interventions. The officials should learn from the family what resources they are able to muster to deal with the problem. The offender should come to realise the nature and magnitude of his or her transgression, particularly its impact on the victim. Victims whether of abuse or of youth offending should learn of the support they have from the family and the wider community.

- *Satisfaction*. The family group conference is an opportunity to speak and to be heard. The abused and the victim of the young offender should feel vindicated by having been heard and having heard the family group conference's condemnation of the offender and expressions of contrition by that person. Their own healing should be expedited by this experience, by their having been able to contribute to determination of the penalty, by being able to forgive if they can and by their sense of rightness and justice satisfied.

- *Repair.* The process may act as a model and initiate better family functioning by way of communication, cooperation, supervision and proper exercise of authority. It need not be a mere episode such as other official proceedings are bound to be but can be the beginning of a more productive and satisfying way of relating and problem solving within the family. It can bring together family members who have lost touch and restore legitimate authority that has undergone attrition.

- *Truth.* The truth may be found more readily in a forum in which evasions, prevarications and lying can be challenged by those familiar with the behaviour of the perpetrator.

- *Privacy.* The realisation of these benefits may be assisted by the fact that the proceedings are not public or recorded.

- *Effectiveness.* The family, knowing its members and what can be expected of them, will make plans that are more likely to work.

As well as advantages, the family group conference model presents certain risks. The principal risks are the reciprocal of the advantages and can be presented under the same headings:

- *Continuity.* There may be no real change brought about by a conference of people already familiar with one another and set in destructive ways of relating. The abuse or offending may then continue, the only change being that it is better concealed.

- *Pride.* Pride in membership of an abusive or criminal subculture may be reinforced.

- *Ownership.* The autonomy of the family group conference can be made a sham by officials dictating the outcome, either directly or indirectly, consciously or inadvertently, through overbearing behaviour, agenda setting and failure to fully inform the conference.

- *Extension*. If effective solutions are not found failure to deal with family matters and a sense of failure may be reinforced and perpetuated.

- *Meaningfulness*. The familiarity of the surroundings may lead the participants to not take the process seriously or hold in contempt the authorities who have been unable to impose their will by more coercive means.

- *Learning*. Families with an entrenched dysfunctional method of operation may learn nothing from a family group conference.

- *Satisfaction*. By seeing official sanction given to the authority of a family that has been responsible for their abuse, children and victims of young offenders may feel trapped and helpless. By contrast in another forum, representing a wider community view, they may be able to feel vindicated. They may not be heard because of entrenched autocratic or intimidatory styles of family functioning. There may be injustice done through lack of due process.

- *Repair*. The process is apt to reopen old wounds within the family and can become grounds for new antagonisms between family members and between factions within the extended family so that divisions are worsened and prolonged.

- *Truth*. The benefit that, say, a court offers in the assembly, presentation, challenging and weighing of evidence by experienced people under established rules is not available in a family group conference and there may be a failure to arrive at the truth.

- *Privacy*. The lack of recording and public scrutiny of the family group conference process may increase the likelihood of injustice.

- *Effectiveness*. The family's plans may be based on unrealistic expectations of members that are derived from family mythology, wishful thinking and pressure to solve the problem rather than practical experience and reason.

The child protection and youth justice services and, most importantly, their officials who coordinate and participate in family group conferences have a heavy responsibility to maximise the advantages and minimise the risks. Their role is crucial in helping to bring about satisfactory outcomes and in determining the credibility of the process. The inherent qualities of the people doing the work, the quality of their training and the support they are given by their service and by the public all contribute. If any or all of these are unsatisfactory, serious harm can come to children, families and communities. The role of the official coordinators of the process and of the social worker or police officer who attends the family group conference is sometimes misunderstood.

There is a well-known danger in child protection practice of insufficient action being taken by a social worker who has been lured into a false belief in the child's safety, a phenomenon loosely called 'family capture'. Dingwall and others (Dingwall, Eekelaar & Murray, 1983) describe three means by which this occurs and label them 'cultural relativism', 'natural love' and 'the rule of optimism'. Knowledge of these traps, training in recognising and responding to them and adequate supervision minimise the risk. The family decision-making model is certainly not exempt from these dangers and if it is misunderstood by protection and enforcement services as meaning their withdrawal once the family group conference is in session or after it has concluded, the risk is enhanced (Hassall, 1993). Family decision-making does not relieve the state child protection and law enforcement agencies of their duty to see that children who have come to notice are reasonably safe and that any sanctions imposed on young offenders have been complied with.

While not interfering with the family decision-making process, the child protection social worker or member of the police at the family group conference must be satisfied that the plans which are made comply with the objectives and principles of the Act. To do this the plans must include adequate monitoring. It has been said that monitoring gives a mixed message that undermines the family autonomy model. The authorities having said 'You decide', proceed to check up on the outcome. However, such checking is an entirely consistent and necessary part of the model. This needs to be made this clear to families, social workers and the public.

The family group conference model is compatible with a number of views of society. One vision it offers is that of restoration of family and community integrity. The idea of repair of families and communities that have undergone some degree of disintegration that has rendered them incapable of protecting and adequately socialising their children is attractive. New Zealand's *Children, Young Persons and Their Families Act* 1989 had a vision at its core: if families are expected by the authorities to act wisely, responsibly and in their children's best interests this could have a salutary effect, activating the natural resilience and resourcefulness of the family, and then the authorities' expectations could become a self-fulfilling prophecy.

References

Atkin, B. (1990-91). Let the family decide: The new approach to family problems. *Journal of Family Law, 29*, 387-397.

Brown, B. J., & MacElrea, F. W. M. (Eds). (1993). *The youth court in New Zealand: A new model of justice.* Auckland: Legal Research Foundation.

Dingwall, R., Eekelaar, J., & Murray, T. (1983). *The protection of children: State intervention and family life.* Oxford: Basil Blackwell.

Department of Social Welfare (1984). *Review of children and young persons legislation: Public discussion paper.* Wellington: Department of Social Welfare.

Department of Social Welfare. (1987). *Review of the Children and Young Persons Bill.* Wellington: Department of Social Welfare.

Department of Social Welfare, Lower Hutt Office. (1988). *Whanau/family decision making. A practitioner view of the implementation of a family empowerment way of working.* Lower Hutt: Department of Social Welfare.

Department of Social Welfare, Panmure Office. (1988). *Family decision making in child protection. A practice paper.* Panmure, Auckland: Department of Social Welfare.

Durie-Hall, D., & Metge, J. (1992). Kua tutu te puehu, kia mau. Maori aspirations and family law. In M. Henaghan, & B. Atkin, (Eds), *Family law policy in New Zealand* (pp. 54-79). Auckland: Oxford University Press.

Geddis, D. C. (1979). *Child abuse.* Report of a national symposium held in Dunedin, September 1979. Dunedin: National Children's Health Research Foundation.

Geddis, D. C. (1993). A critical analysis of the family group conference. *Family Law Bulletin, 3,* 141-144.

Hassall, I. B. (1993). Report to the Minister of Social Welfare on the New Zealand Children and Young Persons Service's review of practice in relation to Craig Manukau and his family. Wellington: Minister of Social Welfare.

Hassall, I. B. , & Maxwell, G. M. (1991). The family group conference. In I. B. Hassall, (Ed.), *An appraisal of the first year of the Children Young Persons and Their Families Act 1989* (pp. 1-13). Wellington: Office of the Commissioner for Children.

Kempe, C. H., Silverman, F.N., Steele, B., Droegemuller, W., & Silver, K. (1962). The battered child syndrome. *Journal of the American Medical Association, 181,* 17-24.

Maxwell, G.M. , & Morris, A. (1993). *Family, victims and culture: Youth justice in New Zealand.* Wellington: Social Policy Agency and Victoria University of Wellington, Institute of Criminology.

Millham, S., Bullock, R., Hosie, K., & Haak, M. (1986). *Lost in care: The problem of maintaining links between children in care and their families.* Aldershot, England: Gower.

Ministerial Advisory Committee. (1986). *Puao-te-Atatu:* The report of the Ministerial Advisory Committee on a Maori perspective for the Department of Social Welfare. Wellington: Department of Social Welfare.

Parliamentary Debates Vol. 497. (1989). Wellington. Government Printer.

Paterson, K., & Harvey, M.(1991). *An evaluation of the organisation and operation of care and protection family group conferences.* Wellington: Department of Social Welfare, Evaluation Unit.

Schmitt, B. D. (1978). *The child protection team handbook: a multidisciplinary approach to managing child abuse and neglect.* New York and London: Garland STPM Press.

Tapp, P. F. (1990). Family group conferences and the Children Young Persons and Their Families Act 1989: an ineffective statute? *New Zealand Recent Law Review, 2,* 82-88.

Trapski, P. J. (Ed.). (1991-). *Trapski's family law.* Wellington: Brooker & Friend Ltd.

3

Family Group Conferencing in New Zealand Child Protection Work

Sarah Fraser and Jenni Norton

The introduction of the family group conference in 1989 changed the face of child protection work in New Zealand. It established a new and exciting balance between the various rights and responsibilities of family groups, agencies with concerns for the well-being of children, the state and the children and young persons themselves. The family group conference was designed:

- to acknowledge that the primary role in caring for and protecting children and young people lies within the family group; and

- to increase family participation in child protection decision-making.

The police and social workers of the New Zealand Children and Young Persons Service[1] have statutory responsibility for investigating and resolving all reported child abuse. Investigations are planned in consultation with local care and protection resource panels set up in each community and comprised of both professional and community personnel. The panels have advisory power only. Once an investigation is completed, the investigating social worker must decide if the child or young person is in need of care or protection according to one or more of the nine

---

1   The New Zealand Children and Young Persons Service was created as a separate business unit of the Department of Social Welfare in 1992.

definitions outlined in the *Children, Young Persons and Their Families Act* 1989. These definitions include harm, neglect, differences between young people and their parents and between the parents themselves, harmful behaviour, offending by children under the age of 14 in certain circumstances, abandonment, and multiple changes of caregivers creating an inability to form healthy relationships. If the investigating social worker believes the situation meets one or more of these criteria, the case is referred to a care and protection coordinator to convene a family group conference. The care and protection coordinator's role is to facilitate the family group conference process and to ensure the spirit and letter of the law are adhered to.

Phases of the Family Group Conference Process

Before the Family Group Conference

The setting-up stage is critical in ensuring that the conference runs smoothly and involves the coordinator making a number of crucial decisions in consultation with a care and protection resource panel. By negotiating decisions on seemingly practical matters, the coordinator begins the process of balancing the rights and responsibilities of the state, the community, the child or young person and the family group. These decisions are:

- *who should attend the conference.* A number of people have legal entitlement to attend the family group conference, including the children or young persons themselves, any member of the child's family group widely defined to include persons having blood, legal, cultural or significant psychological attachment, the coordinator, the person with the care and protection concerns, the child advocate or lawyer and any other person whom the family group wishes to have in attendance. Within this context, the coordinator has to decide who is defined as the family group, whether the child or young person should attend the conference and if there are any entitled persons who should be excluded from attending;

- *where and when the conference should be held and what protocols should be used.* In organising the family group conference the coordinator must, by law, consult widely with the family group about the time, date, place and protocol of the meeting, and must, whenever it is practicable and within the principles of the Act, proceed with the wishes of the family group;

- *what information the conference will need to make an informed decision.* The coordinator has to decide how this information would best be presented and by whom.

All of these decisions can involve extensive consultation and negotiation as the coordinator ensures that people's legal rights are upheld and that the conference is set up in a way that maximises safe decision-making.

The Family Group Conference

As the purpose of the family group conference is to shift responsibility back onto the extended family, the weighting given to the wishes of the family group in the process is significant. The meeting is, therefore, run in three distinct parts.

- *Introduction and information-giving.* The coordinator opens the conference with all the entitled members and any information-givers present. In this section of the conference, chaired by the coordinator, the aim is to give the participants all the information they need to make a responsible decision, including the results of any investigation into allegations of abuse. Information is presented to give a holistic view of the child's life, usually by his or her teacher, doctor, counsellor or social worker.

- *Private family time.* Once all the information is presented, the family group is left in private to consider the issues raised, decide if it believes there is a care and protection concern and make plans to remedy the situation if it does. This part of the conference can take much time, as each family group works together to consider and resolve the issues in its own unique way.

- *Negotiating the plan.* Once the family group has reached agreement and conveyed this to the coordinator, all the entitled members are recalled to hear the family group's plan and recommendations, and negotiate a final family group conference plan. Records from the New Zealand Children and Young Persons Service show that agreement is reached in over 90 percent of cases nationally. In those few cases where no agreement is reached, the coordinator closes the conference and reports the non-agreement to a social worker or police officer who decides if the matter should be put before the Family Court for resolution.

It is the function of the family group conference to ensure that the family group has the first right and responsibility to resolve care and protection issues in relation to its children. It is only when the family group is unable to do this that the state takes over this role. This is a major shift from previous models of either state or multi-disciplinary decision-making. It marks a significant move from professional to family decision-making.

Case Study – The S Family

Background Information

The mother of the S family ran away from home as a teenager. Since that time, she has only had contact with one sister. Her birth family has a history of alcoholism. Her husband comes from one of the Pacific Islands. The eldest child in the family is A. He is 15 years old and had been involved with a troublesome group of teenagers. The social worker's decision to refer A for a family group conference was precipitated by the school's notification that A had arrived at school with a black eye and severe bruising as a result of excessive disciplining by his father. There are two other children in the family – daughter B, six years old, and son C, three years old. Medical reports indicated that these two children were undernourished and developmentally delayed. The mother told the social worker that she had been hitting the children out of frustration and feelings of despair.

Two months prior to the referral, there was a violent argument between the parents and, as a result, the mother experienced suicidal thoughts. The mother was beaten by the father two weeks prior to the referral. Both were intoxicated at the time and incapable of signing an agreement for the children to come into temporary care until the situation stabilised. There were further concerns about the family's financial and living situation. The initial referral for this family came from the social worker who had been involved with the family in a supportive role over a number of months and was accompanied by documentation of the investigation and assessment of son A's injuries.

Setting the Stage

Setting up the family group conference appropriately is critical for the success of any conference. For the S family, this meant completing a series of tasks. First, the coordinator needed to obtain appropriate advice about cultural protocols for setting up and holding the family group conference. This was done by working with the local care and protection resource panel, a worker from the Ministry of Pacific Island Affairs and a local community leader respected by the family. These resource people helped identify issues that would cause particular tensions within the family and would need to be addressed sensitively in the meeting process to ensure success. One of these issues was that the father was the eldest son of the family living in New Zealand and as such there were cultural expectations on him to act as guide and mentor for his younger brothers. There was much shame for him in his brothers learning what was happening in his family and being asked to assist in making decisions about protecting his children. On the advice of the resource people, the coordinator decided the conference would be opened with an acknowledgment of the father's status and the particular difficulty for him of being in this situation. The issue would be addressed directly so as to enable the family to openly support him throughout the process. In this way, it was hoped that he would be able to be more honest about the difficulties he was facing and the kinds of assistance he would need to regain his family's respect and to care appropriately for his children.

The second task was to locate and approach the extended family and gain their support for the family group conference (the father's three brothers and their partners, the mother's two sisters and a brother from some distance away). Other members of the family were unable to attend – including the children's maternal grandmother. She sent one of her children (uncle to daughter B and sons A and C) to the conference to represent her. The senior uncle in the father's family chose to phone his relatives in their home country to gain their views and support prior to the meeting. This was to be critical in terms of the outcome for the eldest child.

Initially, the children's mother was very angry to learn about her family's involvement and the family itself was upset to hear, through the coordinator, what had been happening to the children. The coordinator's role here, at the family's request, was to ensure they had the time and privacy to deal with these issues before coming to the formal conference. Arrangements were made for the mother's family to arrive several days before the family group conference and stay close to her. During this time, much of the challenging and healing of past difficulties was done and the family members were then ready to begin to work together constructively for the best interests of the children.

The next task in setting the stage for the conference involved collecting reports from the agencies to ensure that the families had all the information they needed to accurately assess the situation. Reports were obtained from the social worker, school, day care centre, doctor and several voluntary agencies who had worked with the family. The final task was to ensure the families were supported at the meeting. Therefore, at their request, the coordinator invited the community leader, the minister and his wife, and the Pacific Island Affairs worker to attend.

The Conference

The opening of the conference was essential in setting the tone for the meeting. The coordinator had negotiated with the various branches of the family to make sure they were happy with the order and nature of the ceremony. The community leader welcomed the family to the meeting place and then the Pacific Island minister blessed the meeting in his own language. Following this, the coordinator set the parameters for the conference by explaining the three phases of the meeting; the necessity of securing the agreement of the New Zealand Children and Young Persons Service and those agencies or individuals named in the plan to provide services or support; and the process that would be followed if no agreement was reached.

The first phase of the meeting (information-giving) was very difficult and tense as the extended family members were angry that they had not been informed earlier of the difficulties faced by the S family. They expressed anger and shame about the situation and strongly challenged the rights of the various agencies to be involved. The assistance of the minister was invaluable at this stage in assisting the coordinator to acknowledge the family's feelings and move them on to work through the process. Instead of the professionals telling the family what to do, the family began using the professionals' experience and knowledge to extend their understandings so they could go on to make good, safe decisions for the children. The professionals and agency people then left and the family began their private deliberations – the second phase of the conference.

The family's discussion took a full day to work their way towards achieving their goal and there were many tears, recriminations and challenges during this time. The support people were vital in assisting the two sides of the family to recognise and address their different cultural expectations and conventions. When they were finally ready, the family called the coordinator and referring social worker back in for the negotiation phase of the conference. The family had clear ideas of what they wanted to happen and it was the coordinator's job to assist them to develop these within the legal frameworks available.

The Plan

The plan for son A was for him to live with his paternal grandparents in the Pacific Islands for at least a year. The family felt this would be a positive move in terms of developing his understanding of his cultural heritage, continuing his schooling, and keeping him safe within his family. They did not believe he could safely return to his parents' care at this time. Because of past concerns about other young people being sent back to the Pacific Islands following problems in New Zealand, there were certain considerations that needed to be built into the plan; the coordinator negotiated these between the family and the branch manager of the Children and Young Persons Service. They included:

(1) an assessment by the Island's social services of the proposed caregivers to ensure that they:

   (a) understood why son A was unable to remain with his parents;

   (b) were willing to undertake the caregiving;

   (c) were realistically able to provide the care that would meet A's needs;

   (d) met the required standards for caregivers; and

(2) a contingency plan in case the placement broke down.

The family also asked the New Zealand Children and Young Persons Service to assist with resourcing the travel and this took some detailed negotiating to arrange.

The family wanted daughter B and son C to be returned to the care of their parents with close family and agency monitoring and support. They also asked that appropriate counselling be arranged for the parents to address the issues of violence, alcohol use and parenting. Again, the coordinator negotiated with the agency which was to provide the counselling and gained its agreement to the plan. Finally, the family requested that the family group conference be reconvened in six months to ensure that the plan was working and progress was being made. Overall agreement to the plan was gained from the New Zealand Children and Young Persons Service social worker and the official plan drawn up. The plan concluded with the statutory requirement that if it broke down at any time, any two entitled members of the conference, or the coordinator, could ask for the meeting to be reconvened.

Summary of the Outcomes

Son A went to live with his paternal grandparents and attended school. At the first review of the plan there were no problems and his school and home reports were excellent. However, later that year the situation deteriorated and a review conference was held to make new plans to take him through to independence. The plans for the two younger children also worked well for the first six months, but then had to be revised when the mother began drinking again. The review conference made the decision then that the children should not be returned to the parents' care until the mother and father had both completed appropriate rehabilitation programmes. During that time, the children were to be placed with family members with the financial support of the state.

Conclusion

As they worked through the conferences, the growing confidence of the extended family in their ability to determine positive, appropriate outcomes for the children became evident. By the end of the coordinator's involvement with this family, they were arranging their own travel and accommodation. The facilitation role for the coordinator decreased as the family took more control of the situation themselves. Initially, the family came with feelings of being required to attend the conference by the New Zealand Children and Young Persons Service; at the last meeting, the Pacific Island family provided a traditional meal at the venue for everyone and thanked the coordinator for coming.

The family group conference provided a setting in which the extended family felt safe and in control of the proceedings. The use of culturally appropriate supports and prayers helped. By virtue of being authors of the plan, the family felt a responsibility to monitor progress and ensure the safety of the children. That is, the family group conference enabled ownership of the outcome as opposed to passive acceptance of state imposed conditions.

Balancing the Tightrope – Practice Issues

As shown in this case study, balancing power is key. Although the process is aimed at empowering the family to take primary responsibility for the care and protection of the young person, some power and responsibility lies with the state. It is important that this power, and the practice issues it raises, is recognised so that it can be exercised creatively in the best interests of the child or young person.

- The family group conference is often convened at the request of the state by way of a social worker or police officer, sometimes with the support of the parents and sometimes in opposition to the parents' wishes. Although the family group conference process has been developed so that decisions can be made without the necessity of court intervention, in some cases emergency actions, such as removal from the home, have been taken by the police or social worker to ensure a child or young person's immediate safety. In these cases, there is a tension between initial state intervention and the family empowerment process which follows. It is the coordinator's task to manage this tension to ensure optimum decision-making for the child or young person.

- The coordinator is an employee of the New Zealand Children and Young Persons Service, the agency making the majority of referrals for a family group conference. Although an employee of the major investigation agency, and an entitled member of the conference, the coordinator is employed as a facilitator of the resolution process. This creates an immediate tension. It is often difficult for the family to divorce the coordinator's role from that of the investigating social worker's, especially when there is conflict between the family and the investigators, as can happen over alleged physical or sexual abuse. The skill of the coordinator in handling this tension is critical; if coordinators feel comfortable with this tension then they will be able to achieve a positive balance in each individual conference.

- The coordinator has the power and responsibility to decide which family members to contact and inform about holding the meeting. In establishing who the family members are so they can decide whether or not they wish to take up their legal right to attend, the coordinator may have to override the wishes of the nuclear family who do not wish other family members to know of its problems. In one case, for instance, the father was adamant that the coordinator should not contact a branch of the family because of a rift that had formed within the family 10 years before. These members included half-siblings of the child involved. However, at least one of the half-sisters had been in touch with the teenage boy who, when he was in trouble, would run away to her. After much consultation, the coordinator contacted those family members to inform them about the family group conference and they chose to attend. The private family time of the first family group conference was fiery and the coordinator was asked on two occasions to come back into the meeting to assist with disagreements. However, in the end, the family, including the father, felt delighted with themselves, as they had not only resolved the family rift, but had also agreed that the child would live as an interim measure with one of the half-sisters. It is sometimes tempting for a coordinator not to make concerted efforts to contact other family members, either because of opposition from within the family, or because of the time and effort required to track them down. However, experience has shown that taking the risk, and putting in the time and effort will, in most cases, pay off for the child concerned.

- Coordinators have the power and responsibility for final decision-making about the time, place and protocol of the meeting, even though, by law, they should consult widely with the family before making these decisions and should put the family's wishes into action wherever practicable. How this power is exercised is very important. A practice example of this is a family for whom the coordinator was asked to convene a second family group conference. There was an allegation of sexual abuse by the father in relation to his two small children. His wife was also drinking heavily and appeared unable to keep the children safe. The first conference had been convened in another district. When the family was contacted, they felt bewildered by the process they had been through and were unsure of what they had decided. They felt they had not been consulted about the cultural protocols of the meeting, nor about the timing of the meeting. This was a large family who all wanted to have input. The first thing the coordinator did was engage cultural advice from the care and protection resource panel. The panel provided a consultant to visit family members and discuss with them the venue, who should be at the meeting and, most importantly, the protocol of the meeting. All family members agreed that they would like local elders to attend the family group conference and for there to be greetings and prayers at the beginning and end of the meeting. Refreshments were to be provided for the conference. It was also decided that this conference should be run over two full days, with the family getting together on their own in the evening. The final outcome was that the children, by agreement of their whole family, were put in the custody of family members, with organised and supervised access to their parents.

- The coordinator, social worker, and counsel for the child (a court-appointed lawyer in those cases where matters are before the Family Court) all have the right and responsibility to agree or disagree with the family's plan. This can be interpreted as a power of veto. In practice, there are a number of things the coordinator can do to ensure that this does not become disempowering to the family group, such as ensuring that the family group is fully informed about all the issues involved, particularly any bottom line the referring agency may hold prior to the family's deliberations. Creativity by the social worker will ensure that the family is given the concerns that need to be addressed, without prescriptions about how this is achieved.

- The coordinator has the power and responsibility of deciding who will be resourced by the state to attend the family group conference, and the social worker has the power of deciding which plans, or parts of plans, will be resourced by the state. Since the implementation of the Act, there has been much debate about what the state should, or should not, resource. The *Children, Young Persons and Their Families Act* 1989 is clear that the state has a responsibility to give effect to the family's plans unless, they are inconsistent with the principles of the Act or are clearly impracticable. However, decisions in this regard sometimes appear to be made according to the budget restraints of individual offices rather than on the merits of individual cases.

Conclusion

It is possible for the family to enter a family group conference feeling powerless if the coordinator and referring worker do not take seriously their responsibility of shifting the power to the family group. The primary job of the coordinator is to convene the family group conference in such a way that the family is able to assume responsibility for ensuring their child is safe and cared for. This is a delicate balancing job.

The skills, training and personal attributes of the social workers and coordinator are absolutely critical to the integrity of the process and, even with guidelines and policies in place, the process is vulnerable and dependent on individual coordinators, social workers and the culture of individual offices. There is no magic formula for coordinators and social workers to follow, and the excitement and challenge for workers is to find ways to assist families creatively and flexibly so they can make safe, stable and practical decisions for their children.

4

Research on Family Group Conferences in Child Welfare in New Zealand

Jeremy Robertson

The introduction of *The Children, Young Persons and Their Families Act* 1989 in New Zealand led to a vigorous debate about the merits of family group conferences in care and protection cases and a number of issues were raised by critics: for example, concern about the ability of families to deal with abuse, especially in so-called 'dysfunctional' families; the lack of professional input; and government cost cutting (Geddis, 1993; Tapp, Geddis & Taylor, 1992). Other commentators have suggested that through empowering families, involving wider family members and working in partnership with practitioners, sound and workable solutions to care and protection problems will be found (Barbour, 1991; Connolly, 1994; Maxwell & Morris, 1993; Wilcox, 1991). Unfortunately, much of this debate has been hindered by the lack of research. Many of the arguments presented are couched at the level of theory and anecdote. In this chapter, after briefly describing those studies that have been conducted, contentious issues surrounding the use of care and protection family group conferences in New Zealand are summarised and evaluated in light of the research, gaps in our knowledge are identified, and suggestions are offered for future research.

Existing Studies

The Department of Social Welfare reviewed the 1989 Act a year after its implementation (Renouf, Robb & Wells, 1990). This report provides a brief review of the operation of the Act and its impact on staff and clients. The report is based on the limited statistics then available and interviews with Departmental staff and other agencies. A more substantive report was published in 1991 by the evaluation unit of the Department of Social Welfare (Paterson & Harvey, 1991). This report presents a national statistical profile of care and protection family group conferences and describes how they were organised and operated, the nature of family group conferences' plans and reviews, and the process used to resource their convening and plans (Paterson, 1993). Samples were drawn from nationally representative districts and two postal questionnaires were completed by care and protection coordinators in each district. The first asked coordinators to supply information on five family group conferences they had facilitated during a specified six-month period. There was a 76 percent response rate and this provided data on 184 family group conferences. The second questionnaire covered coordinators' general experience of using family group conferences for care and protection matters. Fifty-four coordinators replied: a 93 percent response rate. Interviews were also carried out in eight social welfare districts with senior social workers and/or social work teams, care and protection panels, workers from agencies who made referrals to coordinators, and people who had provided information and advice to family group conferences. Renouf and her colleagues (1990) and Paterson and Harvey (1991) caution that their results reflect practice during the first 6 to 18 months of the Act and, since then, policy guidelines have been issued and practice is likely to have changed.

A number of other published papers debate the theory behind family group conferences, explore the meaning of the Act and describe the family group conference process (Atkin, 1991; Barbour, 1991; Connolly, 1994; Geddis, 1993; Maxwell & Morris, 1992; 1993; Tapp et al., 1992). Other papers describe the use of family group conferences in care and protection cases based on the authors' experience, some illustrating their argument with case studies (Alexander, 1993; Connolly, 1994; Fraser & Norton, 1993), and two small-scale studies describe family group conferences from the viewpoint of family members who have experienced them (McKenzie-Davidson, 1994; Rimene, 1993). In 1992, the Ministerial Review provided an appraisal of the Act based on the submissions it received. Commentators have also used statistical information collected by the Department (Department of Social Welfare, 1990-94; Maxwell & Robertson, 1991; Renouf et al., 1990). However, there is still no reliable information system and data have been difficult to interpret (Robertson, 1992).

Do Families Participate in Decision-making?

Are families given the opportunity to take responsibility for their children through family group decision-making? When the idea of using family group conferences in care and protection cases was suggested, a number of concerns were raised. Some felt that families might be too 'dysfunctional' to make use of family group conferences (Barbour, 1991; Connolly, 1994; Geddis, 1993). Others thought the extended family would not want to get involved or that the immediate family might not want them involved (see, for example, Angus, 1991; Wilcox, 1991). One way of testing these claims is to consider what research tells us about who are attending family group conferences and how decisions are being made.

To ensure the participation of the family in family group conferences, family/*whanau* (extended family) members must be informed of and encouraged to attend them. As reported by Fraser and Norton in the previous chapter, coordinators report spending some considerable time identifying and contacting family. Renouf, Robb and Wells (1990) report coordinators spending an average of 3-5 hours preparing for each family group conference; most of this is spent contacting the family. Most of the family/whanau contacted attend the conference, but where this does not happen the coordinator usually attempts to record their views to present at it. Paterson and Harvey (1991) reported that an average of six family/whanau members (other than the child) attended each family group conference; this ranged from none (just the child and supporters) to 19. Although most family group conferences have a range of family/whanau attending, coordinators and social workers have mentioned problems with the relatively small number of family/whanau attending some of them (McKenzie-Davidson, 1994), especially those concerning Pakeha or New Zealanders of European descent (Paterson & Harvey, 1991). Coordinators have acknowledged the tension here between having more family/whanau attend, with the greater likelihood of good decisions and plans, versus the hostility that may arise between family members, thus hampering decision-making.

Despite the apparently high number attending some family group conferences, it is difficult to judge whether or not this is an indication of successful family participation. Simply turning up to the family group conference does not automatically ensure participation in decision-making. More needs to be known about how decisions are made and the extent to which those family members with experience and knowledge to make a major contribution to the decision-making are missing from the meeting. It is not enough to assume that the more family/whanau who attend, the better the quality of the decision and plan.

There are a number of elements to a family group conference which are important for family participation in decision-making, including information available prior to the conference, information available at it, private time for the family to deliberate, negotiation of the agreement and formulation of the plan. Most coordinators try to meet personally with important family members. Those contacted by letter are usually sent information on the Act and the family group conference process. However, there has been some criticism that the information provided to families prior to the family group conferences is inadequate (Mason et al., 1992; Paterson & Harvey, 1991; Renouf et al., 1990), limiting the ability of the family to constructively contribute to the process.

Information is presented to the family group conference by both information-givers and referrers. This generally consists of details about the agency's involvement with the child/family, current care and protection concerns, background details and/or assessments of the child and the family/whanau, and descriptions of services the agency can provide (Paterson & Harvey, 1991; Renouf et al., 1990). Information-givers and referrers often indicate, at the coordinators request, what they would or would not like to see happen to the child, although this typically takes the form of a range of options or comments about the options discussed later in the family group conference. Most coordinators in Paterson & Harvey's (1991) research reported being happy with information-givers, although they were sometimes unhappy when they did not provide factual, clear and specific information or appeared not to support the philosophy of family/whanau decision-making.

When Department of Social Welfare social workers make referrals, there is often discussion prior to the meeting as to what they will accept as the family group conference's decision/plan in order to ensure the child's safety. Social workers interviewed by Paterson and Harvey (1991) did not consider that these preliminary discussions interfered with the independence of the family group conference, indicating that they were usually open to other suggestions. On the other hand, Rimene (1993, p. 64) concluded on the basis of her interviews with families that limits were placed on family decision-making by social workers' use of jargon and their presentation of strong views about final decisions (p. 64). Similarly, the Ministerial Review (1992) reported that many submissions to it expressed a concern that professionals were taking over and distorting the family group conference process (see also McKenzie-Davidson, 1994, p. 10). This goes to the heart of the debate about the use of family group conferences in care and protection: who is effectively making the decision – the family, practitioners, or both? While some argue that the family should be left to make such decisions (Rimene, 1993), others argue for a greater role for practitioners (Geddis, 1993; Tapp et al., 1992). In between these viewpoints is an argument for partnership, where the conference decisions are made by all entitled to attend, both family and practitioners (NZCYPS, 1993). The Act requires this. However, in order to make informed decisions it is important that all those participating in the family group conference have an understanding of both the care and protection concerns and the services and resources available to them. There is a fine line between informing and unduly influencing family decisions. So called 'bottom lines' set limits to family decision-making and detract from the notion of family empowerment although, at the same time, they may be necessary to ensure the protection of the child and to avoid situations where the family develops a plan only to find the referrer disagreeing and having to repeat the process.

Having been presented with information, it is expected that the family/whanau will have time to discuss the issues in private. Research indicates that this does not occur in all cases. Paterson & Harvey (1991) state that no reasons were given by their respondents for missing this stage of the family group conference, although this only seemed to occur when just the parents were present. On occasion, information-givers remain during private time. It is unclear whether or not this has truly been at the family's request or is in response to suggestions from professionals (Paterson & Harvey, 1991; Renouf et al., 1990).

After the private family/whanau deliberations, it is normal for the family to report back to the rest of the family group conference. This is usually followed by further discussion and/or negotiation of the decisions, the agreement or non-agreement of the participants to these decisions and the formulation of a plan or specification of how the decisions are to be carried out. Agreement to the decisions, recommendations and plans was reached in about 90 percent of care and protection family group conferences in 1990 (Maxwell & Robertson, 1991; Paterson & Harvey, 1991; Renouf et al., 1990). A few referrers are reported by coordinators to have disagreed with the plan, usually because they considered that the safety or needs of the child were not met or that the plan was not in the child's best interests. When disagreement with the family/whanau's proposals occur, it is most likely to be dealt with by negotiation and compromise.

Practitioners interviewed by Paterson and Harvey (1991) identified a number of potential concerns about family/whanau participation in decision-making: for example, the offender may have abused others in the family, family members may be estranged from one another or family members may not want to make decisions. Two-thirds of coordinators in this research had experienced hostility, either between family members or directed at the Department of Social Welfare, in at least some family group conferences as demonstrated by shouting, verbal abuse, or physical violence. Over half felt that participants' safety had been threatened in at least one family group conference they had run (Paterson & Harvey, 1991). However, conflict is not necessarily bad when handled properly and a good outcome for both the child and the family may still result (Connolly, 1994; Fraser & Norton, 1993).

On the whole, family/whanau are attending family group conferences and taking part in decision-making. There is a high level of agreement amongst participants, and practitioners are generally happy with family/whanau participation. Further research is needed to examine the relationship between attendance, participation and decision-making at family group conferences. These, in turn, need to be related to some measure of the quality of decisions and plans: for example, whether they are carried out or break down and whether or not they protect the child and provide stable care.

Are Children Participating in Family Group Conferences?

It is a principle of the Act that children should be involved in making decisions affecting them. Paterson and Harvey (1991) found that children were present in 79 percent of family group conferences. However, not all parties agree with involving children. A few of those interviewed by Paterson and Harvey (1991) were concerned about the role of the child at the family group conference, believing that the child had too much power as his or her agreement to the plan was required. Others, however, felt that children had too little say. Various reasons were given for excluding children from the family group conference. The child's age or lack of maturity was often mentioned, as was the fact that the family group conference was dealing with sexual or physical abuse. In these cases, other strategies are possible. In Paterson and Harvey's research, 5 percent of family group conferences resulted in a family/whanau member being specifically excluded, usually because they were the alleged or actual abuser, or the child or family/whanau requested it. Other reasons for excluding children concerned their likely response to the meeting: for example, the child might be too scared or anxious. These are legitimate reasons and children need to be protected. But without further data it is not known whether children are more likely to be excluded from family group conferences than abusers.

Are Children and Young People Being Kept Within Families, Community and Culture?

One of the principles of the Act is to rectify past practices of removing children from their families when care and protection issues arose. Relatively high rates of abuse in care, frequent changes of caregiver and placement breakdown have led to moves to keep children in the care of their family (Ban, 1993; Connolly, 1994; von Dadelszen, 1987). However, some commentators (Barbour, 1991; Worrall, 1994) have cautioned against the assumption that kinship care is best, suggesting that this must be examined empirically.

The introduction of the Act in New Zealand led to dramatic reductions in the number of children and young people in out-of-family care. For example, Angus (1991) reported a decrease in the incidence of removing children and young people from their families and an increase in placements with extended families. Renouf, Robb and Wells (1990) found that, although 50 percent of family group conferences lead to a new caregiver, this person was usually a family member. These figures are similar to those in Maxwell and Robertson (1991).

Despite the decrease in residential placement, changes of caregiver between family members may now simply be hidden (Connolly, 1994; Maxwell & Robertson, 1991; Or, 1995). The precise number of children moving from family member to family member is unknown. Worrall (1994) reports preliminary findings from a study of kinship care that kin, particularly grandparents and aunts, have taken an increasing role in caring for children. The lack of preparation, support or financial help offered these caregivers is a matter of concern (Worrall, 1991).

Do Family Group Conferences Result in Plans Which Adequately Protect the Child's Interests?

Concern has also been expressed about family group conferences and the 'potential imbalance in the competing interests of child protection versus family autonomy' (Geddis, 1993, p. 142). For example, some believe it is dangerous to put 'into the hands of the family group who abused the child the final responsibility for making decisions regarding the future protection and well-being' (Tapp et al., 1992, p. 178). Other commentators (Angus, 1991; Hassall & Maxwell, 1991) have noted that this issue is often raised by those sceptical of the family group conference model and argued that the child's best interests are served by involving the wider family.

Does research support these assertions? The requirement that the referrer, usually a Departmental social worker, and the coordinator agree to the family's decision provides a check on its quality. The relatively high rate of agreement at family group conferences (Maxwell & Robertson, 1991; Paterson & Harvey, 1991; Renouf, Robb & Wells, 1990) suggests that these practitioners are usually satisfied that the child's best interests are being met by the plans. This level of agreement may reflect a decision-making process where 'bottom lines' are being set by practitioners and communicated to the families prior to their deliberations. On the other hand, this may reflect the pressure exerted on practitioners not to disagree with the decision-making of the family, in line with the spirit of the Act. We do not know how much negotiation and compromise is necessary between the family and the worker before agreement is reached.

Some data are available on practitioners' satisfaction with family group conferences. Paterson and Harvey (1991) asked both information-givers and referral agencies how they felt about participating in family group conferences and also about their outcomes. They were generally happy with both, although a number had mixed reactions and experiences. The range of concerns they identified were: being uncomfortable about saying 'negative things' about the family; attending a poorly facilitated family group conference; finding family group conferences time consuming and emotionally draining; ensuring the child's safety; lack of follow-up or support for the family/whanau; and leaving issues unresolved. Social workers also expressed concerns about the roles that they and the coordinator played in family group conferences. In some cases, social workers perceived the coordinator as unsupportive to them or siding with the family. On the other hand, a number of coordinators felt that in some cases the practices and attitudes of social workers or lawyers had undermined family/whanau participation.

Many of the practitioners who attended family group conferences were satisfied. They mentioned the strengthening of the family, increased family support for the child and the likely positive effect of the outcome on the child; and they made positive comments about coordinators and their facilitation skills. These comments highlight the importance of the role of the coordinator in successfully managing the decision-making process (Barbour, 1991; Connolly, 1994; McKenzie-Davidson, 1994). It has been suggested that coordinators are caught between being neutral facilitators and child protection workers (Fraser & Norton, 1993), but coordinators are reported to be positive about family group conferences, believing that they allow families/whanau to participate in decision-making and to take responsibility for their children.

Besides making decisions and plans in the family group conference, a further concern has been that, despite high levels of agreement to plans, a number of decisions or plans are not implemented (Paterson & Harvey, 1991; Rimene, 1993). Plans count for nothing if they are not carried out. It is generally agreed that the plans should include a statement of the date and form of the review. Paterson and Harvey (1991) found that three-quarters of coordinators reported regularly including provision for review in their family group conferences' plans. When plans did not include a provision for review, the coordinators said the family/whanau members often carried out the review themselves.

Family group conferences' plans should also contain a statement about regular monitoring of the child or young person. The plans analysed by Paterson and Harvey (1991) did not always contain this. When mentioned, it was usually assigned to family/whanau, the Department, or other agencies. An issue here is who should be responsible for this monitoring – the state or the family? Since there has been no research on the follow-up of family group conferences' plans and/or decisions, it is not known if reviews or monitoring actually take place as scheduled. Renouf, Robb and Wells were led to conclude from their interviews that, 'to date, there seems to have been limited social work monitoring of decisions made at the Family Group Conference and little practical support given to these decisions' (1990, p. 15). Since family group conferences' decisions often require close social work oversight and assistance to prevent breakdown, this lack of monitoring must be of concern. This is confirmed by the findings of Paterson and Harvey that 'decisions were not carried out, (that) reviews were not carried out, and (that) family/whanau members were unclear about, or did not carry out, their individual responsibilities after the FGC' (1991, p. 46). If family group conferences' plans are not being adequately implemented, and this is not being picked up because of lack of monitoring and review, then the plans are failing to meet children's interests. Whether this is due to a fault in the process itself – for example, families are not able to carry out agreed plans – or to poor practice and lack of coordination and communication has yet to be adequately determined.

Are Family Group Conferences Being Used Appropriately in Care and Protection?

According to Connolly, 'the legislation does not make clear what it means by "serious" (abuse or neglect) and hence "severity" and the threshold for calling a Family Group Conference is determined by the workers involved in the assessment' (1994, p. 91). Given the apparent discretion given to social workers, the threshold for cases referred to family group conferences may be too high − that is, they do not get referred for a conference when they should − or too low, in which case the net is widened to include marginal cases (Geddis, 1993; Tapp et al., 1992). Since most cases dealt with in family group conferences do not go to court, there is no real test of whether or not the care and protection concerns warrant state intervention or the degree of intervention. However, some (Alexander, 1993; Angus, 1991) have argued that as the actions and reasoning of practitioners are open to the scrutiny of the family and because practitioners must provide clear information to the family group conference, this helps focus social work practice and avoids perpetual involvement in marginal situations (Barbour, 1991). It has also been suggested that family group conferences may not be suitable for all care and protection cases: for example, cases of intra-familial sexual abuse (Barbour, 1991) or disputes about custody (Connolly, 1994).

In New Zealand, the Children and Young Persons Service (the service agency of the Department of Social Welfare) is using informal family/whanau meetings as well as, or instead of, family group conferences. These family meetings are convened by social workers and usually involve a narrower range of family members. Generally, they are used when the child is not judged to be at immediate risk, funding is not needed, the family/whanau are cooperative, or the legal authority of a family group conference is not needed to ensure that plans are implemented (Paterson & Harvey, 1991, p. 11). Coordinators have commented positively on the use of these family/whanau meetings; social workers tend to see them as less intrusive than family group conferences and justify their use under the minimal intervention principle of the Act. However, these meetings are not mentioned in the legislation and hence do not have the protections associated with family group conferences. For example, it is unclear who is entitled to attend, who must agree to the outcome, and what happens when no agreement is reached. There is a danger that they may be used in those marginal cases that would not stand up to formal scrutiny at a family group conference. Rimene (1993), for example, concluded from her interviews that the lack of extended family involvement in these meetings was disempowering and isolating for the families involved.

Data from the Department of Social Welfare indicate that despite the increasing number of notifications over the past five years, the number of family group conferences held has remained constant. This suggests that the threshold for holding a family group conference in care and protection cases has moved higher. There are no data dealing with cases that go on to a family group conference and those resolved by other means, such as family/whanau meetings, referral to another agency, or minimal social work intervention.

Are Families Supported?

Family group conferences have, at their core, the notion that the extended family can assist the child and his/her immediate family to deal with care and protection issues, both by helping with decision-making and implementing decisions. Some argue rather that placing responsibility on families could be seen as a government cost-cutting exercise (McKenzie-Davidson, 1994; Tapp et al., 1992; Connolly, 1994). An indication of the degree of family and state support in implementing family group conferences' decisions is given in the detail of their plans. Paterson and Harvey (1991) analysed copies of plans from the 142 family group conferences and found that:

- three-quarters (77 percent) of the plans mentioned the provision of financial assistance, although few specified how much was to be spent;

- counselling or assessment was mentioned in 45 percent of the plans;

- social work or other professional assistance was mentioned in 38 percent of the plans;

- other services mentioned included travel assistance, clothing for the child, board payments, care allowances and foster parent payments, unspecified financial assistance, health care costs, personal development courses, education, social and recreational costs, and other services to family/whanau or caregivers and the child;

- 13 percent of plans did not include any services at all;

- the agency funding services was usually the Department.

Renouf, Robb and Wells (1990) report that the Department of Social Welfare had a continuing service or funding role in almost 1200 of the 1734 cases (69 percent) they studied that involved a family group conference and Maxwell and Robertson (1991) found that the Department agreed to resource 61 percent of the family group conferences they examined. Data in the annual report of the Department of Social Welfare indicate an increasing number of family group conferences result in an ongoing service role for the New Zealand Children and Young Persons Service – it had increased from 48 percent in 1992 to 64 percent in 1994.

While the Department is providing funds to approximately three fifths of family group conferences, concerns have been raised about the level of funding provided. Renouf, Robb and Wells found that 'fear of operational over-expenditure is making districts very cautious about expending monies for running conferences. There are concerns that the attitude is too parsimonious with some families and that these families are not getting sufficient help for members to attend the conference' (1990, p. 14). As regards the funding of family group conferences' decisions/plans, they also noted that, in some instances, district offices were being overly cautious about agreeing to expend monies to purchase services for the family. Given Rimene's (1993) finding that the families she interviewed lacked resources of their own and were not getting them from the Department, it is probable that some family group conferences' decisions are being made on the basis of affordability rather than need.

Monitoring family group conferences' decisions also requires state assistance. While Paterson and Harvey hold the view that the state has a continuing responsibility for monitoring, this is also limited by the resources allocated to care and protection work. These authors noted:

> Continued state involvement in the care and protection of children requires resourcing, particularly in terms of personnel. The comments of some of those interviewed suggested that there was inadequate follow-up because of lack of DSW [Department of Social Welfare] staff resources (1991, p. 47).

Are Family Group Conferences Culturally Appropriate?

Family group conferences are designed to be flexible enough to allow for culturally appropriate processes and solutions (Hassall & Maxwell, 1991). It was felt that allowing the family group conferences to be held in a culturally appropriate setting would assist family participation. Paterson and Harvey (1991) report that 37 percent of the family group conferences in their sample were held at a district or area welfare office, one fifth (20 percent) were held in community rooms and about one sixth (16 percent) were held at the home of a family/whanau member. Unfortunately, these data are not presented by ethnic group and there is no indication of whether or not families were comfortable using departmental offices as venues. Coordinators indicated that the selection of venue was usually based on the wishes of the family/whanau, but some agencies and information-givers mentioned problems with the venue and expressed a preference for marae (traditional Maori meeting places) and Departmental family homes rather than Departmental offices (Paterson & Harvey, 1991).

Coordinators aim to run family group conferences in a culturally appropriate manner, for example, by having the meeting conducted according to Maori protocol (*karakia*/prayer, welcome and introduction/*mihimihi*). To obtain cultural input, coordinators indicated that they consulted a number of different sources to get information, including family/whanau, cultural advisors, community resource persons, and the local care and protection resource panel (Paterson & Harvey, 1991). Paterson and Harvey also highlighted a number of cultural issues that concerned coordinators:

> Those [cultural issues] mentioned most often were the ethnicity of the Coordinator being different to that of the family/whanau (mentioned by five Coordinators) and issues associated with having culturally appropriate people present at the FGC, for example, how to identify such people and such people not always being available (mentioned by five Coordinators). Other issues mentioned by Coordinators included how to consult the family/whanau in a way which is culturally appropriate, how to be culturally sensitive, and how to deal with differences between family/whanau members of different ethnic groups with regard to how the FGC should proceed (1991, p.24).

It can legitimately be asked whether or not such strategies transcend tokenism.

Other Practice Issues

Referring agencies have reported concerns about the time taken to respond to notifications, the skills of some departmental social workers and time delays in convening family group conferences. These problems can discourage agencies from making referrals. Paterson and Harvey (1991) report that two-thirds of family group conferences were convened within five weeks of the referral date, while one sixth took more than two months to convene; the average was 36 days. This timing was largely due to locating, contacting and consulting the family/whanau. Coordinators reported a tension here between ensuring that as many family/whanau members as possible attend the family group conference and convening it as quickly as possible. Paterson and Harvey's (1991) survey found that 84 percent took only one session to complete, 89 percent were held on a weekday and less than one fifth started after 4:35 p.m. The average time taken was 3.5 hours although this ranged from 1 to 11 hours in length. Starting late or lengthy family group conferences sometimes created problems for agency representatives, as they often had other meetings or appointments to keep.

A number of research studies have reported variations between districts/offices in the use, convening and running of family group conferences (Barbour, 1993; Connolly, 1994; Maxwell & Robertson, 1991; Paterson & Harvey, 1991; Rimene, 1993; Thornton, 1993). This may be due partly to the lack of clear national guidelines to practitioners in the Department. It may also be an inevitable consequence of the family group conference model itself in that it allows for decision-making processes to be determined by those taking part. However, given earlier comments about the importance of the role of the coordinator and the risk of practitioners directing families, these differences may reflect the different practices of practitioners rather than differences in family decision-making.

Future Research

The Children, Young Persons and Their Families Act 1989 arose partly out of the realisation that previous care and protection practices were not effective and, at worst, caused more harm than good (Barbour, 1991; Connolly, 1994). Changes in social work theory and practice called for a new system, one involving partnership with families to address the care and protection of their children. Partnership was to be achieved through the use of family group conferences, where extended families would meet with a limited number of practitioners to discuss children's care and protection and formulate plans.

The research that has been conducted so far indicates that families are being involved in family group conferences, children are being kept within their extended family and there is agreement between family and practitioners on decisions/plans to protect children. But these conclusions beg the most important question: are family group conferences' decisions meeting the care and protection needs of children and young people? There are no follow-up data on outcomes and, in fact, research indicates that there is little monitoring of family group conferences' decisions.

A number of other issues have been identified which have yet to be adequately addressed by research. Both Ban (1993) and Connolly (1994) have raised the issue of family decision-making and gender roles. Given traditional roles within families, is the family group conference decision-making process simply reinforcing gender inequities? Are men making the decisions and leaving it to women to implement them? Is the family group conference process fair for all who participate? Do all participants get a fair hearing? These questions can only be answered by further research.

With limited exceptions, research has yet to interview the children, young people and their families about their experience of care and protection family group conferences. The core question must be: what are the outcomes for children, young people and their families? Connolly in reviewing the Act, reaches a similar conclusion:

> Although these early findings are encouraging, as yet there has been no research evidence to test the quality of Family Group Conference decisions. The quality and measure of success have hitherto been based largely upon anecdotal information from workers involved in the process . . . Research into the long-term experiences of children exposed to the decision-making process will therefore be particularly important if children's permanency needs are to be safeguarded (1994, p. 94).

The Ministerial review of the Act recommended that 'the Commissioner for Children be empowered to undertake independent, longitudinal research to evaluate the outcomes for the children, young persons and their families affected by the Act' (1992, p. 193). Along with the Department, the Commissioner has recently produced a research specification for a study of outcomes under the Act. The results of this research may well provide answers to many of the questions about care and protection family group conferences which remain unanswered.

References

Alexander, R. (1993, December). The effect of legal changes, 1986-1993, on DSW therapy services. *New Zealand Psychological Society Bulletin*, 31-32.

Angus, J. (1991). The Act: One year on – Perspectives on the Children, Young Persons and Their Families Act 1989, *Social Work Review, 3*(4), 5-6.

Atkin, W. (1991). New Zealand: Let the family decide: The new approach to family problems. *Journal of Family Law, 29*(2), 387-397.

Ban, P. (1993). Family decision making – The model as practised in New Zealand and its relevance in Australia. *Australian Social Work, 46* (3), 23-30.

Barbour, A. (1991). Family group conferences: Context and consequences. *Social Work Review, 3*(4), 16-21.

Connolly, M. (1994). An act of empowerment: The Children, Young Persons and Their Families Act (1989). *British Journal of Social Work, 24*, 87-100.

Department of Social Welfare. *Annual Reports, 1990-1994.* Wellington, New Zealand: Department of Social Welfare.

Fraser, S., & Norton, J. (1993). *Walking the tightrope – the New Zealand family group conference way.* Paper presented at the Fourth Australasian Conference on Child Abuse and Neglect, Brisbane, Australia.

Geddis, D. (1993). A critical analysis of the family group conference. *Family Law Bulletin, 3* (11), 141-144.

Hassall, I. B., & Maxwell, G. M. (1991). The family group conference: A new statutory way of resolving care, protection and justice matters affecting children. In *The Office of the Commissioner for Children, An appraisal of the first year of the Children, Young Persons and Their Families Act 1989: A collection of three papers* (pp. 1-13). Wellington: The Commissioner for Children.

Mason, K., Kirby, G. & Wray, R. (1992). *Review of the Children, Young Persons and Their Families Act, 1989: Report of the Ministerial Review Team to the Minister of Social Welfare Hon. Jenny Shipley.* Wellington: Department of Social Welfare.

Maxwell, G. M., & Morris, A. (1992). The family group conference: A new paradigm for making decisions about children and young people. *Children Australia, 17*(4), 11-15.

Maxwell, G. M., & Morris, A. (1993). *Family group conferences: Key elements.* Paper presented at the Mission of St James and St John, Australia.

Maxwell, G. M., & Robertson, J. P. (1991). Statistics on the first year of the Children, Young Persons and their Families Act 1989. In *The Office of the Commissioner for Children, An appraisal of the first year of the Children, Young Persons and Their Families Act 1989: A collection of three papers* (pp. 14-23). Wellington: The Commissioner for Children.

McKenzie-Davidson, M. (1994). *Family decision making as a preventative solution in child protection.* Paper presented at the 10th International Congress on Child Abuse and Neglect, Kuala Lumpur, Malaysia.

New Zealand Children and Young Persons Service. (1993). Critical analysis of FGCs: A response. *Butterworths Family Law Journal, 1*(1), 7-8.

Or, A. (1995). *"They can really claim the child"; Factors affecting the decision to place children under the legal responsibility of foster parents. A feasibility study.* Thesis MA (Applied) in Social Work, Victoria University of Wellington.

Paterson, K. (1993). Evaluating the organisation and operation of care and protection FGCs. *Social Work review, V*(4), 14-18.

Paterson, K., & Harvey, M. (1991). *An evaluation of the organisation and operation of care and protection family group conferences.* Wellington: Department of Social Welfare.

Robertson, J. (1992). How many abused and neglected children? *CHILDREN, 7,* 5-6.

Rimene, S. (1993). *The Children, Young Persons and Their Families Act 1989, from a Maori Perspective.* Thesis MA (Applied) in Social Work, Victoria University of Wellington.

Renouf, J., Robb, G., & Wells, P. (1990). *Children, Young Persons and their Families Act: Report on its first year of operation.* Wellington: Department of Social Welfare.

Tapp, P., Geddis, D. & Taylor, N. (1992). Protecting the family. In M. Henaghan, & B. Atkin (Eds), *Family law policy in New Zealand* (pp. 168-209). Auckland: Oxford University Press.

Thornton, C. (1993). *Family group conferences: A literature review.* Lower Hutt: Practitioners' Publishing.

von Dadelszen, J. (1987). *Sexual abuse study: An examination of the histories of sexual abuse among girls currently in the care of the Department of Social Welfare.* Department of Social Welfare, Research Series No. 7, Wellington.

Wilcox, R. (1991). *Family decision making: Family group conferences: Practitioners' views.* Lower Hutt: Practitioners' Publishing.

Worrall, J. (1991). Foster care in the 1990s. *Social Work Review, 3*(4), 15.

Worrall, J. (1994). *The CYPF Act and kinship care.* Paper presented at the IYF Family Rights and Responsibilities Symposium, Wellington, New Zealand.

5

Family Group Conferences with Young Offenders in New Zealand

Trish Stewart

The family group conference developed in New Zealand as a new and flexible method for making decisions about the way in which the state would become involved in the lives of children and young people in a range of situations. For youth justice, the importance of the procedure lies in the extent to which it can be used to:

- increase the range of diversionary options through which young offenders can be made accountable for their offending;

- ensure a shift in philosophy from one of unilateral state intervention in the lives of children, young people and their families to one based on partnership with the state;

- enable culturally diverse processes and values to be recognised and affirmed; and

- involve victims in the decisions about outcomes for the children and young people who have offended against them.

This chapter sets out a description of the roles of all the entitled participants in the youth justice family group conference process in New Zealand and then describes the convening and facilitation of a conference and post-conference procedures. It focuses on the coordinator's role, describes tasks carried out by other youth justice staff, and concludes with two case studies.

Key Actors and Their Roles

The legislation defines those entitled to attend a family group conference. These are: the child or young person; their parents, guardian or carer; members of the family, whanau, or family group of that child or young person; a representative of an iwi or cultural authority in whose care the child has been placed; the youth justice coordinator; a representative of the police; any victim of the offence or alleged offence to which the conference relates or a representative of that victim and a supporter of the victim; any barrister or solicitor or youth advocate or lay advocate representing the child or young person; a social worker in certain defined situations and any other person whose attendance at that conference is in accordance with the wishes of the family, whanau, or family group.

Children and Young Persons

The stated objects of the legislation in respect of young offenders are described on page 13 in Chapter 2 of this book. They can be summarised as aiming to ensure that where children or young persons commit offences:

(i) they are held accountable, and encouraged to accept responsibility for their behaviour; and

(ii) they are dealt with in a way that acknowledges their needs and that will give them the opportunity to develop in responsible, beneficial and socially acceptable ways.

Young persons at the conference, like all participants, need to have been well-informed before the meeting. They need to know in advance that victims may forcefully express their hurt and anger, and that it is their right to do so without interruption. How the young person reacts or responds to the victim's statement will influence the outcome of the conference for all. Management of this stage of the conference is a crucial task for the coordinator. The young offender, along with the other entitled participants, has a right to agree or disagree to conditions of the plan. In extreme cases, where agreement cannot be reached, the Youth Court judge will be required to make a decision.

Families

The role of the family is crucial in the family group conference process: the New Zealand legislation was drawn up after lengthy consultation with Maori, and states as a general principle that 'wherever possible, a child's or young person's family, whanau [extended family], hapu [families linked by marriage and identifying with a particular home ground – a sub-tribe], iwi [tribal groupings tracing their descent from the same ancestor] and family group, should participate in the making of decisions affecting that child or young person', and that 'wherever possible, the relationship between a child or young person and his or her family, whanau, hapu, iwi and family group should be maintained and strengthened'. This principle recognises the social structure of the indigenous people; children belong to kin groups beyond their immediate families. Where families have become alienated from their tribal roots as a result of land confiscation, displacement and other social circumstances, the legislation enables coordinators to liaise between families and tribal organisations and assist with reconciliation processes, thus conforming to the principles set down. For Pakeha families (New Zealanders of European descent), grandparents, aunts and uncles, family supporters such as sports coaches, school counsellors or church colleagues and close family friends are potential resources who may contribute to and accept responsibility for supervising plans made for the young person. Their involvement also demonstrates to children and young persons how many people care about them, and assists them to develop a sense of accountability and responsibility to their social circle and consequently to society.

Some families require considerable encouragement to involve people other than the young offender's parents, for reasons of pride and privacy, not wishing to make demands on others, or believing that their son or daughter is solely responsible and should therefore be solely accountable. Considerable work before the conference needs to be done with these families. Young people themselves may nominate possible participants who are not family members though parental approval may be sought for the invitation of such persons. The often quoted influence of 'peer pressure' can be used constructively by the inclusion of a friend of the young person who can offer support and encouragement during the period of the implementation of the plan. In practice, conferences for minor offending are often held with only the parents and young person present. If, however, the young person has come to notice before, or the offending is multiple or serious, then every effort is made to ensure attendance of the wider family group. It is the policy of the New Zealand Children and Young Persons Service to consider the provision of financial assistance to enable family members who live at a distance to attend the conference, particularly if they are influential in the family circle or are likely to be instrumental to the outcome.

Because the concept of families being involved in the decision-making process is a new experience for many, careful preparation is of vital importance. The truth of the old adage 'knowledge is power' is particularly relevant in family group conferencing and practitioners must be meticulous in providing full information to families and in supporting and encouraging those who have been long used to being powerless when dealing with bureaucracies. The empowering of families has necessitated considerable surrendering of bureaucratic power, and this has sometimes been a challenging process for practitioners more used to being in control of decision-making.

Victims

New Zealand enacted legislation defining the rights of victims of offences and victim support groups are now established in most main centres. Victims' details such as names and addresses and, if applicable, a Victim Impact Report prepared by police are made available to the coordinator by the youth aid officer or the prosecutor.

Victims may attend the conference or convey their views, either verbally or in writing, to the coordinator who will present them on the victim's behalf. The legislation originally stated that any victim *or* their representative was entitled to attend the family group conference. This meant victims could decide against attending a family group conference if expected to do so alone. In practice, most coordinators permitted victims to bring supporters. This practice has now been endorsed by a 1994 amendment to the *Children, Young Persons and Their Families Act* 1989 which stipulates the right of the victim to bring supporters and, in addition, to be consulted as to a suitable time, date and venue for the family group conference. Police information normally names one victim per offence. In practice, however, the victims of an offence such as house burglary include all residents of the home, and parents occasionally bring their children whose fears following the burglary can often be allayed by meeting the offender, being offered apologies, and observing and participating in the process of the family group conference.

The concept of restorative, as opposed to adversarial, justice was probably not a foremost concern of the original legislators, but this has emerged from practice as a key factor in dealing with juvenile offenders. Children and young people have a very strong sense of what is 'just', and the opportunity to observe and participate in a process which they can agree is 'fair' bodes well for healing victims' hurts, and creates the opportunity for children and young persons to express their remorse and, hopefully, to be less likely to re-offend. In practice, a conference without victims' participation can become another exercise in adults lecturing young people with little lasting effect.

Victims' confidentiality is maintained by not revealing details of absent victims to offenders, and fears of any recrimination to victims following a family group conference have proven groundless by the experience of the past five years. Victims should be informed of family group conference's decisions, even where they do not attend, and of the eventual outcome of the plan. Coordinators can offer travel assistance or other expenses involved in victims' attending family group conferences, such as loss of wages or the cost of child-care.

Information-givers

The legislation states that the youth justice coordinator should take all reasonable steps to ensure that all information and advice required to carry out conference functions are made available to the conference and that an information-giver 'may attend the conference for that purpose, but may otherwise attend the conference only with the agreement of the conference'. This clause enables a coordinator to invite, for example, a school counsellor who can give information about the young person's schooling, attainments, attitudes, and any areas of concern. Usually, such information-givers are excused from further participation once they have provided their information. They have no role in the decision-making process itself.

Occasionally, the services of an interpreter may be required and the coordinator needs to contract with an appropriate person to carry out this task. It is not desirable to use a family member to interpret, as the responsibility of translating will detract from that person's ability to participate fully in the conference. The interpreter must understand the conference process, and therefore needs to be fully briefed by the coordinator. Decisions need to be made before the meeting as to whether the interpreter will translate sentence by sentence or simply convey the meaning of the discussion. The coordinator and the interpreter must have a good understanding and be able to demonstrate a compatible working relationship. The interpreter does not participate in the family deliberations, but may need to assist the family in presenting their proposal to other members of the conference after their private deliberations.

The Police

In New Zealand, front-line police officers who have investigated offences and apprehended a young offender refer the file to the Youth Aid Section. A large proportion of juvenile offending is handled by youth aid officers who make home visits to children and young persons and who may divert them by warning, arranging apologies, making financial reparation, or imposing other minor penalties by agreement with families and victims. However, if the young person re-offends, if the offending is serious, if reparation claims are large or if the family or young person are not cooperative at this level, then the officer may refer the matter to a youth justice coordinator for discussion about the possibility of a family group conference. Young people may also be arrested in certain defined circumstances or for very serious offences. They will then appear in the Youth Court and the prosecutor's file will be made available to the youth aid officer.

The primary role of the youth aid officer at the conference is as an informant, representing the police, and also, in the absence of victims, representing their interests. The officer reads the official 'Summary of Facts' of the offending, and may alter details in it following consultation with the offender and victim. The officer then determines whether the young person admits or denies the offending. youth aid officers usually have some knowledge of young persons from previous dealings with them and may convey to the families their concerns or highlight areas of the young person's behaviour which may need to be focused on, such as drug or alcohol abuse or undesirable associates.

Youth aid officers also have a role in educating front-line police officers about the legislation. Although police trainees now receive intensive training in the legislation, initially, front-line officers perceived family group conferences as a 'soft option', since they were intended to reduce the number of young persons appearing in court and the number inappropriately held in custodial placements. Some officers felt the new measures would not be sufficiently punitive. The legislation clearly stipulates the rights of young offenders and suspects in any investigation – rights which had previously existed but which were not clearly understood, were often not adhered to, and were not subject to scrutiny. A residue of opinion of family group conferences as a 'soft option' still exists, but as more officers are exposed to the process and see that young offenders frequently incur penalties and restrictions which are more comprehensive than under the earlier legislation, that outcomes are monitored and that consequences follow non-compliance, resistance on the part of the police is diminishing. Recent amendments to the sections in the 1989 Act on the rights of young persons when being questioned were drafted in consultation with the police, whose ability to investigate offending was, they believed, hampered by the previous statutory requirements. These amendments should further reduce police misgivings about the Act.

Youth Advocates

Following arrest and subsequent appearance in the Youth Court, the court appoints a youth advocate to represent the young person in the proceedings. A family may engage a barrister or solicitor privately but this is rare in practice. The Act states that where the court appoints a youth advocate, 'it shall, so far as practicable, appoint a barrister or solicitor who is, by reason of personality, cultural background, training, and experience, suitably qualified to represent the child or young person'. It further stipulates that where possible the same advocate should be appointed in any later proceedings. The advocate is paid by the court without means or asset testing the family.

The role of the youth advocate is to represent the child or young person in the proceedings and to ensure that the legal rights of the alleged offender are protected. The advocate may attend the conference if requested to do so by the young client. Practice varies, but youth advocates, trained in adversarial methods, initially found the conciliatory nature of the family group conference challenging and, at times, difficult.

Most youth justice family group conferences result from consultation and referral from youth justice coordinators and youth aid officers rather than after an arrest and referral by the Youth Court. If these family group conferences result in successful outcomes, the offender is not then prosecuted through the Youth Court. Consequently, no youth advocate is appointed and it sometimes becomes incumbent on the youth justice coordinator to assume the advocate's role and ensure that the young person's legal rights are protected. If coordinators have concerns about a legal issue, they may invite a youth advocate to attend as an information-giver. In this situation, the youth advocate is not engaged to represent the young person but to give information to the conference on legal issues.

Lay Advocates

The Act states that the Youth Court may 'appoint any person not being a barrister or solicitor, to appear in support of that child or young person in those proceedings'. These are called lay advocates and so far as is practicable they should be 'a person who has, by reason of personality, cultural background, knowledge and experience, sufficient standing in the culture of the child or young person . . . to enable that person to carry out his or her duties under the Act'. The functions of the lay advocate are:

- to ensure that the court is made aware of all cultural matters that are relevant to the proceedings; and

- to represent the interests of the child's or young person's whanau, hapu, and iwi (or their equivalents (if any) in the culture of the child or young person) to the extent that those interests are not otherwise represented in the proceedings.

In practice, this provision is little utilised, perhaps because the interests of the family are represented in the proceedings by its own members. But it does present an opportunity for elders expert in cultural matters to be included in the process.

The court or the coordinator may also order a cultural assessment, in addition to medical, psychological, psychiatric, and social work reports. This assessment requires the person providing it to report on:

- the heritage and the ethnic, cultural, or community ties and values of the young person's family, whanau, or family group; and

- the availability of any resources within the community that would, or would be likely to, assist the child or young person or his/her family, whanau, or family group.

Again, this provision is not widely utilised. Where such reports are used, it is often because the young person or family/whanau are alienated from tribal roots, and they can be useful in assisting staff identify the young person's iwi connections.

Social Workers

New Zealand Children and Young Person Service staff in all but very small districts are employed either as care and protection or youth justice social workers. In small offices, staff may be required to work generically across both specialities. Where a child or young person has issues of care and protection, is in departmental custody through a Family Court order or is under state guardianship, the care and protection social worker is entitled to attend the family group conference. A youth justice social worker may also attend the conference where a child or young person is in departmental custody following arrest and appearance in the Youth Court and where bail has not been granted. In addition, in districts where youth justice social workers assist the coordinator with convening tasks, the social worker may also attend at the request of the family/whanau, particularly where there may be social work involvement following the family group conference. Examples of this would be identifying for the family/whanau available community resources and liaising with such groups. The role of the social worker is one of assessment, information-giving and liaison.

There is a clear division in the legislation between the needs and the deeds of the child or young person. While the Act differentiates between the 'welfare model' and the 'justice model' of dealing with juvenile offenders, the interface created where a young offender exhibits care and protection issues is an area of ongoing concern. Workers in youth justice experience frustration in engaging care and protection social workers to act on the care and protection issues unless the needs are overwhelming. This is a reflection of the difficulties faced by care and protection social workers carrying heavy case-loads and tending to give priority to younger children whose care and protection needs are seen as more urgent. As a result, some youth justice conference plans do contain provisions to cover care and protection needs, in addition to those elements aimed at the offending behaviour. It is in the provision of subsequent social work services that difficulties may arise. For example, families and young persons in some situations might become involved with two social workers with different roles, a situation which can be confusing for them. Occasionally, a young person's care and protection issues are so clearly predominant that the Youth Court can refer the young person to a care and protection coordinator. In such a situation, the Youth Court has the power to discharge the charges or invite the police to withdraw them.

Social workers are responsible for arranging custodial placements when custody is ordered, and for providing a report on the situation to the coordinator before the conference. They are also required to provide social work reports to the court. The coordinator has the power to delegate facilitation of a family group conference and other tasks to a person believed to have the necessary skills and abilities, and a social worker may be occasionally asked to accept such delegation.

Youth Justice Coordinators

The positions of both care and protection and youth justice coordinators were created by the 1989 Act which stated that such appointees should have the personality, training and experience necessary to exercise or perform the functions, duties, and powers conferred on them by or under the Act. Other prerequisites for appointment included experience with young offenders and the ability to promote co-operation between individuals, groups, and organisations providing services to young persons and their families, whanau, hapu, iwi and family groups. In making the initial appointments, the Director-General of the Department of Social

Welfare made it clear that these positions were not necessarily to be promotions for existing social work staff, but that applicants from outside the department with the requisite skills, life experience and aptitude were to be given preference, and that special attention should be given to making culturally appropriate appointments.

Only a few of the original appointees are still practising, and there is a noticeable tendency to make new appointments from within the Department. This is probably justifiable in that some youth justice social workers will have acquired the necessary skills, training and experience, and may, from time to time, have facilitated conferences under delegation from the coordinator.

The duties of coordinators under the Act are to receive reports from the police and explore with them the possibility of dealing with the matter by means other than criminal proceedings, to convene family group conferences in accordance with the legislation, to record the decisions, recommendations and plans made or formulated by the family group conference, and to make that record available to all entitled people. The job description of coordinators is a comprehensive one and includes the requirement to develop and maintain functional relationships with iwi and cultural authorities, voluntary sector organisations, police, judiciary, youth advocates, lay advocates, and the care and protection coordinators.

Within the structure of the New Zealand Children and Young Person Service, coordinators do not have direct line-management responsibility. Supervision of staff is not required but coordinators must liaise well with the youth justice team, and be able to access care and protection staff where necessary. The position is an unusual one, with considerable autonomy; coordinators may at times find themselves having to challenge departmental policy or practice if it seems to contravene the legislation. In most districts, coordinators are responsible directly to their office manager, who is frequently also their supervisor. Some coordinators receive supervision from people outside the Department of Social Welfare. Occasional regional conferences enable coordinators to meet with their colleagues and, to date, there has been one national conference for coordinators. As many districts have only one youth justice coordinator who is, therefore, working in isolation, these gatherings are important and valuable.

The number of family group conferences per week varies considerably. In the largest centres, where the convening tasks are carried out by youth justice social workers, some coordinators may facilitate six conferences per week, although most state that five is the optimum number. In smaller districts, where coordinators do their own convening, three per week is described as optimum.

The Process

Before the Family Group Conference

In most areas, youth aid officers and coordinators consult weekly about each young person the officer wishes to refer to a family group conference. The coordinator reviews information on the case, explores options and alternatives to a family group conference with the officer and tries to ensure that the police are, in fact, prepared to prosecute. If the referral is accepted, the coordinator contacts the family and sets up an appointment for a home visit. At this visit, the process of the family group conference is explained to the young person and family, and a determination is made about whether the young person is going to admit or deny the charge. The worker assesses the attitude of the young person to the offence, and prepares them for participation in the conference, particularly with regard to the victim's presence. Possible elements of the plan to deal with the offending are discussed with the family and they are encouraged to prepare for the conference by exploring a suitable time, date and venue.

Most family group conferences take place during normal working hours, but can be held in the evening or on weekends to suit employed family members. For victimless offences, such as possessing drugs or driving offences, family group conferences can be held in the young offender's home. In cases where victims are involved, a neutral venue is sought to ensure the victims are not intimidated. Where it is feasible and appropriate, a family group conference may be held on the offender's marae (tribal meeting ground, including a meeting house). In such cases, marae protocols will be observed. Where the offender is Maori and the victims are not or are from another tribe, the worker may need to spend time explaining the protocols and re-assuring the victims if they are unfamiliar with the marae setting. In any cross-cultural conference, the coordinator must ensure that no participant feels disadvantaged and must possess the skills, or be able to involve appropriate people, to ensure that difficulties in cross-cultural communication do not detract from the purpose and outcome of the conference. If victims are adamant about not wishing to attend a particular venue, further negotiation with the family is necessary. This seldom occurs. Ideally, a neutral venue is chosen, such as a local hall, community house, school or church hall. Conferences in Departmental buildings are now avoided as they can disadvantage families who may be intimidated by the surroundings of 'the system'. The venue needs to be large enough to seat all participants in a circle, to have another room available where victims and officials can adjourn while the family deliberates privately, and to have facilities for refreshments.

Where young persons have offended together and are facing charges from the same incident, joint family group conferences may be undertaken. These require greater organisation, but spare victims the inconvenience of attending several meetings and eliminate the possibility of a young person disclaiming responsibility for a particular offence by incriminating his or her associate, only to have that associate assert the opposite at a later meeting. The right of each family group to private deliberations can be maintained by requiring a venue which offers sufficient rooms for this to happen. The reporting-back session, where the family puts their proposed plan to victims and police, should also be done separately, since it is not necessary that the plans should be identical in every detail.

The Family Group Conference

The coordinator should arrive at the venue before the other participants, in sufficient time to arrange the seating and organise the refreshments. A circular arrangement of chairs without tables or other obstructions works best, enabling all participants to make eye contact and the coordinator to observe everyone without shifting position. As people arrive, the coordinator introduces her/himself and ensures that people feel welcome. The coordinator should check with the family about whether or not they wish to open with a prayer, blessing, or other protocol. As the participants gather, victims must not be left stranded or left to feel threatened in the presence of the offender and her/his family. When all are present, the coordinator welcomes everyone, and the meeting may open with a prayer, appropriate protocols in a marae, or an opening statement from the coordinator thanking people for their attendance, acknowledging that people are experiencing a wide range of emotions and anxiety, and expressing the hope that, through the process of the conference, people will be enabled to feel comfortable and satisfied. The coordinator ensures that introductions are complete, makes a statement about the reason for the meeting, and describes the process which will take place. A typical statement might be:

> The reason we are doing this today is set down in the law called the *Children, Young Persons and Their Families Act*. What we are going to do today is try to make a plan that everyone agrees with, to deal with the matter. The whole idea is that you, Tony (the offender) should be

responsible for what you have done. This is how we are going to do it. First, Constable Smith will read you the summary of facts. This is the story of what the police say happened. It is put together from what you, the victim, and other people have told the police. You need to listen very carefully when it is read to you, and tell Constable Smith if there is anything wrong in it, because he may be prepared to change it. What he will not change is the "charge" – the name of the crime the police say you did, and when you both have the story right, he will ask you if you admit or deny the charge. If you deny it, we will not discuss it any more. The police can then take the matter to a "defended hearing" where a lawyer will represent you, and a judge will decide whether or not you are guilty after he hears all the evidence. But if you admit the charge, then we will carry on.

When we have dealt with all the charges, the victims will be invited to speak to you about how your actions affected them, how they felt at the time, how they feel now, whether you owe them money, or anything else they might want you to do to make things right between you and them. They may be very angry, but I expect you to listen to what they have to say without interrupting. They may want to ask you questions too, and you will answer them if you can. Your family may have something to say too. When they have finished, Mr Johnson, your school counsellor, will tell the meeting how you are doing at school. Constable Smith may want to tell the meeting of his concerns too. When everyone has finished and you and your family have no questions to ask anybody, we will break up and leave you and your family to have a private discussion, and put together a plan saying what you all think should happen. When you are ready, we will join you again and hear the plan, and check with the victims and the police about whether they agree to it. We may have to do some more talking to get it exactly right, and we will decide when you should get everything done by.

If we all agree, and if you do the things by the date we decide, then the bargain you are making with the police is that they will not take you to Court for this. Of course if you decided not to carry out your plan, you could find yourself telling a judge why not, and the judge might order you to do certain things. Now, Tony, we are all here because of you, and the meeting is about you, so it is very important that you take part in it, and that you understand everything that is being said here. If you do not understand, or have a question, then please let me know so we can answer it for you. I have to inform everyone that what takes place in this meeting is confidential and that this confidentiality is covered in the Act by allowing heavy fines for people who break it.

I ask that we all agree to speak one at a time; if you have any comment to make then probably we all need to hear it; I will ensure that everyone is able to speak. Okay Tony, do you have any questions to ask about all that? No? Anyone else? Then I will ask Constable Smith to read you the summary of facts.

This may read as a long introduction, but it does give all participants a clear understanding of the why the conference is occurring and what will happen. As well, it gives time for participants to 'settle in', provides the coordinator with an opportunity to observe the participants and gauge their reactions and state of mind, helps to engage the young person and the other participants, and creates confidence in the coordinator's ability to facilitate the process. Like an overture, it sets the stage and the tone for what is to follow.

Having responded to any questions, the coordinator then invites the police officer to proceed. The summary is read and the admission is sought. Since this is the beginning of the visible process of the young person accepting responsibility, it is important that the admission is given clearly; the young person may need encouragement to make an audible admission. When the charges have been dealt with, the victims are invited to speak to the young person. Where there is more than one, it may be useful to invite the angriest person to speak first, giving less assertive victims the opportunity to observe the young person's reaction and to be reassured that it is all right to express anger openly. Victims often ask why the offence occurred. Circumstances leading up to the offence can then be examined. When victims finish speaking, an emotionally charged silence often occurs. This is the crucial moment of any conference. All eyes are on the young person, awaiting a response. After a time, if there is no response forthcoming, the coordinator should quietly ask the young person, 'How do you feel now about what you did to these people?' At this point, even the most inarticulate and embarrassed young person can say, or more likely mumble, 'I feel ashamed'. Enquiring as to how the offender feels produces a more visible and honest response than asking if the young person has anything to say, as this query may produce an apology which sounds rehearsed or insincere at this point. Some young persons of course may express their remorse and offer an apology spontaneously, but many are too embarrassed to be able to do so immediately. Having elicited from the young person an admission of feeling bad, the coordinator may agree that 'Yes, you should be feeling bad about what you did. Would you do it again, now that you have heard how your actions affected the victims?' 'No.' 'Why not?' This question gives the young person the chance to indicate that they had not thought about how their actions impacted on the victim and that, having heard about that impact, they realise that their behaviour was wrong. Generally, an apology is now forthcoming. This whole interaction is usually emotional. Voices are low; silences, particularly following the victim's statement, are important because, if victims observe genuine remorse in the young person, then they can move on from anger to forgiveness. Healing has begun, and the young person's 'penance' and progress toward reconciliation can commence. It is not uncommon for tears to be shed during this emotional process, not only by the young person.

It is important for the coordinator to be sensitive, empathetic, unbiased and supportive of both victims and offenders in this interchange as it will colour the rest of the proceedings. When the apology is offered, the coordinator enquires from the victims whether or not it is acceptable to them, and may enquire whether or not they will accept a hand-shake on it. If so, the coordinator then invites the young person to cross the floor and shake hands with the victims. This will not always be appropriate, of course, particularly if the offence is a physical assault, but it can assist the young person to articulate the apology again and, by having to physically move from what is by now probably a slumped and dejected posture, the young person can be assisted to prepare for the next part of the process. The coordinator may now enquire whether the young person's family wishes to speak. In some cultures, other than the predominant Pakeha one in New Zealand, the family group leader may customarily offer a formal apology from the entire family. Where this is not necessarily a cultural custom, a parent may endorse the young person's apology. Since one of the principles of the Act is to maintain and strengthen family relationships, it is useful at this time to enquire what steps the family has taken to deal with the young person since the offence. Most families will have restricted their youngster's freedom and imposed other sanctions such as the removal of privileges. The conference needs to hear of these steps, to take them into account in planning the outcome, and to reassure victims and the police that the family disapproves of the behaviour.

When all victims and information givers have been heard, and all matters for the family's consideration have been presented and the family has no questions to ask victims or the police, usually the coordinator calls a break for refreshments and excuses the further attendance of information-givers. When the conference resumes, the family group meets privately to discuss what they have heard. The other participants wait in another room. When the family indicates that they are ready, the full conference resumes. A member of the family presents their proposal; this generally covers three main elements. First, 'putting things right' between the victims and young person by giving and accepting an apology. The family may decide that the young person should add to the verbal apology with a follow-up letter to the victims present and letters to absent victims. The second element is addressing any reparation. This may be done in a variety of ways. The family may propose a regular payment from the young person's earnings from a part-time job or by selling an asset such as a bicycle or stereo. The family may pay the reparation and have the young person work within the family to repay the debt; or they may offer the young person's services to the victim in lieu of reparation. Victims take a variety of attitudes to the debt they are owed. They may require full repayment and accept weekly payments; they may waive the full claim if they have received insurance and settle for the cost of the excess on their policy. They may accept a portion of the claim, they may ask for a donation to a charity, or they may waive the claim entirely taking into account the young person's circumstances and ask that in return the young person promises not to re-offend. It is not unknown for a victim who is an employer to have a young person work unpaid for them, until the debt is expunged, and then put the young person on the payroll if his or her work is satisfactory.

The third element of the plan is the penalty. This varies depending on the nature of the offending but often involves the young person doing unpaid community work; the number of hours will be agreed upon by the conference. Again, this is usually offered first to the victim or a group or organisation the victim nominates. If this is not acceptable, then the family may propose a group of their choosing, sometimes with suggestions from a social worker. Community work can be carried out in creative ways with the most successful venues providing opportunities for the young person to gain constructive skills and knowledge while carrying out the work. Plans may also include measures aimed at preventing reoffending, for example, a curfew, a requirement not to associate with certain persons or an educational course. The potential for creative penalties is limited only by the imagination of the participants.

All the elements are covered by the mediation process involving the family, victims and the police. Where victims are present and agreeable to the family's proposals, the police usually assent readily to the agreed plan. When the process is concluded, time-frames are set. The vast majority of plans are in place for three months. The nature of the offence dictates whether a shorter or longer period is required. The coordinator checks that the written plan is correct in all details, ensuring that individuals having particular responsibilities or tasks are identified and that dates are stipulated. A review date is set, generally one week before the date by which the plan is to be completed. It is useful to invite participants to make any final comments. This is a valuable closing procedure. Victims will usually wish the young person well; family members often affirm their support for the young person and offer thanks to other participants for their attendance and contribution. The meeting then closes, with a prayer where appropriate, or with a closing statement from the coordinator acknowledging individuals and their input, reminding the young person that, if he or she carries out the plan by the closing date, the files will be closed and the matter ended.

Conferences following court appearances will also discuss how the plan might be framed within the orders available to the Youth Court. These may include an adjournment for discharge on completion of the plan. Other orders range upward in severity, covering admonition, the young person coming before the court if called upon within 12 months so the court may take further action, a fine for the young person or the parents, paying the costs of prosecution, a reparation order against the parents or the young person, a restitution order, forfeiture of property, driving disqualification, confiscation of a motor vehicle, placing the young person under the supervision of the Director-General of Social Welfare for up to six months, a community work order, a supervision with activity order, a supervision with residence order, or conviction of the young person and transfer to the District Court for sentencing.

After the Family Group Conference

The coordinator is responsible for preparing a report of the plan, recommendations and decisions made by the conference and for ensuring that copies are sent to all participants. Responsibility for monitoring the plan now passes to the youth justice social worker whose tasks may involve assisting with setting up the community work, organising reparation payments, or organising assessments and counselling. Should the plan break down, two of the conference members may request the coordinator to reconvene the meeting: an infrequent occurrence. At the review date, if the social worker reports that the plan is not complete, some coordinators write a warning letter to the young person reminding him/her of the possibility of prosecution if the plan is not completed. Normally, however, at the expiry date the coordinator notifies the young person, family and victims that the matter has been completed and the files closed. Alternately, due to non-completion, the referral is returned to the police for their action. In such a case, the police can refer the offender to the Youth Court. The judge may then make any of the available orders.

Case Studies

Case 1: John

The youth aid officer requested a conference for John, a 15-year old accused of twice breaking into a supermarket through a sky-light and stealing $1200 of cigarettes. John sold them to friends. He was attending school and had been cooperative during the investigation. In the past 12 months, youth aid officers had dealt with him for graffiti and shoplifting. His parents were concerned that John was drifting into a pattern of offending. The police were prepared to prosecute. The coordinator accepted the referral. A home visit was made to John and his family and information given about the family group conference process. The family asked that the grandparents, John's married sister and her husband, and John's teacher be invited. The manager of the supermarket agreed to come to the meeting. A booking was made in a community house convenient for the family and the manager, and the meeting date was set. The teacher agreed to attend to give information.

At the conference, John was repentant, saying he had done the burglaries to get money. The supermarket manager accepted his apology. The teacher said that John did not cause concern at school, that his work was generally adequate, and that he had observed that John had difficulty making friends. John agreed that some boys now admired him for doing the burglaries, were keen to buy cigarettes cheaply from him, and wanted to be his friends. After their deliberations, the family proposed that John sell his stereo and contribute the proceeds to the reparation, undertake 50 hours of community work and be curfewed. It was also proposed that the family would regularly check with the school to ensure John's homework was done. John's grandfather proposed to take him fishing regularly so that they could spend more time together.

The manager agreed to John doing his community work at his supermarket and proposed that John should appear to be an employee like the other school boys employed packing shelves. He was to call for a job interview and be given an appointment. His working hours would then be arranged. The manager also accepted the offer to sell John's stereo, so that John would 'feel the pinch', but asked that John purchase from the proceeds the required black trousers and white shirt to work at the supermarket and donate the remainder to the Children's Hospital. He further stated that when John had completed his 50 hours unpaid work and, providing he was punctual and worked satisfactorily, he would then be given part-time employment. Only the manager and John would know the circumstances of his working at the supermarket. John was visibly happy about these arrangements, as was his family. The police agreed to the plan and agreed not to prosecute if it was completed by the three months' expiry date. John fulfilled all conditions of his plan.

Case 2 : Tama

Tama, a 16-year old Maori boy, appeared in the Youth Court following his arrest on two charges — assault with intent to injure and robbery. His co-offenders were aged 19 and 23 and they appeared in the District Court. The offence took place at 12.30 a.m., in a darkened city street. The victim was 18 and had been accosted by the offenders with a demand for money. When he refused, one pulled a knife and the attackers then took his wallet, jacket and shoes, punched and kicked him and ran off. All three offenders were apprehended drinking in a city park at 3:00 a.m. Tama had spent the remainder of the night in a police cell until his appearance at the Youth Court at 10.00 a.m. The youth advocate interviewed him at 9.30 a.m. The judge remanded Tama for two weeks in the custody of the Director-General of Social Welfare and ordered a family group conference to consider the questions of custody and jurisdiction (that is whether the matter should be dealt with in the Youth Court or the High Court). No plea was entered at this time. Tama was placed in a Departmental residence and work began to locate his family whose whereabouts were unknown, although he said they lived in a country town.

The coordinator contacted a local elder of Tama's likely tribe who identified the family, confirming they resided in the country town. Telephone contact was made with an aunt in the town who informed the coordinator that Tama's father had died when Tama was ten. Tama had run away from home about two years ago; his mother had since moved and her whereabouts were unknown. He had a large extended family still living in the country town. The aunt expressed concern for Tama and agreed to visit him in the residence. The youth justice social worker met with Tama, who said that after his father's death his mother had taken a partner whom he hated so he had run away to the city where he survived on the streets, moving constantly and committing petty offences. Tama admitted to using alcohol, marijuana and pills. He had sniffed glue and drunk methylated spirits. He had no close attachments and did not know his co-offenders well; the offence had occurred after they had been drinking and wanted money for more.

A conference was convened to consider Tama's placement while in custody, to determine his plea, and to make recommendations about jurisdiction. If he were to admit the offence, the conference would also consider a possible sentencing outcome, although detailed planning would not be undertaken at this stage. The coordinator then visited the victim and his family and explained the legal processes and the purpose of the family group conference. The victim was making a good recovery from the attack and had not sustained any lasting physical injury, but his attackers' ethnicity was the subject of derogatory remarks from his family. Tama, meanwhile, attempted to abscond from the residence and was placed in the secure unit there. It was decided to hold the conference at the residence, to lessen the temptation for him to attempt to abscond again. Arrangements were made for four family members, including his aunt, to come to the city and be accommodated overnight. The victim and his parents agreed to attend.

The coordinator arranged for lunch to be available at the conference, which was likely to be long. Before the meeting, an emotional re-union took place between Tama and his whanau, and Tama dropped his tough facade and cried as he was greeted and embraced. The whanau included a respected elder (Tama's great uncle) who opened the meeting with the customary *mihi* or welcome. In his speech in Maori, he identified himself with the canoe in which his ancestors arrived, with his local mountain, his river, and thus acknowledged his family's ancestral link to the land. He acknowledged Rangi, the Sky Father, and Papatuanuku, the Earth Mother, and invoked them and the spirits of the ancestors to bless the proceedings. He acknowledged the local people and the meeting place. He welcomed the victim and his family individually, and the officials present, and then spoke a prayer of invocation. He translated his speech into English, and then his family stood to affirm his speech with an appropriate song in Maori. He then concluded his speech and handed the proceedings to the coordinator. The coordinator acknowledged the opening and proceeded, adding to the usual opening remarks information about the particular tasks of the conference to consider custody and jurisdiction. The youth advocate had consulted with the young person and reported on the police evidence; the young person subsequently admitted the offence with a slight alteration to the summary of facts, which was not disputed by the victim.

The victim then spoke of the effect of the attack on him; his words had a visible effect on Tama, particularly when the victim pointed out that there was only two years between them and that he too had got into trouble with the law as a young teenager. His parents also added their comments and asked Tama why he had removed himself from his family connections. They were clearly impressed by what Tama's uncle had said and by his manner and bearing, but also challenged the family for having lost track of

Tama. On the question of custody, the victim and his family took the view that Tama should lose his liberty for a short period, to teach him what that would mean if he earned a prison term. They expressed the view, however, that he should not be imprisoned for this offence, that the matter should remain in the Youth Court, that the orders available to that court should be used and that a detailed plan should be prepared. The police took the view that because of the serious nature of the offence and public concern at the increasing frequency of similar offences, the matter should go to the High Court.

Tama followed the discussion closely. He then stood and made a sincere and spontaneous apology to the victim. He also assured him that he would never do such a thing again. Family members praised him for the manner of his apology. The victim and his family also complimented him. They then pointed out to the police officer that the co-offenders were 'getting off lightly' by comparison to Tama, as they did not have to face the victim, and that the police should take this into account. The conference broke for lunch and all the parties mingled in a relaxed way. The family and Tama then deliberated privately to consider all they had heard. Their proposal to the meeting was that, in regard to custody during the remand, Tama should remain in the residence. He had given them his word that he would not attempt to abscond again. Although they would have liked to take him home, they acknowledged that the logistics of travel for court appearances and an alcohol/drug assessment which they also proposed would be too complicated to be practicable. They recommended that jurisdiction remain in the Youth Court, as they agreed with the victim that reunion with the family and rehabilitation were more desirable than a prison term which would harden and alienate Tama further. They acknowledged the seriousness of the offence, but submitted that he had been under the influence of adult associates. They were prepared to cooperate with the Department, as were the whanau back home, to develop a comprehensive plan for a supervision with activity order and subsequently a supervision order. The whanau also asked that, during the remand period, Tama be enabled to visit his whanau at home.

The victims agreed with this proposal, but the police disagreed and preferred the court to make the decision on jurisdiction. The family expressed their understanding of the police point of view and that they would accept the judge's ruling just as Tama would. The conference was then closed by the elder with a prayer and a song in Maori, in which most participants joined.

Subsequently a visit was arranged and Tama was taken by the coordinator and a social worker to visit his whanau in his home town. The whanau had also located his mother who came to the town to meet him. In all, 43 family members gathered at his aunt's to meet him, including a great-grandparent with whom Tama had spent a lot of time. The coordinator informed the family of all the circumstances, and they undertook to identify a Maori-based programme, preferably in the bush country where Tama could undertake a structured rehabilitation programme under close supervision, removed from access to drugs and alcohol. The focus would be on physical activities, survival skills, and guidance from Maori tutors knowledgeable in cultural matters.

At court, for which whanau again travelled North, the elder rose and spoke his *mihi* (speech of acknowledgment) to the judge who acknowledged the elder and the whanau. He then carefully pondered the report of the conference and listened to submissions from the youth advocate and the police. After deliberation, he gave a judgement in favour of Youth Court jurisdiction, based on the whanau's submissions and the views of the victim. He indicated that he would consider a detailed plan for supervision with activity but told Tama and the whanau that he still had the option to convict him and transfer him to the District Court for sentence. He then further remanded Tama in the custody of the Director-General of Social Welfare for planning and reports to be done.

A forestry camp programme was identified that agreed to admit Tama. Detailed plans were prepared by the social worker and funding submissions were approved. The plan included arrangements for Tama's whanau to maintain contact with him. At the next court appearance, the judge accepted the plan but took an unusual step. He imposed a supervision with activity order (3 months) on the assault with intent to injure charge, but on the second charge remanded Tama for three months and ordered that he appear in court with a progress report from his supervisor. If this was good, then on the second charge he would impose a supervision order, but, if Tama had not responded to the programme, then he was liable to be convicted and transferred to the District Court for sentence on the remaining charge.

Three months later Tama returned to the court. The change in his demeanour was immediately apparent to all. His chin was up, his voice was confident, and his appearance was clean and tidy. The progress report was excellent and the judge made a supervision order for six months to dispose of the outstanding charge. Tama acquired forestry skills during his sojourn at the camp and found employment with the camp when his time there expired. He has maintained contact with his whanau and, now almost 20, he has never reoffended.

6

Research on Family Group Conferences with Young Offenders in New Zealand

Gabrielle Maxwell and Allison Morris

This chapter discusses critical questions which have been raised about family group conferences for young offenders. In particular, it discusses whether or not family group conferences result in rational and fair decisions, are a soft option which allow young people to escape accountability, are mechanisms that widen nets of social control, coerce families and oppress cultures, adequately protect the rights of young offenders, meet the welfare needs of young people, and truly provide restorative justice. It also examines issues related to the implementation and practice of family group conferences and concludes by presenting some new data on the re-offending of young people who have been involved in family group conferences. Overall, it examines the potential, practice and subsequent dilution of family group conferences within the New Zealand youth justice context.

Research in New Zealand on family group conferences with young offenders has been mainly carried out by the authors of this chapter (Maxwell & Morris, 1993; Morris, Maxwell & Robertson, 1993; Olsen, Maxwell & Morris, 1995). From August 1990 to May 1991, a team of 10 researchers followed what happened to nearly 700 young people who came to attention for offending in one of five different areas of the country. They attended, wherever possible, the family group conferences that were arranged for just over 200 of these young people and interviewed the young people, their families, the victims of their offences and the professionals who were involved with them. When the young people were arrested (there were 70 of these), the researchers interviewed the arresting officer and followed through what happened in the Youth Court. They followed up what happened subsequently for most of the family group conference sample, by interviewing families and checking files three to six months after they first entered the sample. They also collected relevant statistics from national data bases and compiled statistics from the files kept by police, welfare services and the courts. Throughout, the research was bicultural. Maori advised the researchers in the planning stages, helped with the design of questions, interviewed Maori young people and families, advised on the analysis of the data and wrote or advised the research team on issues relating to Maori. A Samoan researcher also participated in the interviews of Pacific Island families and commented on the report.

Other information on the practice of family group conferences is contained in the report of a Ministerial Review (1992) carried out under the Chairmanship of Judge Mason, a report by Jackie Renouf and others in the Department of Social Welfare (1990), a briefing paper edited by Maxwell (1991), recent commentaries (Maxwell & Morris, 1994; Maxwell, 1995), the annual reports of the New Zealand Children and Young Persons Service and the newsletters published by the Office of the Commissioner for Children (*Children*) and the Youth Justice Association (*Te Rangatahi*).

Do Family Group Conferences Provide a Rational and Fair System?

Early writings around the development of the New Zealand *Children, Young Persons and Their Families Act* 1989 (Doolan, 1988) identified equity and proportionality as key organisational principles. Warner (1994), however, has challenged the possibility of achieving a rational and fair system of justice through family group conferences on the basis that they will inevitably breach these ideals. This proposition can be tested by examining the outcomes of family group conferences. Maxwell and Morris (1993) carried out a multiple regression to examine the factors that influenced the severity of the outcomes recommended at family group conferences. This identified as important offence-related factors – the seriousness of the offences committed, the number of offences committed and prior offence history – indicating that the same factors are influential in family group conferences as in more traditional systems. The proportion of variance accounted for by these factors was 29 percent, which indicates that non-offence factors also played an important role. This is equally true of adult courts; the amount of variance accounted for by offence factors in

Maxwell and Morris (1993) is very similar to that in another New Zealand study of the sentencing of adults in the district court (Deane, 1995).

Equal outcomes may not, however, be the most appropriate test of rationality or fairness. Another way of judging whether or not the system is rational and fair is to examine the views of those affected by the offence. Maxwell and Morris (1993) were able to assess whether or not family group conference outcomes were agreed to by all participants, the satisfaction of those involved with these outcomes and the extent to which the court endorsed or modified those family group conference decisions brought before it. They report that 95 percent of the family group conferences studied reached agreed decisions and the national figure reported by the government in 1990 was 90 percent (Maxwell & Morris, 1993). Satisfaction of participants with family group conference outcomes was also reported to be generally high: over 80 percent for all participants except victims. There are two points to note about lower levels of satisfaction by victims. There is no comparable information on victims' satisfaction levels with court outcomes and so this apparently low figure could be a mark of relative success and, to a large extent, victims' views of outcomes were influenced by dissatisfaction with the process external to family group conferences, including such factors as the failure of professionals to inform victims about what happened after the family group conference and to make the necessary arrangements for reparation. Finally, another test is provided by information on the extent to which the Youth Court endorsed the family group conferences' plans for those cases it dealt with. Maxwell and Morris (1993) found that, in 81 percent of these cases, the unmodified recommendations of the family group conference were followed by the Youth Court. In only 11 (17 percent) of Youth Court cases was an order made at a higher level than that recommended by the family group conference.

Are Family Group Conferences Soft Options?

There is little support from research for the suggestion that family group conferences are soft options. Table 6.1, derived from Maxwell and Morris (1993), shows that most young people dealt with in family group conferences received 'active' penalties.

When apologies are added, 95 percent of all cases dealt with by family group conferences involved 'active' penalties, an apology or both. Moreover, these figures contrast with sanctions before the 1989 Act: a similar proportion of young people appeared before the court then as appear now at family group conferences, but only 60 percent of them received an 'active' penalty and apologies to victims were rare.

Table 6.1: Recommendations of Family Group Conferences (N= 199)

		N	%
Active penalties			
	Custodial	3	1
	Supervision	14	7
	Financial	65	33
	Work	82	41
	Restrictions of liberty	5	3
	Sub-total	16	85
Apologies and reprimands		19	10
Welfare only		9	4
No action		3	2
TOTAL		199	100

Whether or not these penalties can be considered 'soft options' for the most serious offenders is a matter of judgement. Although custodial or residential penalties were only recommended by family group conferences in 3 percent of cases, the penalties for other serious offenders often involved quite large numbers of hours of work in the community. A more important question is what, if anything, would have been achieved by a greater use of the 'tough' options of custody and residential placement. Research generally indicates that these more severe penalties do not deter (Roeger, 1995).

Do Family Group Conferences Widen the Net of Social Control?

In developing a new diversionary system, there is always the danger that young people who might otherwise have been dealt with by more informal processes will be drawn into the criminal justice process. One way of examining this is to determine the proportion of young people now dealt with by family group conferences. Table 6.2 provides comparative data on young people dealt with by the police, family group conferences and courts over the period 1991-1993.

Table 6.2: Clearance of police offences for fiscal years 1991-1993

YEAR	TOTAL N	WARNED %	YOUTH AID %	FGC %	COURT %
1991	36084	20	62	9	8
1992	36797	26	55	11	9
1993	36278	25	56	10	9

Source: New Zealand Police

This table shows that about a quarter of the offences committed by young people and reported as cleared by the police were dealt with by a warning from the apprehending officer, that between 55 percent and 62 percent were dealt with through diversionary action by police youth aid officers and that only between 17 percent and 20 percent were dealt with in a family group conference (either through direct referral by the police or by referral from the Youth Court). It also shows that this proportion has remained relatively stable over the period for which data are available.

It is difficult to compare this pattern with patterns in the past when there were only two possibilities: warning by the police or referral to the court. Diversion of juvenile offenders by the police was used through the 1980s and approximately 50-60 percent of young people were dealt with in this way before the 1989 Act. The rest, at most 50 percent and at least 40 percent, were processed through the Children and Young Persons Courts (Morris and Young, 1987). Thus, since 1989, diversion by the police has increased and also family group conferences have replaced court hearings for about three-quarters of those who might otherwise have appeared in court. This suggests that net-widening is not occurring.

Another strategy for examining the issue of net-widening is to compare the type of offenders dealt with in various ways. Examining the characteristics of offenders for whom family group conferences are used within the New Zealand system can also answer questions raised in other countries about the level of seriousness of offences that can suitably be dealt with by family group conferences. Table 6.3 describes some of the characteristics of the offenders in Maxwell and Morris's (1993) sample. This demonstrates that it was the young people committing relatively serious offences, older offenders, young people with previous offence histories and those committing a large number of offences who were dealt with through direct referral to family group conferences, in comparison with those dealt with by police diversionary procedures. Those arrested (who, on the whole, were committing even more serious offences and who were also older, more experienced and more prolific offenders) were also referred to family group conferences. This again seems to refute suggestions that the use of family group conferences necessarily encourages the referral of less serious offenders into the system.

While the probability of an 'active' penalty has increased and some of these penalties are moderately severe, the point to note is that the formality of the intervention has decreased markedly. Fewer cases now appear in court: the rate of court appearances has decreased on average

Table 6.3: Comparison of Police Diversion and Police-Referred FGC Cases Compared to Arrest Cases

	POLICE DIVERSION (N=415)	POLICE-REFERRED FGCS (N=187)	ARREST (N=69)
AGE	%	%	%
Under 13	38	26	0
14-16	62	74	100
SERIOUSNESS OF OFFENCE			
Minimum	70	16	10
Medium/minimum	9	11	21
Medium	20	66	51
Medium/maximum or maximum	1	7	18
TYPE OF OFFENCE			
Assaults/robbery/sexual	4	14	22
Burglary	13	35	29
Car conversion	8	16	16
Theft/fraud, etc.	53	26	16
Drugs/anti-social	6	3	4
Property damage & abuse	15	3	0
Other, including traffic	1	3	12
PREVIOUS HISTORY			
Yes	31	83	90
No	69	17	10
NUMBER OF OFFENCES			
1	92	68	57
2	5	17	31
3	2	5	6
> 3	1	10	7

from 63 court appearances per 1000 young people aged 14-16 in the three years before the Act, to a rate of only 16 per 1000 – a decrease of nearly a quarter on average from pre-Act figures. Fewer young people appearing in court now receive court orders. Before the Act, 39 percent of cases were dismissed, withdrawn or discharged; this contrasts with 1990 when half the recorded cases were dismissed, withdrawn or discharged and only 2 percent involved residential detention. Comparative figures on sentences involving residential placements before the Act are not available but some indication of the change is provided by the fact that while there were 200 places in residences for young offenders before the Act, there are now only 76. Thus, fewer young people are receiving sentences of supervision with residence, the sentences are generally shorter (maximum three months) and fewer young people are remanded in custody. Sentences which involve custody are much less frequent now than before; there were on average 374 cases per year sentenced to imprisonment or corrective training before the Act compared to 112 in 1990: less than a third of the average number in the preceding three years. Overall, young people are now much more likely to be dealt with by informal means, within the community and without a record of a conviction.

Do Family Group Conferences Coerce Families and Increase State Control?

Families, young people and victims are all now key decision-makers. However, there is another important party to the decision-making – the state. It is the professionals who represent the state who make the arrangements for family group conferences, invite the participants to them, manage the process and must agree to the decisions. There is little doubt, therefore, that the state's interests are being served too. The family group conference is a process for ensuring that young people are made accountable to the state as part of its responsibility for dealing with offending. To this extent, family group conferences are part of the system of social control. The involvement of families in decision-making can be seen, cynically, as an effective way of expanding the system of social control by making families instruments of the state in this task. Even when families report that they are satisfied with family group conferences' outcomes, the reality of this can be questioned.

Certainly a number of findings in Maxwell and Morris (1993) give cause to doubt that families were always free to choose: it was almost invariably the professionals who provided the informational basis for decisions, families were not always allowed time to deliberate on their own, and, sometimes, professionals argued strongly against family preferences. The fact that the police were generally satisfied with outcomes suggests that outcomes were, at least on occasion, pitched relatively high compared with those that a court may have given. On the other hand, the involvement of families can lead to solutions different from those which would have been imposed by a court and potentially more meaningful for the young people concerned. Maxwell and Morris (1993) certainly report a more diverse range of penalties used by family group conferences than in the previous system. Families also reported feeling involved in the decisions and being satisfied with the outcomes; this cannot be lightly dismissed. The argument that involving families in decisions merely increases the power of state control is fundamentally untestable. A system which produces outcomes that satisfy young people and their families and, at the same time, reduces the numbers of young people in court and in custody does not seem to us to be one which has increased social control.

Questions have been raised about whether or not family group conferences may be yet another method of sustaining men's dominance in critical-decision-making procedures. No formal measurement of the participation of women compared to men has been made in the research on family group conferences. On this point, Maxwell (1993, p. 292) comments that family group conferences are, in practice, 'places where women's voices are heard'. The reality of family life is that women usually decide about children and this often advantages them in a conference which involves decisions about children. Indeed, arguably, of the variety of dispute resolution fora currently available, the family group conference, on the whole, reproduces less of the traditional disadvantages experienced by women involved in disputes.

Are Family Group Conferences Culturally Responsive?

Keeping faith with indigenous peoples is an issue that is currently widely debated. In New Zealand, the demands of Maori are based on the Treaty of Waitangi which guarantees to Maori sovereignty over their people and culture. Translating these claims into modern idiom signifies, at the very least, participation by Maori in all decisions affecting them, including those related to criminal justice. A key issue here is the extent to which Western systems of criminal justice can accommodate elements of an indigenous approach. To be truly responsive to the needs of different cultures, there has to be a different way of reaching decisions, a different type of spirit and underlying philosophy and, potentially, different outcomes from those traditionally available in criminal justice contexts. In each of these respects, the practice of youth justice in New Zealand shows both limitations and successes.

The family group conference is an attempt to give a prominent place to culture in reaching decisions. But research (Olsen et al., 1995) has shown that although family group conferences could transcend tokenism and embody a Maori process, they often failed to respond to the spirit of Maori or to enable outcomes to be reached which were in accord with Maori philosophies and values. Nor has there been any discussion at all in this context of how paying one's penalty might be given a cultural meaning and significance. On the other hand, there are difficulties in knowing what this might mean. Traditional Maori methods of justice were not always benign; utu (a traditional system of redressing wrong) could involve death, slavery or exile. And even today, there are varied views on what it means to talk about justice the 'Maori way'.

For Maori to develop their own systems requires the commitment of resources. With respect to the provisions of services, the Government has failed to honour its commitment to provide the iwi and cultural services described in *The Children, Young Persons and Their Families Act* 1989. Several marae do offer services for Maori families and young people but, for the most part, without adequate funding, although new protocols for iwi services are currently being negotiated.

In summary, therefore, the new system remains largely unresponsive to cultural differences. However, there is at least the potential for family group conferences to be more able to cope with cultural diversity than other types of tribunals. This is best summed up in the words of the Maori researchers involved in the project coordinated by Maxwell and Morris (1993):

> We feel that the Act for the most part is an excellent piece of legislation which promises exciting possibilities for the future. When the processes outlined in the Act were observed, Maori families were indeed empowered and able to take an active part in decisions concerning their young people. It is not difficult to see the beneficial influences that the Act may eventually exert on wider Maori, Polynesian and Pakeha society. Maori society could gain immensely from legislation that acknowledges and strengthens the hapu and tribal structures and their place in decisions regarding the wellbeing of young people and from legislation that provides them with an opportunity to contribute to any reparation and to support those offended against. The same scenario would apply to Pacific Island peoples. [The whole of] society would also benefit from a process which acknowledges the family and gives redress to victims (p. 187).

Do Family Group Conferences Protect Young People's Rights?

Informal systems, such as police diversion and family group conferences, can encourage young people to admit offences to get matters over and done with quickly and, hence, to forgo due process protections. Research by Maxwell and Morris (1993) showed that the police did not always ensure the presence of an adult before taking a statement and did not always inform young people of their rights. In the family group conference, there is no mechanism for ruling out evidence obtained improperly, nor in Maxwell and Morris (1993) did the youth justice coordinators always check that the child or young person agreed with all the details contained in the summary of facts before admitting their offending.

The rights of young people can be protected through the provision of legal representation. However, most young people do not have legal advice or representation because they are dealt with by police warning or by direct referral to family group conferences. Discretionary decision-making does take place at these points, but these young people miss out on advice or representation. In Maxwell and Morris (1993), there were no examples of youth advocates becoming involved in non-court cases. Thus there was, in practice, no opportunity for young people attending non-court ordered family group conferences to have legal advice about whether or not they should admit the offence or the consequences of any admission. Nor did young people have legal advice in the family group conference when they wished to question details in the summary of facts. Following the Ministerial Review (1992), the Government agreed to extend the role of youth advocates to meet such situations although there is little evidence that this is in fact happening. Even in those cases where the court ordered the family group conference, only 59 percent of family group conferences in Maxwell and Morris's (1993) study were attended by youth advocates although in all cases where charges were laid in court a youth advocate had been appointed. Many of the youth advocates served their clients' interests well. In other cases, clients received a token service with little effective consultation and representation. Some youth advocates were not well-versed in the Act. Others appeared unaware of the details and background of the case. Others still appeared to be arguing in the interests of justice in general or on behalf of the victim rather than on behalf of their client.

Some of the problems identified here could be remedied by improved practice but others are inherent in the current procedures. It would be possible to require checklists to be filled out at the start of a family group conference to record whether or not police followed the agreed procedures and to ensure that issues of denial and agreement were canvassed. However, the pressure on a young person to admit offences and get matters over and done with is a very real one. Other research (Maxwell, Robertson & Morris, 1994; O'Connor & Sweetapple, 1988; Wundersitz, Naffine & Gale, 1991) demonstrates that, rhetoric to the contrary, these pressures are part of the youth court system in Australia and the adult courts in New Zealand. The cost of denial is often long delays and additional expense and these factors affect offenders' decisions in all jurisdictions. These unacknowledged costs may be aggravated for young people because of their lack of sophistication, limited access to resources and pressure from parents.

Do Family Group Conferences Respond to the Needs of Young People?

Welfare issues are a prominent focus of many youth justice systems. The rationale for this comes from two themes: social justice and crime prevention. Certainly there is evidence within New Zealand (Fergusson, Horwood & Lynskey, 1993), and overseas (Farrington, Ohlin & Wilson, 1988), of the link between childhood disadvantage and offending. Most persistent young offenders lack adequate family support, skills and opportunities and providing for their welfare needs can be an appropriate way of redressing social inequality and increasing the chances of crime prevention. The 1989 Act, however, explicitly prohibits bringing young people into the youth justice system solely to ensure that their welfare needs are addressed though its objects and principles refer to enhancing the well-being of young people. Maxwell and Morris (1993) report a number of tensions around addressing welfare issues in a youth justice setting. Because the main focus in the family group conference is accountability, the welfare needs of the young person may not be discussed at all.

In theory, young offenders with specific needs can be referred for a care and protection family group conference. Many of the cases referred there from the youth justice system are not, however, dealt with, partly because of other priorities and partly because there are different opinions about whether these matters should be dealt with by a care and protection coordinator or a youth justice coordinator. One example of such a case was where a group of four young people from two nearby families became involved in regular offending. All four had previously been under the supervision of Department of Social Welfare but were no longer considered the responsibility of the care and protection social workers because they were older and had offended. Their parents provided little supervision and the local schools were unable to manage them. Despite referrals for care and protection, no help was provided during the period of the research. Furthermore, the tasks agreed on at the youth justice family group conference were not completed and the young people were involved in further vandalism and petty theft in the local area.

A further issue that emerged from the Maxwell and Morris (1993) research was that some parents reported seeking the help of the Department of Social Welfare when they began to have difficulty managing their children and before any offending had occurred. However, they reported that the Department was unable to help them. Even those families who attended family group conferences for their children found that the necessary services were not always provided. Some young people were referred to an overloaded counselling service which had a waiting list of several months. Others had long waits for vocational and anger management programmes. Job training programmes have been cut several times since the 1989 Act came into force with the result that the few remaining schemes were asked to take several young offenders at once, potentially recreating the conditions for a school for crime. Although there has been an increase in the variety of programmes offered in some areas, there is little evidence of improvement in the overall availability of programmes to young people and their families.

Are Family Group Conferences Restorative?

One of the most important claims made for family group conferences is that by involving families and victims, they allow damage to be healed and social harmony to be restored. Criteria for determining the achievement of such goals include whether or not offenders, their families and victims attend the meetings, whether or not they see the process positively, whether or not they feel involved in the decision-making and how satisfied they are with the outcomes. Attendance rates at family group conferences in New Zealand are generally high. In Maxwell and Morris (1993), almost all young people and their immediate family attended and their extended family or whanau attended in two fifths. On the other hand, victims actually attended in less than half the cases when they could have been present. This failure of victims to attend, however, was largely due to poor social work practice. Only 6 percent of victims said that they did not want to meet the offender. When invited at a suitable time and with adequate notice, victims attended.

Family group conferences seem to have met with some, though not complete, success in involving young people. Maxwell and Morris (1993) showed that a third of the young people in their sample felt involved, a few more said that they had felt partly involved and around a fifth felt that they had been a party to the decision. Traditional expectations that adults rather than young people make decisions may explain why these figures are not higher. On the other hand, the involvement of young people in family group conferences is, without doubt, much greater than in the courts. Families are very definitely involved in family group conferences. In practice, they almost invariably attend and participate and it is usually possible to find relatives, friends or neighbours who can provide some support. Two-thirds of the parents interviewed in the Maxwell and Morris research said they felt involved and almost two-thirds said they were one of those making the decision. Thus, in contrast to past failures to involve parents in youth justice decisions, family group conferences provide a way of giving parents a real part in decisions about both repairing the damage caused by their child and the future of their child and family. Fears that the process would not work because so many of the families are 'dysfunctional' or would not attend and play an effective part have not been realised.

As already indicated, most families and young people were satisfied with the family group conferences' outcomes. They saw them as fair and fitting, giving them an opportunity to repair the damage that had been done and placing the responsibility for the offence back on the young person. Even when the outcomes were relatively severe, they were seen as satisfactory by 74 percent of the parents and 70 percent of the young people. About 60 percent of the victims interviewed in the Maxwell and Morris research found the family group conference they attended was helpful, positive and rewarding. Generally they said they felt involved and felt better as a result of participating. The meeting with the offender was sometimes described as a cathartic experience; negative feelings about the offence and the offender could be released. Victims also commented on two other specific benefits for them: providing them with a voice in determining appropriate outcomes and meeting the offender and the offender's family face-to-face so that they could assess their attitude, understand more why the offence had occurred and assess the likelihood of it recurring.

Other victims, about a quarter, said they felt worse as a result of attending the family group conference. There were a variety of reasons for this. Perhaps the most frequent and important was that the victim did not feel that the young person and his or her family was truly sorry. Other less common reasons included the inability of the family and young person to make reparation, the victims inability to express themselves adequately, the difficulty of communicating cross-culturally, a lack of support, feeling that their concerns had not been adequately listened to and feeling that people were disinterested in or unsympathetic to them. Only half the victims in the Maxwell and Morris research were satisfied with the outcomes. Sometimes this was because they saw the decision of the family group conference as too soft or too harsh but sometimes it was because the promised arrangements fell down afterwards. The responsibility for this lay as often with the professionals as with the young person and his or her family. Some victims were simply never informed about the eventual outcome of the family group conference. Also, victims may have had inappropriate expectations, especially with respect to reparation, and this may have increased their dissatisfaction. Overall, as a system of restorative justice, family group conferences are not always successful.

However, it is unrealistic to expect that remorse for the harm caused and the healing of victims can always be achieved. That positive and constructive outcome occur at all can be construed as a considerable achievement in contrast to the failure of criminal courts to achieve restorative goals.

Issues of Implementation and Practice

Appropriate arrangements for the management of family group conferences are critical for ensuring that the youth justice system is effective. Key issues are timeliness, funding and resourcing of the agencies involved in arranging the family group conferences, the training and commitment of professionals to the philosophy and objectives of the Act, inter-agency cooperation, the location of youth justice services and monitoring and feedback on both process and outcomes. These are discussed below.

Timely Management of Youth Justice

The issue of the length of time taken for the resolution of a case is important for youth justice systems since actions to deal with offending may lose their impact when they occur some time from the original events. In many jurisdictions, especially when offenders plead not guilty, delays in court hearings are considerable and, when the offences are serious, young people can be held in custody before trial and sentence for lengthy periods. This is still the case in New Zealand when young offenders charged in court with serious offences plead not guilty. In contrast, young people referred directly by the police to family group conferences are dealt with relatively speedily. In the Maxwell and Morris research, 85 percent of such referrals were resolved within six weeks and 95 percent were resolved within nine weeks although non-denied family group conference cases referred through the court took twice as long. These time spans are not unreasonably long but some of these cases were in breach of the statutory time frames originally set in the 1989 Act which were 14 days from referral for court-ordered family group conferences and 21 days for direct referrals. Time limits have now been extended to accommodate Departmental practice. The new time frames in the *Children, Young Persons and Their Families Amendment Act* 1994 allow one month for family group conferences to be convened, and 'convened' has now been interpreted to mean the setting of a date rather than the holding of the family group conference. The impact of these changes has yet to be determined.

Funding Youth Justice

Criticisms have been levelled at the reduction in the number of staff managing the family group conference process, in the budgets available to set up and resource family group conferences and in the availability of programmes for young people and families. 'Funding starvation' is now a term used in relation to youth justice. Data on budgets provide considerable support for these claims. In the first full year after the implementation of the Act (1990-91), 5900 family group conferences were held. To manage this case-load, 48 youth justice coordinators were appointed and, by 1992, they were supported by a staff of approximately 200 youth justice social workers. Since then, the number of family group conferences has increased to 7,500 for 1993-94, the number of full-time youth justice coordinators has risen to 50 and the number of youth justice social workers has increased to about 230. On average, each youth justice coordinator now manages 136 family group conferences per year compared with 123 in 1990-91.

The role of the youth justice social workers is also changing. Until 1994, they played an integral role in arranging and organising family group conferences as well as supporting and providing follow-up to young people and their families after the family group conference. Increasingly, the role of assisting in arranging family group conferences is being phased out in favour of an emphasis on providing support services as required after the family group conference has made plans and recommendations. It is likely that all of this has led to fewer people being present at family group conferences, to more time being taken to arrange family group conferences and to jeopardising the quality of the decisions reached at family group conferences.

The total budget for youth justice has dropped from 34.5 to 27.5 million between 1991 and 1994 and, of this, the amount allocated for operational expenditure has declined even more dramatically, from 11.5 to 4.5 million. The data show that financial resources in the operational budget specifically earmarked for arranging and financing plans decided at family group conferences have consistently and markedly decreased each year. Over the same period, the number of conferences held has increased so that the gap between funds and demand has increased. Overall, the resources available for family group conferences have probably diminished by a factor of nearly four since the first year of the Act's operation, and possibly by much more. Youth justice coordinators now report that they have no more than $100 on average to resource each family group conference. In practice, this means that they are unable to ensure that family from out of town can attend and assist in reaching solutions, to resource community placements or to respond to families' requests for help and support. The savings inevitably made by fewer young people being processed through the courts, sentenced to residences, and sentenced to imprisonment or corrective training have not been reallocated to provide for the children and young people coming into the youth justice system.

Training and Staff Commitment to Philosophy and Objectives

Adequate performance of the complex roles expected of professionals involved in the youth justice system demands good intake training and effective ongoing training. This was discussed extensively in the Ministerial Review (1992). Judge Mason and his colleagues commented on the inadequacies in both the initial skill levels of staff within the youth justice system and the training provided to them in setting up the new system. Little has changed.

One of the main tasks of training in a new system is to ensure that staff understand its philosophy and the implications it has for their practice. Without this, staff who have worked in the former system are likely to operate very much as before and there will remain dissonance and potential resistance to the changes. A number of commentators (Hassall & Maxwell, 1990; Maxwell & Morris, 1993) have described this problem with respect to police officers, social workers and youth advocates during the early years of the Act; police continued to arrest young people for relatively minor offences, social workers continued to advise families on what they should do and youth advocates failed to consult adequately with their clients and assist them to participate in proceedings. Youth justice coordinators, youth aid officers and Youth Court judges all found that they needed to develop new skills, especially in relation to working with victims, communities and different cultural groups and, on occasion, the quality of professional practice and the skills of professionals were not adequate to the tasks asked of them. Such problems should have lessened over time, but there is no information on this.

Inter-agency Cooperation

The extent and effectiveness of collaboration among the agencies dealing with young offenders has varied throughout New Zealand. Notable failures have occurred in some districts. For example, the police have criticised social workers for being unavailable to take custody of young people and for releasing young people they perceive to be serious offenders into the care of their families, for failing to deal adequately and speedily with young people who are in need of care and protection and for failing to monitor family group conferences' outcomes. At the same time, the police have been criticised for failing to refer young people for family group conferences because of the alleged ineffectiveness of the system or social workers, and for arresting and charging offenders who could have been dealt with through direct referral for a family group conference. Particular problems have arisen around the determination of policy makers to reduce institutional places beyond levels seen as appropriate in some sections of the professional community and debates have occurred about the provision of and grounds for secure care, especially when young people abscond from open institutions. Delays in resolving cases when young people continue to offend can lead to inter-agency allegations of inefficiency and the media have often been quick to seek scapegoats which has often exacerbated the problems. In addition, some police officers and the Police Association (the union for police officers) have been persistently critical of the philosophy inherent in the Act.

Although inter-agency cooperation is an object of the Act, in practice, achieving this has been left to local initiatives and this has had variable results. Many of these difficulties are not particular to family group conferences but are endemic to criminal justice systems more generally. By their nature, professionals develop different cultures, philosophies and views (Gelsthorpe, 1994) and working together effectively remains a challenge in many settings.

Location and Management of Youth Justice

In New Zealand, the management of family group conferences is located in the New Zealand Children and Young Persons Service which also has responsibility for care and protection and adoption. This raises issues about the independence of the process and its practitioners. There is also a continual threat to the integrity of the system as management decisions re-order the relative priorities given to staffing and funding processes within the youth justice system. The extent to which the two systems, care and protection and youth justice, should share resources or be separate has been continually reassessed in the many restructurings that have occurred since the Act (Maxwell & Morris, 1994). This has undoubtedly affected the quality of service provision.

A critical issue is the position of the youth justice coordinators in the management structure and the extent to which they are given responsibility for the budgets needed to ensure that outcomes meet specific goals such as diversion, protection of young people's rights, accountability and responding to the needs of young people and their families. Budgetary controls, as well as funding cuts, influence the functioning of family group conferences and the speed and autonomy of decision-making is jeopardised when permission must be sought from managers for plans and recommendations agreed at family group conferences which have financial implications. The greater these budgetary strictures, the less energy coordinators have in attending to other responsibilities such as ensuring family participation, encouraging family decision-making and providing support for young people and victims.

Monitoring and Feedback About Process and Outcomes

Another important element in maintaining the integrity of any system is the quality of information available to managers, related agencies, public groups and individuals. The New Zealand system has been handicapped by the progressive decline in the amount of regular information available on policing, social welfare and justice matters since 1990, the period immediately after the introduction of the 1989 Act. There were a number of reasons for this: the failure to change the statistical categories used for recording actions in line with the new legislation and new procedures, the removal of some of the earlier data-capturing systems in the interests of economy, and delays in the development of new systems. Moreover, there has been little evaluative research since 1990 and there has been no research on the longer term outcomes of family group conferences.

Reoffending

From time to time, media stories reflect a moral panic about youth crime – it is getting out of hand, it is getting more serious, and so on. Headlines in the New Zealand press have claimed that there was 'NO BETTER TIME TO BE CRIMINAL', it is 'TIME TO GET TOUGHER WITH YOUNG CRIMINALS', there is a 'HARD CORE OF LAWLESS YOUTH' and that 'BAD JUVENILES NEED LOCK-UPS'. These headlines can certainly be matched in other jurisdictions, regardless of the system for responding to juvenile crime. They reflect both continual concern about the inability of society to prevent offending and re-offending and to accept that this will never be completely possible. In our view, the real measure of the success of family group conferences is the extent to which they represent a fair, humane and acceptable method of dealing with young offenders. At the same time, we also accept that it is legitimate to expect such a system to lessen the chances of re-offending.

Anecdotal evidence has been used to claim both remarkable successes and devastating failure for family group conferences. It is not, however, possible to accurately determine the impact of the new system on reoffending because there is no adequate information on the reoffending rates of juveniles before the Act. And even if there was sufficient information, there would still be problems. Reoffending rates based on criminal reconvictions are not a good indicator of the success or failure of any changes in the criminal or youth justice system. Some young people may offend and yet not be detected; some may be detected committing an offence but are not charged or convicted of it and so appear not to have reoffended. Many other factors which also change over time, such as population patterns, unemployment, social and economic difficulties or migration, affect reoffending as much as, if not more than, the ways in which the criminal justice system impacts on offenders.

Given these qualifications, some data are available on the reoffending of a sample of young people involved in family group conferences in 1990. Morris and Maxwell have been able to follow-up 193 of these young people who were still in New Zealand four years later. Of these, 42 percent had no later convictions for either criminal or serious traffic offences recorded against them in either the youth court or an adult court. Whether this is a mark of success or failure is impossible to say. There are no base-line data against which to compare this figure. One possible comparison is with a cohort of men aged 24 whose offending histories were checked in 1981 (Lovell & Norris, 1990); 25 percent of this group had appeared in either the juvenile or adult court on one occasion and of those appearing once, 53 percent appeared on at least one other occasion. Though precise comparisons cannot be made, the recidivism rate of the family group conference sample is certainly no worse.

Perhaps a more important and interesting finding is the proportion of the sample who went on to become persistent offenders. Of the total sample, about a quarter (24 percent) were categorised as persistent offenders who had appeared on moderately serious criminal charges on at least three different occasions over the four-year period (Morris & Maxwell, 1995). The data were examined to determine whether any factors could be identified that might differentiate between those who persistently offended from those who had not. Those factors which were predictive of both re-offending and persistent offending were, in general, the same although their power to predict re-offending was generally greater when the contrast was between persistent offenders and non-offenders. The young people who became re-offenders or persistent re-offenders were more likely to have originally committed a larger number of offences and to have had a previous history when they entered the family group conference sample; they were more likely to have been older at the time and Maori; and they were more likely to have been placed in custody, to have had provisions made for their welfare and to have had whanau or extended family involved in their family group conference. The finding of greater offending by Maori is a distressing one. It may reflect the greater stigmatisation and likelihood of Maori coming to police attention pointed to by Fergusson et al. (1993); it may also reflect their greater socio-economic disadvantage compared to Pakeha.

There was some evidence that the variables that assessed family group conference process were predictive of recidivism. Victim satisfaction was least often reported for persistent recidivists and this group were also least likely to have completed the tasks agreed to at the family group conference. Regression analysis also suggested that those who failed to apologise were three times more likely to reoffend than those who had apologised. These findings hint at the possibility that restorative justice outcomes may actually reduce the chances of reoffending.

Some of these data are in line with other studies which show that offence histories are the most powerful predictors of re-offending. They also confirm the findings of others (Roeger, 1995) that those who are sentenced to custody are more likely to re-offend. But while severe sanctions did not appear to deter, neither did welfare provisions seem to rehabilitate. One explanation for these findings is that severe sanctions, welfare provisions and a family group conference attended by extended family members only occurred when the offending pattern had already become well established. Such an interpretation fits with the finding that, unlike other studies, older offenders at the time of the family group conference were more likely to re-offend than younger offenders. Since these data were collected from research designed for different purposes, it was not possible to examine evidence for protective factors such as success in school, finding a job or establishing a stable partnership.

Another way of examining re-offending is to compare offending rates over time. A number of factors affect crime rates including changes in the number of police officers, patterns of offending, the focus of police operations (for example, the priority given to burglaries, family violence and so on), and instructions about recording and the computerisation of information. Since the Act, juvenile offending remained relatively stable initially but increased more recently when there were also increases in the overall offending rate. However, juvenile and young adult offending rates have not increased as much as adult offending. This has been cited as a positive consequence of the Act. We would be more cautious about this attribution; much of the increase in crime rates is in violent offences, family violence in particular, which are more characteristic of older offenders. That said, it is quite clear that the new system has not led to dramatic increases in the recorded crime rate of young people and young adults.

Conclusion

The principles underlying family group conferences are new, radical and exciting. They emphasise diversion, restorative justice and responding to the needs of young people through strengthening families and acknowledging cultural differences. They have impacted considerably on practice. Diversionary outcomes have been achieved for the great majority of young offenders. At the same time, nearly all young people involved in offending that is considered sufficiently serious to warrant a family group conference are held accountable for their offences. Families are, for the most part, participating in the processes of decision-making and are taking responsibility for their young people. Extended families are also often becoming involved in the continuing care of their kin and as an alternative to foster care and institutions. Families, professionals and young people record high levels of satisfaction with outcomes. Greater acknowledgment is being given to the customs of different cultural groups and, in some instances, traditional processes have been used to reach agreements. Victims are also involved to a greater extent than they were before and than is customary elsewhere. And many of the victims involved in family group conferences report being satisfied with the outcomes.

However, critical questions have been raised about the fairness of the system, its potential coerciveness and its ability to achieve the ideals of diversion, restorative justice and cultural appropriateness. Although an examination of practice demonstrates, as might be expected, imperfections, it also demonstrates the potential of family group conferences to achieve these goals to a greater extent than the more traditional process of court hearings. Much depends on practice, resources and the systems that support the processes. Poor practice can fundamentally undermine outcomes, fiscal restraint can starve the system of the necessary resources in terms of both staff and services and inadequate structures can impede the delivery of quality services. There is little doubt that giving effect to the goals of the Act is being hampered by deficiencies in these respects.

References

Children. A newsletter from the Office of the Commissioner for Children. Wellington.

Deane, H. (1995, March). *The effect of gender and ethnicity on sentencing.* Criminology Aotearoa/New Zealand. Newsletter from the Institute of Criminology, Victoria University, No. 3.

Department of Social Welfare (1992). *Review of the Children Young Persons and Their Families Act, 1989: Report of the Ministerial Review Team to the Minister of Social Welfare* (known as the Mason Report).Wellington: Department of Social Welfare. [See also "Ministerial Review Team"]

Doolan, M. (1988). *From welfare to justice: An overseas study tour report.* Wellington: Department of Social Welfare.

Farrington, D., Ohlin, L., & Wilson, J. (1988). *Understanding and controlling crime: Toward a new research strategy.* London: Springer-Verlag.

Fergusson, D. M., Horwood, J. L., & Lynskey, M. (1993). Ethnicity and bias in police contact statistics. *Australian and New Zealand Journal of Criminology, 26*(3), 193-206.

Fergusson, D. M., Horwood, J. L., & Lynskey, M. (1993). *The childhoods of multiple problem adolescents: A 15 year longitudinal study.* Unpublished report. Christchurch Child Health and Development Study.

Gelsthorpe, L. (1994, October). *Inter-agency aspects of crime prevention.* Criminology Aotearoa/New Zealand. Newsletter from the Institute of Criminology, Victoria University of Wellington, No.2.

Hassall, I., & Maxwell, G. M.(1990). The family group conference. In G. M. Maxwell (Ed.), *An appraisal of the first year of the Children, Young Persons and Their Families Act 1989* (pp. 1-13). Wellington: Office of the Commissioner for Children.

Hassall, I. B., & Maxwell, G. M. (1994). The family group conference: A new statutory approach to dealing with child care and protection and young peoples offending. In N. Wigg (Ed.), *Ensuring our children's future: The fabric of childhood in Australian society* (pp. 199-214). Adelaide: Proceedings of the 1991 CAFHS Conference.

Lovell, R., & Norris, M. (1990). *One in four: Offending from age ten to twenty-four in a cohort of New Zealand males.* Study of social adjustment: Research Report, No 8. Wellington: Department of Social Welfare.

Maxwell, G. M. (1995). Rights and responsibilities: Youth justice. In A. Else (Ed.), *Children and families: rights and responsibilities* (pp. 61-69). Papers from the International Year of the Family symposium on rights and responsibilities of the family. Wellington: International Year of the Family in association with the Office of the Commissioner for Children.

Maxwell, G. M. (1993). Arrangements for children after separation? Problems and Possibilities. In *Women's law conference papers: 1993 New Zealand Suffrage Centennial.* (pp 289-296). Wellington: Victoria University of Wellington.

Maxwell, G. M. (Ed.). 1991. *An appraisal of the first year of the Children, Young Persons and their Families Act 1989.* Wellington: Office of the Commissioner of Children.

Maxwell, G. M., & Morris, A. (1993). *Families, victims and culture: Youth justice in New Zealand.* Wellington: Social Policy Agency and Institute of Criminology.

Maxwell, G. M., & Morris, A. (1994). *Rethinking youth justice: For better or worse?* An Occasional Paper – New Series – Number 3. Wellington: Institute of Criminology, Victoria University of Wellington.

Maxwell, G. M., Robertson, J. P., & Morris, A. (1994). *The first line of defence: The work of the duty solicitor.* A report to the Legal Services Board, Wellington, New Zealand.

Ministerial Review Team (1992). *Review of the Children Young Persons and Their Families Act, 1989. The Government's response to the report of the Ministerial Review Team to the Minister of Social Welfare*, Wellington: Department of Social Welfare.

Morgan, J. (1984). Unpublished internal reports on police files supplied by Inspector D. Drummond, Police Headquarters, Wellington.

Morris, A., & Young, W. (1987). *Juvenile justice in New Zealand: Policy and practice.* Study Series 1. Wellington: Institute of Criminology, Victoria University of Wellington.

Morris, A., Maxwell, G. M., & Robertson, J. P. (1993). Giving victims a voice: A New Zealand experiment. *The Howard Journal, 32*(4), 304-321.

Morris, A., & Maxwell, G. M. (1995) *Family group conferences and recidivism.* Unpublished paper

NZ Children and Young Persons Service. *Annual reports* of the NZ Children and Young Persons Service, Wellington.

NZ Children and Young Persons Service. (1995). *Children, Young Persons and Their Families Act 1989: Amendment Act 1994.* Information pack. Wellington.

NZ Children and Young Persons Service. (1992). *Profile.* Wellington.

O'Connor, I., & Sweetapple, P. (1988). *Children in justice.* Cheshire: Longman.

Olsen, T., Maxwell, G. M., & Morris, A. (1995). Maori and youth justice in New Zealand. In K. Hazelhurst (Ed.), *Popular justice and community regeneration: Pathways of indigenous reform.* Westport: Praeger.

Renouf, J., Robb, G., & Wells, P. (1990). *Children, Young Persons and Their Families Act 1989: Report on its first year of operation.* Wellington: Department of Social Welfare.

Roeger, (1995). The effectiveness of criminal justice sanctions for Aboriginals. *Australian and New Zealand Journal of Criminology, 27*(3), 264-281.

Te Rangitahi. The newsletter of the Youth Justice Association.

Warner, K. (1994). The rights of the offender in family conferences. In C. Alder, & J. Wundersitz (Eds), *Family group conferencing and juvenile justice: The way forward or misplaced optimism?* (pp. 141-152). Canberra: Australian Institute of Criminology.

Wundersitz J., Naffine, N., & Gale, F. (1991). The production of guilt in juvenile justice system: The pressures to plead. *The Howard Journal, 30*(3), 192.

7

Family Conferencing for Young Offenders: The South Australian Experience

Joy Wundersitz and Sue Hetzel

Introduction

South Australia is one of six States and two Territories making up the Federation of Australia. Located in the southern part of the continent, it has a population of approximately 1.5 million, the majority of whom reside either in the capital city of Adelaide (population 1.1 million) or in several smaller cities and towns concentrated along the coast. Historically, South Australia has always considered itself a trendsetter in the social justice arena – a perception which can, in part, be traced to the fact that, unlike many other Australian colonies, it was established not by convicts but by free settlers who espoused the ideals of social justice and humanitarianism. One area which has constantly been the focal point of innovative reform is juvenile justice. In the late 19th Century, South Australia became the first State in Australia to establish a separate Children's Court system and to adopt a 'child saving' approach to the treatment of young offenders, which aimed to 'reclaim' rather than punish the child. This approach remained in force until the late 1970s when, as a result of a Royal Commission into Juvenile Justice, it became the first State jurisdiction to acknowledge the deficiencies of this welfare model and to advocate for a return to a more formal style of justice, based on the twin notions of just deserts and due process (Naffine, Wundersitz & Gale, 1990). Most recently, in 1994, as a result of yet another major review of its juvenile justice system, it legislated for the introduction of family conferencing as a key component of its formal juvenile justice system. In so doing, it has become the first State in Australia to statutorily embrace a new paradigm of justice for young people – that of restorative justice.

Since the *Children, Young Persons and Their Families Act* introduced family group conferences into New Zealand in 1989, this innovative approach to the treatment of young offenders has attracted considerable attention among Australian juvenile justice reformers and legislators. As a result, in addition to the South Australian programme, modified versions of conferencing are now operating in a number of other jurisdictions, usually as localised, pilot schemes. For example, in several rural communities in New South Wales, conferencing is being used as part of a restructured police cautionary diversion programme, often referred to as the 'Wagga Wagga model' (Moore & O'Connell, 1994). A similar version based on police-mediated conferencing has recently commenced in the Australian Capital Territory, with the aim of targeting not only juvenile offenders but also those adult offenders apprehended for 'drink driving' offences. In Victoria, a non-government youth agency – the Mission of St James and St John – is currently piloting a conferencing programme for those young offenders referred to it by the Children's Court (see Ban's chapter in this book). And in Western Australia, 'family meetings' have been included as a key strategy option available to the newly established youth justice teams (Hakiaha, 1994). Although these meetings began as part of a small pilot programme, they have since been incorporated into Western Australia's new *Young Offenders Act* 1994 and are now operating across the State.

Family conferencing has thus made a significant impact in Australia. This chapter will, however, focus exclusively on the South Australian model. It will describe the position and role of family conferences within this State's restructured juvenile justice system and outline how they operate on a day-to-day basis. Conferences have now been in place in South Australia since February 1994 and by the end of April 1995 some 1592 had been held. The system is therefore sufficiently well established to have identified any teething problems and to have begun the process of developing an operating model suitable for local conditions and needs.

Family Conferencing: The Impetus for Change

During the late 1980s in South Australia, there was growing community concern about youth crime and the apparent inability of the existing justice system to deal effectively with that behaviour. In response to these concerns, in August 1991 the State Government appointed a Parliamentary Select Committee to inquire into all aspects of its juvenile justice system. Evidence presented to the Committee during the course of its 12-month enquiry identified a number of deficiencies within the existing system, including long delays, ineffective sentencing, over-processing and domination by professionals to the exclusion of offenders and victims. Of particular concern was the continuing problem of high Aboriginal over-representation. Although Aboriginal young people made up only 1.7 percent of the State's youth population, in 1992/93 they accounted for 12.9 percent of all people apprehended and 30.4 percent of all people sentenced to detention in a secure care facility (Wundersitz, 1995).

The Committee became increasingly convinced of the need for substantial changes to the way young offenders were processed. In their search for alternatives, attention was drawn to the New Zealand youth justice system, and in particular to the comparatively new concept of family group conferencing. Committee members subsequently visited that country where they sat in on several conferences and conferred with key juvenile justice personnel. They were strongly influenced by what they observed during this visit and in their final report to Parliament (South Australian Select Committee, 1992), they recommended the adoption of a system based closely on the New Zealand model. The Committee's recommendations were subsequently accepted by the government and formed the basis for three new pieces of legislation, the main one being the *Young Offenders Act* 1993. This Act, which redefines the philosophy and structure of juvenile justice in South Australia, was passed through Parliament in May 1993 and proclaimed on 1 January 1994.

Family Conferencing: Structural and Philosophical Issues

Family conferencing is based on the paradigm of restorative justice, which holds that criminal behaviour is primarily a violation of one individual by another. When a crime is committed, it is the victim who is harmed, not the state; instead of the offender owing a 'debt to society' which must be expunged by experiencing some form of state-imposed punishment, the offender owes a specific debt to the victim which can only be repaid by making good the damage caused (Zehr, 1990). What constitutes appropriate reparation is decided through a process of negotiation involving not only the offender and the victim but also their respective families and social networks who have also been harmed by the criminal act. The ultimate aim of restorative justice is one of healing. Through receiving appropriate reparation, the harm done to the victim can be redressed; by making good the damage caused, the offender can be reconciled with the victim and reintegrated back into his/her social and familial networks; and through such reconciliation and reintegration, community harmony can be restored.

Restorative justice thus represents a radical departure from the notions which have underpinned juvenile justice for more than a century. Despite this fact, most jurisdictions, including New Zealand, have attempted to incorporate a restorative justice process – namely family conferencing – into an existing system which is still largely predicated on and geared to deliver state-centred notions of retribution and rehabilitation. This is clearly illustrated by the South Australian situation.

Figure 7.1: Restructured South Australian Juvenile Justice System

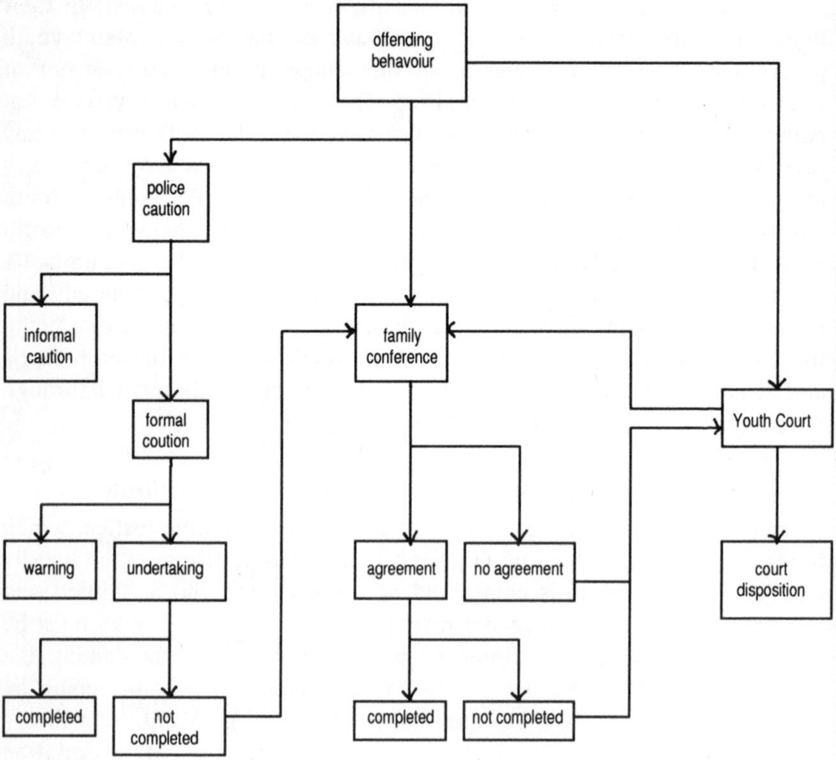

In structural terms, the juvenile justice system now operating in South Australia is outlined in Figure 7.1. As shown, family conferencing represents the second level of processing in a three-tiered system. At the front end is police cautioning, which can involve either an informal, on-the-spot warning or a more formal caution. The latter, in line with the New Zealand model, not only allows police to administer a verbal caution in the presence of a parent or guardian, but also enables them to place a young person on a voluntary undertaking to perform community work, apologise to the victim, or do anything else considered appropriate by the cautioning sergeant. A key reason for giving police these extended powers was the hope that, as in New Zealand, they would be able to deal with at least 60 percent of all apprehensions, thereby reducing the number referred to either conferencing or the Youth Court. This was seen as particularly important given the fact that the volume of cases which conferences can handle is relatively restricted (Wundersitz, 1994, p. 91).

While cautions sit at the 'front end' of the system, and are designed to deal with the least serious cases, the Youth Court has been retained for the most serious offending and for the 'hard-core' recidivists. Unlike New Zealand, where even quite serious matters coming into the Youth Court still have to be rerouted back to a family conference before disposition can occur, in South Australia if a charge is laid involving a major indictable offence, only a judge is legislatively able to deal with those cases. The Youth Court operates very much as any criminal court of summary jurisdiction. Young people who appear before it are formally charged with a criminal offence; they have access to the full range of legal rights normally available to adults; and once guilt has been established, they are subject to a standard range of penalties, including fines, community service orders and detention in a secure care facility.

Positioned between these two levels is family conferencing, designed to deal with those matters considered too serious for police diversion but not serious enough to warrant a formal adjudicated hearing. What we have, then, is a restorative based mechanism positioned between the two structures of police cautioning and the Youth Court, both firmly committed to the delivery of state-centred justice. There is, therefore, an attempt to meld two quite different approaches within the one system, with the overall objective of 'secur[ing] for youths who offend against the criminal law the care, correction and guidance necessary for their development into responsible and useful members of the community and the proper realization of their potential' (*Young Offenders Act* 1993, s. 3). To achieve this aim, the *Young Offenders Act* 1993 (s 3) lists three key factors which those persons exercising powers under the Act must have regard to, namely:

- the need to make the young person aware of the consequences of breaching the law;
- the need to impose sanctions which are sufficiently severe to provide an element of deterrence; and
- the need to ensure that the community is protected against the wrongful acts of juveniles.

Once these factors have been taken into account, decision-makers may give consideration, 'so far as the circumstances of the individual case allow' (*Young Offenders Act* s. 3(3)), to a further five factors. The first of these refers to the victim's right to compensation and restitution. The other four are oriented towards the welfare needs of the young person. These include the need to:

- preserve and strengthen the youth's relationship with his/her family;
- keep him/her within the family environment;
- avoid any unnecessary interruptions to schooling and employment; and
- avoid causing damage to the youth's racial, ethnic or cultural identity.

In effect then, at a philosophical level, the legislation embodies what may be regarded as a tripartite approach. To the twin concerns of justice/retribution and welfare/rehabilitation, which have traditionally dominated juvenile justice in South Australia and elsewhere for most of this century, has been added a third goal – that of a concern for the needs of the victim and the need to restore harmony between the offender and victim (Naffine & Wundersitz, 1994, p. 250).

Family Conferences: The Process

Administrative Responsibility

Under the terms of the *Young Offenders Act* 1993, administrative responsibility for the conferencing process rests with the Courts Administration Authority (which administers all South Australian courts) while the actual task of overseeing and monitoring the scheme rests with the Senior Judge of the Youth Court. In line with this, the legislation stipulates that youth justice coordinators responsible for convening the conferences can only be appointed after consultation with the senior judge and are directly answerable to that judge for the 'proper and effective discharge of their duties' (*Young Offenders Act* 1993 s. 9(4)). To reinforce further the link between family conferences and the court system, the Act provides for all magistrates who are 'members of the Youth Court's principal or ancillary judiciary' to be automatically designated as youth justice coordinators (*Young Offenders Act* 1993 s. 11(1)(b)). In introducing this clause, it was not anticipated that magistrates would be used in this capacity on a regular basis. However, it was recognised that, especially in the more remote areas of the State, specialist coordinators may not be available to convene conferences. By allowing magistrates to undertake this task, the intention was to ensure that young people would not be denied access to conferencing simply because of their residential location. To date, no magistrate has taken up this option of actually convening a conference.

The decision to locate conferencing within the Courts Administrative Authority was a deliberate one. In making this recommendation, the Select Committee was cognisant of the fact that in New Zealand at that time, the Department of Social Welfare (which has responsibility for conferencing in that country) was coming under strong criticism for its tendency to 'take over' and bureaucratise a process which was intended to disempower the professionals. The Committee was also aware of the criticisms being levelled by criminologists and others (see, for example, Sandor, 1994) at those police-controlled conferencing programmes being piloted in Wagga Wagga. The Courts Administration Authority offered an alternative to these two options. On the one hand, it was in keeping with the Act's strong philosophical commitment to 'justice' rather than 'welfare' concerns. On the other hand, because the Authority is not involved in the task of apprehending and charging alleged offenders, it was perceived as a more independent and neutral player in the system than the police, thus placing it in a better position to impart these qualities to the conferencing process.

The Referral Process

As outlined in Figure 7.1, the first option available is to deal with the youth by way of a police caution. The decision regarding the appropriateness of such a response rests entirely with the police – either the apprehending officer (in the case of an informal caution) or a cautioning sergeant (in the case of a formal caution). However, if these officers judge the matter to be too serious for a caution, a decision must then be made as to whether the matter should be referred to a conference or be channelled directly into the court system.

In those cases where the young person has been reported by police or where the youth has been arrested but released on police bail, this referral decision rests with a specialist team of police youth officers. A different process applies to the relatively small number of youths who have been arrested by police and detained in custody. Such cases must be brought before the Youth Court within two working days following the arrest in order to review their custodial status, and, in these circumstances, the court can either choose to deal with the matter itself by way of a formal court hearing or refer it back for either a conference or a caution.

There is a third, but so far little used, route into the conferencing system. If police, in dealing with a case involving a reported or bailed youth choose to send the matter to court, the legislation allows that court, if it considers the referral inappropriate, to overturn that original decision and redirect the case to either a conference or caution. This was one of the important 'checks and balances' deliberately built into the system; the intention was to provide a means of overcoming any tendency on the part of police to inappropriately by-pass the conferencing process by channelling relatively non-serious matters straight to court.

The role of the youth justice coordinator in the referral process is essentially a passive one. If the police or the court choose to refer a case to a family conference, coordinators cannot formally overrule that decision. Under the terms of the legislation, they are obliged to convene a conference, even if they consider it an inappropriate response. It was initially feared that this failure to provide coordinators with gatekeeping powers would result in a large number of relatively trivial matters being sent to a conference, rather than being dealt with by way of a caution. However, this has not happened. The number of police referrals to conferences have been much lower than anticipated, and so coordinators have not been required to accept large numbers of minor matters. In fact, during the first 12 months of operation of the new system, police chose to deal with approximately 40 percent of matters themselves by way of a formal caution and referred only 14 percent to conferences. The remainder (some 40 percent) were directed straight to court.

Factors to be Taken into Account in the Referral Decision

Under the terms of the legislation, both police cautions and family conferences are restricted to dealing with 'minor offences' only. In deciding what constitutes a minor offence, the police officer in charge of the investigation is statutorily required to take into account the following factors:

- the limited extent of harm caused;
- the character and antecedents of the alleged offender;

- the likelihood of the youth reoffending; and
- where relevant, the attitude of the youth's parents or guardians.

None of these criteria make specific reference to the actual type or seriousness of the offence. Nor does the legislation attempt to identify which of the 'minor offences' should appropriately be dealt with by way of a caution and which should go to a conference. The police subsequently developed their own set of guidelines (Police Commissioner's Circular, no. 509), which provided a more extensive definition of what constitutes a minor offence suitable for resolution by family conferencing. These guidelines do have regard to the seriousness of the charge. They include:

- any summary offences not dealt with by way of a caution;
- any minor indictable offence for which the maximum term of imprisonment allowed by statute does not exceed five years, or if five years is exceeded, where the amount of property loss or damage resulting from the offence is more than $5000 but less than $25,000; and
- any drug related offence classified as a summary or minor indictable offence.

All major indictable offences must, according to these rules, be referred to court.

Table 7.1: Most serious offence alleged per offender per conference
1 February 1994 – 31 December 1994

	N	%
Major offence		
Offences against person (exc. sexual)	117	10.5
Sexual	12	1.1
Robbery/extortion	9	.8
Offences against the person		
Burglary	163	14.7
False pretences, fraud, forgery	15	1.4
Larceny, receiving	371	33.4
Offences against property		
Property damage	163	14.7
Offences against good order	134	12.1
Drug offences	115	10.4
Driving offences	2	.2
Other	9	.8
TOTAL	1110	100.0

Source: Crime and Justice in South Australia 1994, Table 6.9. Office of Crime Statistics, Attorney General's Dept., 1995, S.A.

The type of offences actually referred to conferences during 1994 is outlined in Table 7.1. These detail the most serious offence alleged per individual per conference. It should be noted that if two or more young offenders attended the same conference, each is counted separately. As shown, the majority of offences processed by conferences involved property offences (49.5 percent), the main ones being larceny and receiving (33.4 percent) and burglary (14.7 percent). Offences against the person (notably assault) represented 10.5 percent of the offences while drug-related offences (most of which lack a direct victim) accounted for a further 10.4 percent.

The police guidelines also state that, even if an offence falls within the stipulated definition of 'minor', other factors must be taken into account before a referral to a conference rather than court should be made. These include:

- the circumstances under which the offence was committed;
- the youth's prior offending record (including prior cautions and conferences);
- the number of offences involved;
- the attitude of the youth and his/her parents/guardians to the offending;
- the personal circumstances of the youth (including character, age, mental or physical condition and cultural identity);
- the extent to which the victim has been inconvenienced or has suffered emotional, psychological, physical or financial harm as a result of the offence;
- the views of the victim regarding the suggested method of disposition; and
- the public interest.

Some commentators (Simpson, 1994) have questioned the validity of basing referral decisions on such factors because of the danger that certain sub-groups of youth – such as those without supportive parents, those who lack appropriate social and verbal skills, and those from minority sub-cultures – will be unfairly disadvantaged. Whether or not this is the case has yet to be determined.

One final condition must be met before a matter can be referred to a conference; the young person must be willing to admit the allegations. In South Australia, responsibility for this ascertaining rests with the police. At the point of apprehension or during the interrogation process, some indication of willingness to admit may be obtained. It is then the responsibility of the police youth officer to verify this before making a final referral decision. Technically then, by the time a file has been forwarded by police to a youth justice coordinator, the issue of admission should already have been dealt with. In reality, this is not always the case and coordinators generally prefer to confirm this fact for themselves during their pre-conference discussion with the young person.

Pre-Conference

Once the police (or the court) has decided that a matter warrants a family conference, the file is referred to the family conference team, consisting of nine youth justice coordinators and one senior coordinator, backed up by four family conference clerks. Because South Australia's population is concentrated in the capital city of Adelaide, the majority of the staff are based in the city, and, from there, cover about one-third of South Australia. Only two coordinators are permanently situated outside of Adelaide. The professional backgrounds of the coordinators are deliberately diverse: a strategy aimed at increasing their responsiveness to a wide range of families and communities. Because of the substantial over-representation of Aboriginal youths in the criminal justice system, two of the coordinators are Aboriginal. They are able to offer skills vital to the team in developing culturally appropriate ways of conferencing in Aboriginal communities.

Each coordinator convenes approximately five to six conferences per week, although the number can vary according to the amount of preparation and travel time involved. Although the legislation imposes no time constraints on the referral process, the intention is to notify the coordinator of a conference matter as soon as possible following apprehension and then to convene a conference within 28 working days of the date of that notification.

Upon receiving a referral, the coordinator's first task is to contact the key participants. Because of resource limitations, these contacts are normally made by phone. If no phone number is available, letters will be sent, and, if these elicit no response, a home visit may then be made. According to the coordinators, phone contacts are generally as effective as a personal visit. There are, however, some exceptions where a home visit is the preferred method of initial contact. These include cases where an interpreter is needed, or when particularly sensitive offences (such as sexual offences) are involved. The coordinators also make a point of undertaking home visits in all cases where the offender is Aboriginal. While the conference clerks often support coordinators by taking on some of the preparation, it is still considered essential for the coordinator to talk personally to and develop rapport with each participant before the conference. Hence, even when support staff have made the initial contact, coordinators will, wherever possible, follow this up by phoning each participant just prior to the conference.

Inviting the Participants

According to the terms of the legislation, the persons who must be invited to attend a conference include:

- the guardians of the youth
- any relatives of, or any other person who has had a close association with, the youth and may, in the coordinator's opinion, be able to participate usefully in the conference;
- the victim of the offence;
- if the victim is a youth, the guardians of the victim;
- any other persons whom the coordinator, after consultation with the youth and members of his/her family, considers appropriate.

A representative from the Police Department must also be present at every conference.

Of these invitees, the victim (if there is one) is considered the key participant and particular emphasis is placed on encouraging attendance. In most instances, coordinators contact them first to explain what a conference is, what role they could have and what they could realistically hope to achieve or contribute by attending. Although no reimbursement is offered to facilitate their participation, wherever possible both the venue and time of the conference are planned to suit their needs, while offenders' preferences are given secondary consideration. There are, however, occasions when the victim's preferences cannot be met. These include instances where there have already been long delays since the date of offending and where the option of introducing further delays to enable the victim to be present may be unacceptable. When there are multiple victims, it may also be difficult to find a time and place suitable for all of them.

Great care is taken to ensure that victims do not feel coerced into attending. However, if victims express some initial reluctance to participate, a coordinator may agree to make a home visit to discuss the matter further. At times, after such visits, victims change their minds and agree to attend. If they do not, other options are suggested. For example, victims are encouraged to nominate a friend or supporter to attend on their behalf. The team has also developed a close working relationship with the Victims of Crime organisation. This organisation now provides volunteers who, after being briefed by the victim, are able to represent them at the conference. These volunteers can be used in innovative ways. For example, in one case involving two youths who could not be dealt with together, two separate conferences had to be held. The actual victim was able to attend the first but not the second conference. The Victims of Crime volunteer therefore agreed to attend with the victim on the first occasion, in order to gain a 'feel' for the issues which the victim wished to convey and, armed with that background knowledge, then went on to represent the victim in the second conference. Other strategies have also been developed to provide a victim's perspective, including the use of tape recordings made by the victim outlining the harm caused, written victim impact statements, and photographs depicting the damage done. If all these options are rejected, the police officer is considered the most appropriate person to take responsibility for conveying the views of the victim to the offender during the conference. Occasionally, coordinators will perform the task, but this is not considered good practice because it may undermine their neutrality in the eyes of the young offender.

One particular issue facing coordinators when conferences were first established was how to involve and encourage attendance by corporate victims and, in particular, the large department stores, which were the target for many of the larceny offences referred to the team. coordinators began by contacting each store individually, which then led to an invitation for the team to talk with the Retail Traders Association. At this meeting, the department stores agreed to support the process by designating appropriate representatives, usually the store's security officer, to attend conferences. Such support has generally been maintained. Although a detailed evaluation has not yet been undertaken, preliminary evidence suggests that 75-80 percent of those conferences involving a victim-based crime have at least one victim present.

Apart from the victim, the other crucial participant who must be contacted at the pre-conference stage is the young offender. In the first months of operation, the team consulted with a reference group of young people to identify the types of questions young offenders might want answered. These now provide an important guide for coordinators. Young people are always asked who they would like to support them at the conference and, as far as possible, their preferences for significant family members, friends and professionals are taken into account. The fact that the legislation requires the parents or guardians to be invited sometimes makes for difficult situations if the young person is adamant that they do not want a particular parent to be present. This may be the case, for example, where there is family conflict or where the youth has been living away from home for some time. These requests are always taken seriously by the coordinator but, at times, the young person's preferences may be overridden if the parent in question really wants to attend and it seems that such attendance may contribute to a positive outcome.

For young people who are alienated from their families, the task of identifying and contacting members of a 'community of care' (Braithwaite and Mugford, 1994) is often time consuming and not always achievable. However, it is important that there is at least one person present on whom the youth can rely for support. A homeless youth, for example, may be encouraged to nominate a youth worker and/or other 'street kids' who can take the place of family members. Most young people, however, choose not to bring friends, perhaps because of the shame involved. Yet, increasingly, coordinators have commented that ensuring the presence of a peer is perhaps more important than is currently acknowledged simply because, by having someone of their own age at the conference, it goes some way towards redressing the imbalance caused by the presence of so many adults.

One other important task of the coordinator at this pre-conference stage is to verify that the young person is willing to admit the allegations and to ensure that they understand their legal rights, including the right to invite a lawyer to the conference, the right to refuse a conference and have the matter dealt with by the Youth Court, and the right to disagree with any outcomes reached at the conference.

In relation to other participants, if it is culturally appropriate to do so, an elder (esteemed person) from the community will be invited. coordinators are also able to use their discretion, without needing the young person's approval, to invite other adults who either have a particular interest in the welfare of the youth or skills which are likely to be useful in the conference. For example, if a sexual offence is to be dealt with, a counsellor specialised in working in this area is usually invited. Their role in the conference is to assist the young offender understand more about the impact of their actions and how counselling might assist them to make changes. While young people are statutorily allowed to have a lawyer present during the conference to provide legal advice, this is an option most youths choose not to take up. The few lawyers who have attended conferences have generally appreciated the fact that these meetings are informal and non-adversarial and so have tended to assume the role of an ordinary support person, rather than that of legal advocate.

The final participant who, according to legislation, must be present at a conference is a representative of the Commissioner of Police. In Adelaide, this role is filled by a team of 12 specially trained police youth officers. In the country, the officer in charge of the local police station is designated as the 'police youth officer'. Their role in the conference is a crucial, albeit somewhat limited one. They are required to present the facts of the case and ascertain the youth's willingness to admit those facts. They may also play a part in representing the victim's interests if the victim is not present. And finally, they also have the statutory right (as does the young offender) to veto any outcome put forward by the conference.

Selecting a Venue

In addition to organising the participants, another aspect which must be determined at the pre-conference stage is the appropriate time and venue. While most conferences are held during normal office hours, some are scheduled for late afternoon or evening to accommodate those victims who have work or other commitments during the day. No conferences, however, are convened on weekends.

Venues are selected primarily for their neutrality and ease of access. The location must not be seen to favour any participant and should, as far as possible, be in fairly close proximity to the participants' area of residence. It must be a place where both victims and offenders feel safe and secure. Although police stations and the homes or workplaces of victims and offenders have been used, these are considered less desirable than a more neutral zone such as a community centre, youth service or local council. Rooms situated within a court complex are also used because of their accessibility and acceptability to victims. The city offices occupied by the conferencing team has meeting rooms attached to them, but these are not considered ideal by some of the coordinators because of a lack of parking and their somewhat austere atmosphere. They do, however, have the advantage of centrality which makes them useful in those cases where the participants live in quite different parts of the city. On occasions, conferences have also been held in detention centres when the young person has been in custody. While the advantages or disadvantages of holding conferences in such a location have yet to be determined, the fact remains that, under the circumstances, alternative venues are simply not an option.

Conferences for Multiple Offenders

Wherever possible, co-offenders and their supporters are invited to the same conference. This practice was borrowed from New Zealand, and is considered appropriate for several reasons. It is more convenient for the victim(s). It is also easier to get a better understanding of the issues involved and to encourage greater discussion than if each offender is dealt with separately. There is the added advantage that if all co-offenders are present, one individual cannot try to absolve him/herself from responsibility by shifting the blame to the others. Nevertheless, there are some disadvantages in this approach. Some coordinators have noted that, particularly in complex cases, dealing with co-offenders together may mean that insufficient time is available to address the particular issues confronting each offender. The practice is, therefore, currently under review.

Situations involving one offender but multiple victims raise more complex issues. In some cases, for example, a young person may be charged with assault and break and enter, each involving quite different victims. Because of the different nature of these offences, the coordinator may consider it preferable to deal with each as a separate matter. But rather than organising two separate conferences, the alternative is to convene a single conference for the offender and bring each victim in separately at different times. In effect then, the offender sits through several consecutive, but discrete, mini-conferences, each of which is likely to have quite separate outcomes. Organising such multi-layered conferences can become quite complex because of the different set of victims and supporters involved. The effectiveness and efficiency of this approach is yet to be evaluated.

Summary

The work undertaken at the pre-conference stage is of vital importance to the ultimate success of the conference. It allows the coordinators to identify the issues of concern to each participant and to provide a full explanation of what conferences entail, how they are run, what they hope to achieve, and what role each participant has. It also allows clear ground rules to be established in advance. Each participant, for example, is made aware that aggression or violence at the conference is not acceptable; that each participant must be given the opportunity to speak and be listened to; that each person must be treated with respect. It is also vital at this stage to ensure that all participants understand that their role in the conference is an active one, and that it is quite different from the role normally accorded to offenders and victims within the conventional criminal justice system.

Conducting the Conference

South Australian conferences are intended to run along similar lines to those of New Zealand. This is made explicit in the Government's second reading speech, which introduced the new legislation into Parliament. This notes that the task of the youth justice coordinator is 'to bring together, in an informal and non-threatening setting, those people most directly affected by the young person's offending behaviour and, through a process of discussion and mediation, reach consensus regarding an appropriate outcome' (South Australia Parliament, Debates, 1 April 1993: 2853). The need to empower parents by encouraging them to participate fully in the decision-making process is acknowledged, as is the need to include members of the extended family and the need to give victims the opportunity to confront the offender with their feelings of anger and hurt and to have an input into the final outcome. The need to transfer responsibility for decision-making from the professionals to the key protagonists is also clearly recognised. The second reading speech stipulates that 'decision-making . . . will rest primarily with the parents and victims, with the professionals being there to give advice only when needed' (South Australia Parliament, Debates, April 1993: 2853). How have these intentions been translated into practice?

The process usually begins with participants being seated within a circle of chairs. In an attempt to create an informal setting without physical barriers, no tables are used. Some coordinators prefer to control the seating arrangements while others have found that, by allowing the participants freedom of choice, they often gain some important insights into the likely dynamics of the group. For example, a parent of the young offender may deliberately choose to sit away from their offending child, or a victim may opt to sit next to the police officer, or a young person may sit next to their co-offender's parents, rather than their own. To a skilled coordinator, these choices provide clues to underlying issues which may surface during the conference.

Each conference consists of three distinct stages: the introductory stage, the second stage during which the impact of the offence is discussed, and the final stage in which the hoped-for resolution is reached. During the first stage, the coordinator introduces participants and reminds the group of the purpose and structure of the process on which they are about to embark. The option of allowing the participants to introduce themselves has been trialed by several coordinators but rejected because some participants took it as their opportunity to launch into an account of their own story, rather than limiting themselves to introductory remarks. However, this is an area which needs further exploration because, as demonstrated in New Zealand, letting people introduce themselves operates as an important tool of empowerment at this crucial opening stage and provides a clear message that the professionals are not there to direct the process. It is also essential at the beginning to gain everybody's agreement to the ground rules canvassed during pre-conference discussions. In a highly emotional and conflictual conference, it may be necessary to keep reminding participants of these rules. The young person is then reminded of their legal rights, including their right at any stage during the conference to request an adjournment for legal advice, to leave the meeting, or request that the process be terminated if they consider that they are being dealt with unfairly. They are also reminded that they are entitled to disagree with any outcomes put forward by the conference.

At the beginning of the second phase, the police youth officer briefly outlines the details of the offence and seeks the young person's agreement to the facts. The young person is, in most instances, then asked to tell their story of what happened. The decision to focus on the young offender first is a deliberate one because it provides a means of engaging the young person right from the beginning of the conference. As one coordinator noted, if victims are asked to speak first, often subsequent questions directed at the youth elicit only terse, single-word agreement with the victim's account, thereby reducing their involvement in the process. It has also been noted that victims prefer this approach because it conveys a message to the young person that they are being required to account for their behaviour. There are, however, some exceptions. In some cultural groups, it may be considered inappropriate to allow the youth to speak first. If the young offender is Vietnamese, for example, respect must be shown to the youth's father, as head of the family, by giving him the opportunity to have his say first.

Drawing on mediation skills, the coordinator then encourages victims, family members and supporters to speak freely about the offence and its impact, and invites the young person to respond to their statements and feelings. The aim is to establish an atmosphere of respect in which the young person's input is taken seriously, while ensuring that other participants feel free to challenge. To facilitate the young person's participation, various strategies are used, including ensuring that the right support people are present, using open-ended questions which are not too broad and avoiding judgemental questions such as 'why?' It is also necessary to check regularly to ensure that the person understands what is going on and feels part of the process. If there seem to be significant obstacles to participation, the coordinator may choose to take the young person out of the room to talk. In one particularly extreme case, when it became clear that the youth had no intention of participating in the discussion, he was seated in a room by himself while the other conference participants sat in another. This was a very difficult case involving sexual abuse, and the decision to separate the offender was only done with the agreement of the youth and the victims involved. The coordinator moved constantly between the two rooms conveying information to the different parties. A satisfactory agreement was ultimately reached, with the young person undertaking to attend counselling.

It is during this second stage of the conference that the quality of interaction between victim and offender becomes clear and where the groundwork for a successful or positive outcome is laid. The young person is given the opportunity to acknowledge responsibility and feel shame for their actions, while victims are given time to voice their often deep-seated feelings of hurt and damage. Victims and family members often become very emotional as the effects of the offence are revealed. Much of this may come as a surprise to the young offender and tears often flow. It is only after everyone has had the opportunity to express their feelings that the third stage is commenced.

The goal of this final phase is to negotiate a fair outcome which takes into account the victim's need for restitution and reparation, community expectations regarding accountability, and the young person's needs and circumstances. In response to legal concerns that conferences may be more punitive than a court outcome, the *Young Offenders Act* 1993 (s 12(2)) requires family conferences to 'have regard to sentences imposed for comparable offences by the Court'. In reality, however, this is difficult, partly because relevant information on appropriate court tariffs is not available to coordinators and also because such notions of sentencing proportionality do not accord with the principles of restoration on which the conference is predicated. For example, what seems to be a 'tough' outcome may, in fact, be an appropriate response to the level of harm experienced by the victim.

To identify appropriate outcomes, the coordinator usually calls upon the young person first for suggestions about what needs to be done to repair the harm caused. The views of the other participants, especially the victims, are then sought. Again, where it is culturally respectful to ask older family members first, the order of consultation is varied. Negotiation continues until agreement is reached and it is usually at this point that the police youth officer is asked for an opinion. It is considered that, unless the group has no ideas, seeking the police viewpoint too early in the process may hamper discussion, limit suggestions by other participants and put extra pressure on the young person to agree. Originally, it was not planned that the young person and family members should take time out to deliberate options, as is done in New Zealand. However, early feedback from victims and offenders indicated that they would have felt more satisfied if there had been more time to think about the final decision. As a result, the team is currently experimenting with the practice of allowing all parties to take a short break during the third stage to consider outcomes separately.

One of the key tasks of the coordinator during the outcome negotiations is to ensure that the young person does not agree to anything they cannot realistically achieve. The temptation to do so, either to make amends or simply to get the conference over and done with, can be significant. However, the coordinator must ensure that the young person's agreement is entirely voluntary and that he/she is not being set up to fail. Under the terms of the legislation, the young person and the police must agree on the outcome. Failure to do so means that the matter must be referred to court, where the magistrate or judge 'may decide any question, and exercise any power, that could have been decided or exercised by the family conference' (*Young Offenders Act* 1993 s. 11(5)). In effect, a second conference is convened in a formal court setting. The victim, their supporters and the offender's supporters may again be invited, and, after listening to their views, the magistrate hands down a decision. Although the outcome may reflect the wishes of the participants, it is different in that the magistrate is the final arbiter. Youths referred to the Youth Court in this way are not formally charged with the offence and do not acquire a criminal record.

The requirement that police and youths must agree on the outcome has received both support and criticism. On the one hand, it is seen as an important safeguard in those instances when it becomes apparent that there is little or no common ground between the interests of offender and victim. It provides a means for such cases to be resolved without the need for a formal court disposition. On the other hand, there was some initial concern that police would use their power of veto too liberally, either to demonstrate their control of the conference process or to ensure that most matters would be dealt with by the Youth Court. However, this has not happened. Police have used their power of veto very sparingly, mostly in support of victims. Nor have young people used their power of veto very frequently – a fact which may require greater scrutiny. On the one hand, it may indicate that conferences are, in fact, reaching appropriate agreements voluntarily entered into by the young person. On the other hand, coordinators have expressed concern about the potential coerciveness of the process. One of their most difficult tasks, they argue, is to ensure that young people are not disempowered by the large number of adults present, including a police officer and their parents. There is also the problem that young people are aware of the fact that if they do disagree with an outcome, they will be referred to court, where they will have little or no say in the process. Coercion is, therefore, undeniably present and it is the coordinator's task to minimise it as far as possible.

It is during this third stage that evidence of reconciliation between victim and offender often occurs, perhaps in the form of a heart-felt apology or spontaneous handshake. At other times, it occurs either at the end when an agreement has been reached, or immediately afterwards when people linger to chat. On yet other occasions, when there has been no evidence of reconciliation, the coordinator can only hope that the completion of the undertaking, particularly if it involves work for the victim, will allow some healing to occur. However, there are also occasions when reconciliation is not possible, either because the victim is not ready to forgive or the young person has not taken the crucial step of accepting responsibility for their behaviour.

Outcomes

According to the legislation, family conferences have a wide range of options available to them. They may administer a formal caution against further offending or require the youth to enter into an undertaking which may include:

- paying compensation to the victim;

- carrying out a specified period (not exceeding 300 hours) of community service;

- apologising to the victim; or

- doing 'anything else that may be appropriate in the circumstances of the case' (*Young Offenders Act* 1993 s. 12(1)(d)).

The overwhelming majority of conferences result in undertakings which generally involve some element of reparation. Community work is a common outcome, with the largest number of hours so far negotiated being 200. It was originally envisaged that at least 70 percent of the community work emanating from a conference would involve work done directly for the victim. However, many victims are reluctant to have this type of on-going contact with the youth, and to date victims have provided only 25-30 percent of all work placements. As a result, coordinators face the often difficult task of finding appropriate work for the youth. This requires extensive consultation and networking with local community groups, many of whom are either reluctant or lack the resources to become involved. Where a community organisation does express a willingness to take young offenders, subsequent problems may arise (such as a failure by the young person to turn up or to do the work properly), with the result that the organisation may choose to withdraw its support. When appropriate work in the local community cannot be found, coordinators are left with no option but to try to slot the youth into one of the community service order programmes organised by the state welfare department. Because of their generic nature, work offered by such state-run programmes are, in most instances, not directly related to the type of offending involved. Thus, youths brought before a conference for breaking and entering may find themselves cleaning off graffiti. There is also the problem that because the state programmes are designed primarily for youths sentenced to community work by the Youth Court, individuals dealt with at a conference are usually required to work alongside more serious offenders and recidivist youths. While individualised community work organised either directly for the victim or for a local community group is therefore preferable, the task of organising such work is a difficult one.

Apart from community service, another frequent component of undertakings is monetary compensation. Although no data are available, anecdotal evidence suggests that far more compensation is being paid from family conferences than is currently ordered by the Youth Court. Apologies feature in almost one-quarter of all undertaking conditions, while 'other' conditions such as an agreement to attend counselling and participate in training programmes account for almost one half. Not all conferences result in an undertaking. In a few cases, for example, the fact that the youth has participated in the conference process may be regarded as a sufficient 'outcome' in itself. Other conferences have recommended a formal police caution.

After the Conference

The coordinator's post-conference role is to follow up undertakings by arranging community service placements or referrals for counselling, training and employment. Wherever possible, supervisors for specific aspects of the agreement are appointed from among the conference participants, usually either a parent or relative, and it is their task to inform the coordinator if the condition in question has been completed.

The coordinator is also available to assist both supervisors and young people when compliance is threatened. This may occur when a work placement breaks down, or if it is no longer possible for the young person to pay the compensation in time. A young person's life may change dramatically in a short space of time, so it is not unusual for duration and placements to be renegotiated. This is normally done by the coordinator, in consultation with the police youth officer, the young person and the appropriate family member. Victims are not usually consulted, simply because of time constraints.

In the case of certain undertakings, the Act builds in a more formal accountability structure. Section 12(6) stipulates that where the youth agrees to pay compensation to the victim or agrees to complete a number of hours of community work, those undertakings are to be lodged with the registrar of the Youth Court, who is then required to monitor their completion and bring any instances of non-compliance to the attention of the coordinators. To date, however, only compensation is dealt with in this way. All monies are now paid directly to the Youth Court which then assumes responsibility for distributing it to the victims.

In those instances where an undertaking has not been completed within the specified time, no attempt is made to reconvene the conference in order to negotiate alternative outcomes. Instead, the coordinator has several other options: if most of the conditions have been fulfilled, the coordinator, after consultation with the police, may decide to waive the outstanding elements. Or, if the degree of non-compliance is too substantial, the matter will be referred back to the police, who may either choose to waive it themselves or lay charges and refer the matter to court. A formal court disposition will then be imposed. Referrals back to police have not been a common occurrence. Although only preliminary statistics relating to non-compliance are available at this stage (and may therefore be subject to change) these indicate that, of those undertakings which had expired by 30 April 1995, only 10.6 percent were referred back to police. Conversely, 86.0 percent were complied with while a further 3.4 percent were waived because of near-compliance. There were, however, some variations depending on the type of conditions involved. Preliminary figures indicate that, during this same time period, young people were more likely to repay the agreed amount of compensation by the due date (a compliance rate of 84.8 percent) than complete their community work on time (a compliance rate of 73.5 percent). However, coordinators found that giving young people more time to complete their community work often paid dividends, with a further 9.5 percent of the community work conditions being complied with after the due date.

Appropriateness for Aboriginal Young People

One of the reasons for including family conferences in South Australia's new juvenile justice system was its potential to offer a more culturally sensitive mechanism for responding to Aboriginal young offenders who are substantially over-represented in their contact with the criminal justice system. Informal meetings held with Aboriginal mothers during the enquiries of the Select Committee on the Juvenile Justice System revealed that they wanted more say in what happened to their offending children. They also stressed the need for members of the extended family to be included. In many ways then, although the terminology differed, what these mothers were asking for bore close resemblance to family conferences. More than a year on, however, the task of developing culturally appropriate conferencing methods still has a long way to go. In part, this reflects the considerable diversity found within Aboriginal communities. These range from totally urbanised families who have been resident in Adelaide for three or four generations, to rural communities centred on what were historically European-controlled missions and government settlements, through to those communities living in remote areas of the State which still follow a relatively traditional lifestyle.

Conferences in Adelaide and Rural Environments

Conferences involving Aboriginal youth in Adelaide and rural centres are not all that different from those convened for non-Aboriginal youths. Procedures have, however, been modified in some respects. Wherever possible, Aboriginal coordinators convene the conference (as long as the family has no objections) and these coordinators have introduced some different procedures designed to elicit greater Aboriginal participation and empowerment in the process. For example, at the pre-conference stage, contact is always made by way of a home visit as well as by phone or letter. The main reason for this is that Aboriginal people as a rule feel more comfortable with face-to-face communication. It may also require more than one home visit, as well as assistance from local Aboriginal agencies to locate the young people who are often highly mobile, shifting from one relative's house to another within Adelaide or moving from the city to other Aboriginal communities located in rural areas.

The other advantage of a home visit is that it not only enables the coordinator to establish rapport with the families and provide a detailed explanation of what conferencing is about, but it also facilitates the process of identifying those significant others in the young person's life. Even within the urban environment, many Aboriginal families are part of an extended kin network, and often the most important adult in the youth's life, and therefore the one most appropriate to invite to a conference, is not the parent but an auntie, a grandmother or other relative, who has had some responsibility for disciplining and caring for the youth. Identifying such kin in Adelaide is often difficult and time consuming, because families are more dispersed and the Aboriginal community more fragmented than in the country. Other strategies designed to empower Aboriginal participants have also been implemented. Wherever appropriate, for example, respected community elders are invited and, with the young person's permission, a field officer from the Aboriginal Legal Rights Movement is also asked to attend and provide support. These field officers will sometimes take on the added responsibility of transporting the young person and their family to the conference.

In spite of careful preparation, the Aboriginal young person and/or family members may not attend, at least not the first time the conference is organised. Reasons for this include the young person's mobility, the fact that they are required to attend other events which the community considers to be more important (notably funerals) and the disillusionment which they and their families often feel when required to deal with 'the law', which, so often in the past, has failed to respond to Aboriginal people in a sensitive and equitable manner. When such non-attendance occurs, the conference is frequently reconvened at a later date.

In running a conference, Aboriginal coordinators use questioning content and styles which vary in subtle ways from those used in non-Aboriginal conferences. Overall, however, the structure of the conference does not change and outcomes tend to be fairly similar, with most agreements involving some form of reparation or restitution to the victim. Wherever possible, community service placements, if not offered by the victim, are set up within Aboriginal job training programmes and Aboriginal community centres.

Conferences in Traditional Communities

It is in the traditional communities where conferences differ most. These communities of up to 500 people are scattered throughout the far northwest of South Australia in a geographical area extending over a very large distance. Most of the land is owned by the Anangu Pitjantjatjara people and, to gain entry, outsiders must obtain a permit issued by the Anangu Pitjantjatjara Council. The people living on 'The Lands' have maintained many of their traditional customs but the ongoing need to integrate them with 'whitefella' systems can pose great difficulty, especially in relation to the white justice system which generally does not recognise Aboriginal customary law.

The task of convening conferences on 'The Lands' is problematic, not only because of the cultural differences, but also because of the distances involved, the difficulties of locating the participants, and the fact that many are not fluent in English. Preparation for a conference usually requires several visits and much travel over rough dirt roads. On the first visit, much time is spent contacting the relevant parties, consulting with the appropriate family and council members and developing rapport with the community. Considerable effort is also made to ensure that all significant family and community members have been identified and invited to attend. This may, for example, result in a young man having three 'fathers' present. At this first visit, the coordinator explains the purpose of the conference and tries to give the participants some understanding of how they are run, and what they hope to achieve. An interpreter who is acceptable to the family must also be arranged. This is usually a head of the family or a community member whom the family views as holding authority outside of their kin network. Unfortunately, the person chosen by the family is not always the best interpreter, as they tend to appoint a person who has appropriate authority, rather than one who is skilled at interpreting. A suitable time is then organised for the conference to be held. However, it is not unusual for the coordinator, on the return visit, to find that the key participants are not there. Often other 'business', including matters relating to customary law or council business, takes priority and the conference has to be delayed either for a few hours or until the next day.

In pre-European times, traditional ways of settling disputes within Aboriginal communities included lengthy informal discussions between the family groups of the key protagonists. The aim of these discussions was to restore positive relationships between individuals and to decide on appropriate reparation by the 'offender'. In this context, the notion of 'pay-back' was particularly strong and could include some physical 'reprisal' such as a ritual spearing. Shaming also played a key role in maintaining and restoring community harmony. On the surface then, there appear to be many parallels between the values underlying this traditional justice system and the principles of restorative justice underpinning family conferencing. For this reason, conferences have generally received positive support from the people.

The conferences are held outside, such as in a dry sandy creek bed a little distance from the settlement if the family want to keep the matter relatively private, or in an open area in the centre of the town where the whole community can observe what is happening. Although the coordinator assumes responsibility for introducing the conference and for explaining why they are there, in most instances the actual running of the conference is shared between the coordinator and the interpreter, who, as a family or community leader, is well placed to assist participants communicate their concerns and feelings to the meeting. In many instances, the conference is conducted almost entirely in the Pitjantjatjara language.

In relation to those conferences involving property damage or theft, outcomes tend to involve some element of community work or compensation. Those involving petrol sniffing are more difficult to resolve, and often involve removing the youth from the community for a period of time. Some young people, for example, have agreed to go on a camel trek or live for several months on one of the homelands under the supervision of a significant adult.

While some Anangu people have voiced their confidence in family conferences because they have a greater say in decisions affecting their young people than was the case in the previous system, it is too soon to determine whether or not it is possible to evolve forms of conferencing which fit effectively with traditional Aboriginal cultures.

Conclusion

The South Australian family conference system is now in its second year of operation and preliminary indications are positive. For the first time in this State's history, young offenders are being formally confronted by their victims and are being given the opportunity to make direct reparation for the damage caused. For their part, victims now have a direct input into the decision-making process and have the opportunity to express their feelings of anger, frustration and hurt. That victims are supporting the new system is indicated by the high victim participation rate and by the fact that 93 percent of victims contacted during a small pilot study reported that they found participation in the conference helpful (Goodes, 1995).

This is not to say, however, that family conferencing has escaped criticism. Accusations of coerciveness, lack of consistency and proportionality in outcomes, and lack of adherence to the principle of frugality of punishment have been made (Warner, 1994). However, these are accusations which could be levelled against any form of informal processing, not just conferencing. The only real response to these criticisms is to abandon all forms of diversion and revert to a situation in which youths are dealt with unilaterally by way of a formal court hearing – a move which seems unlikely given the enthusiasm with which pre-court alternatives have been embraced in countries such as Australia and the United States.

Thus, despite the implementational and philosophical issues which have yet to be resolved, it seems clear that, at least in Australian juvenile justice systems, family conferencing is rapidly becoming a key component of reform, offering opportunities for reconciliation and reintegration which have not so far been available.

Acknowledgments

The authors would like to acknowledge the support provided by the Family Conference Team: Carlene Barbour, Marnie Doig, Tim Goodes, Eric Kasearu, Jan Kitcher, Amanda Morrison, Bruce Smith, Grant Thomas, Rodney Welch, Vicki Green, Jenny Mercer and Jackie Wake.

References

Braithwaite, J, and Mugford, S. (1994). Conditions of successful reintegration ceremonies: Dealing with juvenile offenders. *British Journal of Criminology, 34*, 139-171.

Goodes, T. (1995). *Victims and family conferences.* Unpublished paper, Adelaide.

Hakiaha, M. (1994). Youth Justice teams and the family meeting in Western Australia: A trans-Tasman analysis. In C. Alder, & J. Wundersitz (Eds), *Family conferencing and juvenile justice: The way forward or misplaced optimism?* (pp. 103-119). Canberra: Australian Institute of Criminology.

Moore, D. B., & O'Connell, T. A. (1994). Family conferencing in Wagga Wagga: A communitarian model of justice. In C. Alder, & J. Wundersitz (Eds), *Family conferencing and juvenile justice: The way forward or misplaced optimism?* (pp. 45-86). Canberra: Australian Institute of Criminology.

Naffine, N., & Wundersitz, J. (1994). Trends in juvenile justice. In D. Chappell & P. Wilson (Eds), *The Australian criminal justice system: The mid 1990s.* Sydney: Butterworths.

Naffine, N., Wundersitz, J., & Gale, F. (1990). Back to justice for juveniles: The rhetoric and reality of law reform. *Australian and New Zealand Journal of Criminology, 23*, 192-205.

Sandor, D. (1994). The thickening blue wedge in juvenile justice. *Alternative Law Journal, 18*(3), 103-112.

Simpson, B. (1994) . . . and the judge wore blue. *Alternative Law Journal, 19*, 207-210.

South Australia. (1992). *Interim report of the select committee on the juvenile justice system.* South Australia: Government Printer.

South Australia. Parliament (1993, April 1). Young Offenders' Bill. *Debates, House of Assembly 47th Parliament, Fourth Session.* South Australia: Government Printer, pp. 2851-2858.

Warner, K. (1994). Family group conferences and the rights of the offender. In C. Alder & J. Wundersitz (Eds), *Family conferencing and juvenile justice: The way forward or misplaced optimism?* (pp. 141-152). Canberra: Australian Institute of Criminology.

Wundersitz, J. (1994). Family conferencing and juvenile justice reform in South Australia. In C. Alder, & J. Wundersitz (Eds), *Family conferencing and juvenile justice: The way forward or misplaced optimism?* (pp. 87-102). Canberra: Australian Institute of Criminology.

Wundersitz, J. (1995, in press). Juvenile justice. In K. Hazlehurst (Ed.), *Australian criminology textbook*. Sydney: Law Book Co.

Zehr, P. (1990). *Changing lenses: A new focus for crime and justice*. Scottsdale, PA: Herald Press.

8

Implementing and Evaluating Family Group Conferences with Children and Families in Victoria, Australia

Paul Ban

Background

Interest in the use of family group conferences in Australia was shown as early as 1988, and in 1992 the first pilot project was initiated by the Mission of St James and St John, an Anglican family and child welfare agency in Victoria. This paper describes the development of care and protection family group conferences in Australia, presents the results of the first pilot project, outlines other projects in progress and discusses some of the key issues which have been debated.

The Mission took the lead and received funding from a philanthropic trust to conduct a pilot project to test the family group conference technique. The Mission's pilot project commenced in October 1992 and ran for two years. An evaluation was conducted of the first 19 of the 40 family group conferences completed (Swain, 1993a; 1993b). The intention of the pilot was to work with the Department of Health and Community Services, the statutory child welfare agency, to apply the technique to case planning with child protection referrals. Following the success of the pilot,

Health and Community Services funded the Mission of St James & St John to conduct a further 40 conferences in the metropolitan area over a one-year period, and provided additional funding to a Health and Community Services region to conduct another 40 conferences. These 80 family group conferences will be completed by July 1995 and an evaluation made of their outcomes.

Other experiments with care and protection procedures have been occurring in Australia. Statutory child welfare authorities in Tasmania, Queensland and South Australia are adapting their case planning practice to become more participative by actively seeking and including extended family members to plan for their children. The South Australian government legislated in the *Children's Protection Act* 1993 for family care meetings to take place before care orders are made by a magistrate in the Children's Court. The facilitators of the family care meetings are employed by the Children's Court rather than the statutory child welfare agency. Legal recognition of family care meetings in South Australia has led to the statutory child welfare authority revising its commitment to involve extended family in participative case planning. While there has been no significant recognition of family group conferences by the statutory child welfare authority in New South Wales, two non-government family and child welfare agencies are jointly ready to establish a pilot project with private funding similar to that undertaken by the Mission of St James & St John in Victoria.

The rapid interest in family group conferences in Australia has occurred at the same time as changes in the child welfare legislation and the growing belief that the state can only protect children from harm if it works in partnership with family networks and community resources. Family group conferences are increasingly being seen as an effective and comprehensive tool in achieving this aim.

Implementation and Evaluation of the Mission of St James & St John 's Pilot Project

The intention of the pilot was to work within the existing case planning guidelines of the Department by substituting family group conferences as the decision-making technique rather than traditional case planning where the Department makes all the decisions. Two metropolitan regions of the Department of Health and Community Services provided referrals to the project staff.

The goals of the project were:

- to consider the relevance of family group conferences to the Victorian and Australian context;

- to keep children who have been or are suspected of being physically, sexually or emotionally abused or neglected within the extended family network, provided this meets with the best interests of the child;

- to empower families to make decisions about their children's well being, bearing in mind that they may require adequate resourcing if they are to care for the child;

- to assist children who are currently in non-relative care to return to their family of origin if that family is able and willing to care for the child;

- to promote power sharing and responsibility for child welfare decisions between professionals and family groups.

The proposed methodology for evaluation included the following components:

- a review of the evaluation of the first 12 months of the New Zealand program with the purpose of comparing and contrasting the similarities and differences between the families and child welfare authorities in New Zealand and Australia;

- an examination of historical and demographic data relating to the children and families referred to the project;

- direct observation of family group conferences by the evaluator;

- interviews with family members, referring workers, information providers and senior Health and Community Services staff who attended the conferences (Swain, 1993a).

The evaluation covered family group conferences held between March and August 1993, and covered 19 conferences involving 13 families and 23 children. Of the 23 children, 10 were under a protective investigation by Health and Community Services and six were subject to temporary care orders. The remaining seven were subject to supervision or guardianship orders. For the majority of the families, the referral was made to engage the extended family in either determining the future care arrangements for the children or to galvanise support for the care of the child within the immediate or wider family. While these were the explicit reasons for the referral, the more pragmatic one was that all other interventions had been tried and family group conferences presented as a fresh approach.

A review of case plans before and after each of the 19 family group conferences found that in only six instances did the case plans remain unchanged (Swain, 1993b). In seven instances, for example, the case plans changed from a protective placement (non-relative) to a family-based placement (with either the immediate or extended family) and, in one case, the previous permanent case plan (long-term placement with a non-relative) was replaced with a planned return of the child to parental care with supervision and support: a dramatic change in plan for the family. Overall, more than two-thirds of the family group conferences resulted in changes to the case plans for the children.

One of the earliest concerns in Australia about 'importing' family group conferences from New Zealand was that the Australian extended family had broken down and that family members were unlikely to attend. In fact, an average of six family members (the median was 7) attended the first 19 conferences, indicating that extended family will participate in planning meetings if they are sufficiently prepared by the facilitator (Swain, 1993b). Another concern was that family group conferences would be expensive, with relatives wanting money to cover their travel and accommodation costs to attend. The evaluation report of the first 19 family group conferences showed that 97 of the 116 family attendees lived in metropolitan Melbourne, 10 attendees lived within the State of Victoria, and only 9 attendees lived elsewhere. Financial help was given to the out-of-State attendees, but in most cases this was a partial contribution toward their expenses rather than full reimbursement. Experience has shown that family members are more than willing to spend their time and money if they believe that their attendance and contribution at a conference will be valued by professionals and will benefit the child. The time taken by the conferences averaged three hours. This was greater than the normal case planning process, but the results in terms of changes to case plans to involve wider family in the child's life, combined with the family's satisfaction that it was 'their' decision, is likely to lead to less involvement by welfare authorities in the long term.

Despite the limitations of a small sample, the evaluator found that there was a widespread feeling across all participant groups that their experience was considerably better than traditional case planning meetings. The majority of those who participated stated the key difference was that family members had control over decision-making. Overall, the strong perception of participants – especially family members – was that children would be better off and that more adequate and sustainable plans would be achieved with family participation in and control over the planning processes. The clear message from family members was that, overall, the family group conference process enabled them to make a real contribution to the planning for their children. Over 80 percent of family members expressed satisfaction with what took place and the outcomes of the family group conference they attended. As one family member commented:

> With everyone there they [the agencies] couldn't fob you off . . . it had to be the truth and they had to look you in the eye and commit themselves. We got six months work done in one meeting because everyone was there and willing to make a commitment. . . (Swain, 1993b).

Despite the limited number of conferences held during the evaluation period, the Victoria project produced anecdotal evidence that the plans produced by family group conferences appeared to be long lasting.

The Department of Health and Community Services' Pilot Project

On 1 August 1994, the Department of Health and Community Services commenced funding for a second phase of the pilot aimed at integrating family group conferences into the child welfare system by conducting 40 family group conferences in each of two regions: one metropolitan and one rural. The two regions selected were considered representative testing grounds for determining the impact of the conferencing process. A significant difference between the two regions was that family group conferences in the metropolitan region were to be conducted by independent facilitators from the Mission's project team, while those in the rural region were to be conducted by an experienced staff member of the Department of Health and Community Services, trained and supervised by the Mission's team.

A key assumption of the project is that there are strong links between extended family members, despite the fact that they do not live under one roof or in close proximity. The primary goals are:

- to divert children and young people from the child welfare system where appropriate;

- to involve family members in decision-making about a child or young person and to confirm the responsibility of the family for their children;

- to facilitate families mobilising their own network and resources to care for a child and to strengthen their ability to provide care, protection and discipline;

- to ensure that decisions reached do not contravene the intention of the *Children and Young Person's Act* 1989 for ensuring the safety of the young person and timely decision-making;
- to ensure the child's ongoing protection and, when statutory involvement is required, to explore the least intrusive option for involvement.

In addition, the objectives of the conferences are to ensure that welfare agencies assist in the process of empowering families; that welfare workers are appropriately educated about the aims and procedures of family group conferences; that appropriate referral processes are in place to facilitate the referral of families to the program; and that the broader community is educated in relation to the role of both immediate and extended families in supporting and assisting vulnerable families.

The evaluation entails reviewing Health and Community Services files about the nature of cases referred and interviewing referring workers and their supervisors. As Health and Community Services have time limitations on their evaluation, it is unlikely they will obtain answers to questions about long-term outcomes. However, they should develop a clearer picture of the characteristics of the families who find the process successful and should be able to collect more information on the use of the technique at various intervention points in the life of the cases. The sample of 80 cases should be sufficient to identify trends and develop useful knowledge for practice. As the two halves of the project have both an internal facilitator and an external facilitator, the evaluation will assess perceptions of this difference by both the professional participants and the families.

Proposal to Implement Family Group Conferences at a Women's Prison

A third pilot project will introduce family group conferences into a new context. Staff of a Children in Prison program in Victoria, which aims to maintain mother-child relationships while the mother is serving a prison sentence, were aware that they had limited information form which to make decisions based on the best interests of the child. They expressed a concern that children under the age of five placed in prison with their mothers were not receiving adequate assessments as to whether or not this placement was in the child's best interests. As a result of these concerns, it has been decided to trial family group conferences as a method of making placement decisions.

The prison allows children to live in prison based on an assessment by the prisoner's case worker and, if the decision is approved, the prisoner mother assumes full responsibility for the care and the management of her child for the duration of her sentence of imprisonment. There were a number of weaknesses in the existing process of considering applications to care for children.

- There was no expertise in the Prison Branch in the area of child care, child development or child protection; therefore, decisions related to children being cared for in prison were not grounded in specialist knowledge or experience in determining the best interests of the child.

- The assessment of applications by mothers to care for their children in prison were based on the mother's perspective and wishes for the child. Family members were generally not involved in the assessment or decision-making process, particularly where conflict or potential conflict existed between family members.

- The assessment and decision as to whether or not a child can be cared for in prison by his or her mother was based on the immediate and short-term interests of the child while the mother was in prison. Little thought or consideration was given to the long-term needs and interests of the child after the mother was released from prison.

- The Prison Branch only has the authority to determine whether a child can be cared for in prison by his/her mother and cannot determine or even influence the placement of a child in the community if the decision is not to place the child with the mother in prison. Therefore, decisions are sometimes made to allow the child to be cared for in prison with the mother on the basis that the current placement does not appear suitable in some way. The Prison Branch did not have the authority to explore alternative placements for the child with extended family members.

After discussions with the Mission's project staff, the Prison Branch decided that family group conferences might be a better way of determining the child's best interests because it involves the wider family network and significant others in the decision-making and placement process for the child. The two main objectives of the proposed pilot are:

- to ensure that the best interests of the children of prisoner mothers are met, both in the short and long-term, by giving family networks the opportunity to have significant input into planning for the child who may be at risk.

- to prevent children of prisoner mothers from requiring statutory intervention (almost a quarter of children in prison were involved with Health and Community Services) due to neglect or abuse. This is to be achieved by mobilising family networks to make plans for the child.

The pilot project began in October 1995. Family group conferences occur in each case when a prisoner makes application to care for her child in prison and where there is some potential for the family to work together for the child's interests. Where the family group conference cannot agree on a decision, the reasons for the disagreement will be noted and the General Manager, Prison Operations, will determine whether or not the child will be cared for in prison.

The evaluation of the conferences will be undertaken externally to the Prison Branch, will involve consideration of both process and outcomes and will include the following components.

- *Participants' feedback.* All participants of family group conferences will be interviewed within two weeks of the conference to ascertain their perceptions and views of the process, the outcome, the benefits and weaknesses in relation to the needs and interests of the child and the impact on family relationships. They will also be interviewed one year after the conference to ascertain their perceptions of the benefits and weaknesses of the conference outcomes for the child and family relationships.

- *Analysis of the children's placements.* An analysis of each child's placement before the conference and one year after the conference will be made in terms of changes in placement from non-family to family placement, and the number of placements one year before the conference will be compared with the number of placements one year after the conference.

- *Children's contact with other family members.* An analysis will be made of each child's frequency of contact with family members before the conference compared to the frequency of contact after the conference, regardless of whether the child is

147

in the mother's care in prison, with other family members or in a community placement.

- *Children's contact with the Department of Health and Community Services.* Interviews will be carried out with regional Health and Community Services staff who have had contact with children of prisoner mothers to assess the effectiveness of the conference in reducing statutory intervention in children's lives.

- *Time taken for Family Group Conference process.* An assessment will be made of the time taken for the preparation of conferences and their conduct.

Practice Issues

Independence and Neutrality of the Facilitator

The model of family group conferences initially presented to Australians from New Zealand had the facilitator or coordinator as part of the Department of Social Welfare, the same statutory authority responsible for child protection investigations. Some concerns were raised in Australia about the appropriateness of this arrangement, particularly in light of the perception of families that the coordinator is on-side with the protective worker (Barbour, 1991; Connolly, 1994; Patterson & Harvey, 1991). The initial pilot project in Victoria used independent facilitators, and there was strong support for their independence by both the family members and professionals who attended.

To date, the use of an independent facilitator in Victoria has ensured that families perceive the statutory authority as a key information provider rather than as a controlling agent. The roles of the representative of the statutory authority and the facilitator have been quite distinct. Representatives of the statutory authority state the legal basis for the intervention, their assessments, their non-negotiable 'bottom lines', and the resources they can provide to assist the family. During the preparation phase before the conference, the facilitator has the opportunity to discuss and clarify the information and opinions of the professionals. While the conference is in progress, the facilitator's role is to assist the family to understand the information provided by the professionals. Evaluation of the first 19 conferences suggests that the presence of an independent facilitator may have encouraged families' attendance and participation.

Those on one side of the debate argue that independence is not the issue and that a skilled facilitator can overcome any bias perceived by the family. Those on the other side take the position that independence is the key to the success of both process and outcomes, that this overcomes families' feelings of powerlessness which arise from situations where there has been statutory intervention in their lives in the past and that this empowers as much as possible families to take control of the situation and to develop a child protection plan. The evaluation of the second phase of the family group conferencing project involves both an independent facilitator and a facilitator from the statutory child welfare authority, each conducting family group conferences in two different regions over a 12-month period. This will enable comparisons to be made of this difference in process.

Professionals' and Families' Resistance

Family group conferences have generally been welcomed by professionals, but at the same time there have been barriers imposed to fully implementing the conferences. An example of this is that those making referrals set a high threshold and only families seen as possessing good decision-making skills tend to be referred. This means that protective workers often fail to consider the option of involving extended family members and giving them information and power to make decisions. The shift in practice for Health and Community Services staff from sole decision-maker to information and resource provider is difficult, and there are circumstances where families do not want to meet and make decisions. It remains to be seen whether or not these families are in the minority and whether or not family group conferences can be used in a wide variety of circumstances.

There have also been logistical problems in fully implementing family group conferences in Victoria. Experience has shown that the total amount of time spent preparing and conducting conferences can be up to 20 hours. On average, this is in contrast with the shorter time taken in the current system where professionals involve only a few family members before making the final decisions. Most of the extra time is spent preparing the family and the professionals before the family group conference, and this greater investment of time is considered part of a process which leads to more comprehensive and longer-lasting decisions.

Project staff in Victoria have found that family members may resist participating in conferences by scapegoating other family members as the problem (a parent may blame a teenager and sees him or her as the sole person in need of help) and may only wish to participate if it is accepted that they are not 'the problem'. In addition, key family members who are locked into coping with the impact of problems do not initially see how other family members can help. The most common line of resistance is to say they are 'too busy', 'not interested', or that there has been no contact with other family members for a long time. Once the facilitator has permission from the key family members to contact the wider network, approximately half the work required in preparation for the family group conference has been completed. It is essential to assure the most vulnerable members of the family network that it is 'their meeting' and that they will be helped to find 'their solutions'. Factors such as an appropriate neutral venue, timing of the conference to suit the family's needs, child care, refreshments and an opening statement at the conference affirming the empowering intention of the process, all contribute toward overcoming natural suspicion and resistance by the family.

Conclusion

A common reaction to family group conferences by workers in the helping professions is that its principles and practice are basic to social work training and to community development work. While the values underpinning the principles of family group conferences have not been challenged, there have been challenges to the notion of individuals being connected to a network of people through blood ties. For some this connection is an accident of birth; the relevance of kinship networks has been relegated to pre-industrial tribal societies and is not considered significant in post-industrial societies. The challenge of working with this technique is for professional staff to consider their own identities and family ties. When they are challenged by families as to why they are pursuing an individual's connection to their network, the worker involved is required to have thought through his/her own position. Consequently, it becomes very difficult for a worker who does not acknowledge any sense of connection to the notion of wider family to be able to prepare and conduct a family group conference. To run family conferences effectively requires an acceptance of values consistent with the application of the technique and the use of appropriate skills.

Although information about family group conferences has been available in Victoria for over six years, and considerable interest has been expressed in the application of the technique, only a handful of professionals have actually attempted to conduct a family group conference. Interested professionals have had their enthusiasm dampened by a welfare environment that has not rewarded their efforts to empower families. Evaluative data are required to satisfy financial managers that family group conferences are a more cost effective way of planning for children. Changes to accommodate family decision-making practice in Australia will initially occur slowly. But evidence of the benefits of family group conferences is emerging in a number of fields and this is likely to have a lasting impact on the helping profession's responsibility to respect and empower extended family networks.

References

Barbour, A. (1991). Family group conferences: Context and consequences. *Social Service Review. 3*(4).

Connolly, M. (1994). An act of empowerment: The Children, Young Persons and Their Families Act (1989). *British Journal of Social Work, 24.*

Patterson, K., & Harvey, M. (1991). *An evaluation of the organization and operation of care and protection family group conferences.* Interim Report of the Evaluation Unit, Wellington: Department of Social Welfare.

Swain, P. (1993a, April). *Implementation report of the family decision making project.* Melbourne: Mission of St James & St John.

Swain, P. (1993b, November). *Safe in our hands — The evaluation report of the family decision making project.* Melbourne: Mission of St James & St John.

9

Family Group Conferences in Child Welfare Services in England and Wales

Peter Marsh and Gillian Crow

In England and Wales, the principles of the *Children Act* 1989 and the research underpinning this Act provide the backdrop for family group conferences. After some small-scale experiments, an organised programme of training has been coordinated and supported since 1992 by the Family Rights Group, with research support from the University of Sheffield. This chapter describes this backdrop to the programme, outlines some of the key areas now being examined, and provides a brief descriptive account of the current stage of the development of family group conferences in England.

The Children Act 1989

The *Children Act* 1989 'represents the most comprehensive and far reaching reform of child law which has come before Parliament in living memory' in the words of the Lord Chancellor as he introduced the Bill in the House of Lords. The Act has affected almost every aspect of child welfare in England and Wales, uniting the law for divorce and child protection with common principles, court structure and orders, and has helped both to promote and to shape the introduction of family group conferences. The Act emphasises: children's need for families; families' need for support; a strong preference for voluntary rather than imposed services; users', including children's, views in key service decisions; and consideration and respect for a family's culture and cultural heritage.

These areas provide a sound framework for the introduction of family group conferences, although the gap between the conference's approach and current practice (as distinct from legal specification) should not be under-emphasised. Some of the key links between the Act and family group conferences are partnership, limits on compulsion, family support services, and the importance of respecting cultural diversity. The family group conference programme and the associated research has concentrated on these areas.

Partnership and the Children Act 1989

Although the word 'partnership' does not appear in the Act, it is a key principle throughout the voluminous Guidance that accompanies the Act, and it is clearly at the heart of current child welfare policy and practice (Marsh, 1993; Packman, 1993). The 10 volumes of Guidance that indicate best practice under the Act propose a variety of ways in which the partnership principle should be established: users should be consulted about policies, parents should be consulted about services, and children and young people should be directly involved in decision-making wherever possible (Department of Health, 1989). In child protection work, the Guidance (Department of Health, Home Office, Department of Education and Science, Welsh Office, 1991) has emphasised partnership primarily by means of parental participation in statutory meetings, especially the multi-professional child protection conferences which are the key decision-making bodies for child protection plans.

In order to implement the Act, there has been a substantial investment in training and funding for local and regional training programmes. Implementation of the Act has, rightly, been regarded as a major task (Coffin, 1993) to be undertaken over many years. Research on the family group conference programme is also pursuing this emphasis, and it is, therefore, looking very carefully at the successes and limits of implementation, especially the links between policy and training.

Limited Compulsory Intervention

The Act emphasises voluntary agreements, rather than compulsory legal orders, as the desired basis for child welfare activities. An unusual clause in Part 1 s. 1 of the Act states that 'where a court is considering whether or not to make one or more orders under this Act with respect to a child, it shall not make the order or any of the orders unless it considers that doing so would be better for the child than making no order at all'. In addition, and in contrast to previous legislation, if children are provided with residential or foster care, this is to be regarded as the provision of accommodation and is not subject to any compulsory controls (unless a court hearing makes an order). The emphasis is on the need to try and reach negotiated agreements in the best interests of the child and to use services to support these without taking away any of the rights of the parent or child. Family group conferences have therefore been developed in both compulsory and voluntary contexts, and the way this is experienced, especially from the point of view of families and professionals, is a second theme in the research.

Family Support

The Act stipulates that if a child is to be accommodated, the first priority is to do so within his or her family. It also provides the principles, if not necessarily the resources, for a comprehensive service of family support, introduces the concept of 'children in need', and suggests that social services must be clear about the priorities for supporting these children as a matter of both overall policy and individual practice. The principles are generally good, but commentators have been concerned that they will come up against tight budgets (Packman & Jordan, 1991) and be affected by the substantial investment in child protection investigation, so that 'in need' will be effectively limited to 'in need of protection' (Cooper, 1993; Hughes, 1995). In order to reflect these issues, the third theme of the research is a description of the services that have been provided following family group conferences. In a second stage of the programme, the research will focus specifically on the way that conferences may play a role in making sure that 'in need' has a wider meaning than 'child protection', in accord with the spirit of the Act.

Race, Religion, Language and Culture

All decisions taken under the Act must conform to a 'welfare check list', which makes the child's welfare the 'paramount consideration' and which must involve consideration of the child's wishes and feeling, and their age, sex, and background. While this will, in the best examples, involve culturally sensitive practice, only in a few sections does the Act specifically mention the need to consider 'religious persuasion, racial origin, and cultural and linguistic background'. The need to make services aware of cultural and discriminatory factors is, therefore, part of the Act, but there is still some way to go to make this the central concern that the partnership orientation requires. The way that cultural diversity is, or is not, respected is a key issue within the development of conferences, and forms a fourth theme of the research.

Children's Rights

As mentioned, the Act makes explicit and clear the need to ascertain the views and wishes of children and young people and to consider them 'in the light of their age and understanding'. There are also a number of specific requirements to consult children and young people. The Act's general ethos is to support some limited rights for children, and it stands out from the rather poor record of England and Wales generally. 'Power' and 'empowerment' are key issues being explored in the research. It is intended to assess these concepts using measures being developed elsewhere (Koren, DeChillo, & Friesen, 1992) and thus to contribute to their development in child welfare in general.

Child Welfare Research

There has been a major investment in child welfare research in England and Wales and, in a major review of it (Department of Health, 1991), the Chief Inspector of Social Services stated that research 'has played a fundamental part' in bringing about the changes contained in the Children Act. This review, and a previous one (Department of Health and Social Security, 1985), were able to draw on many studies, covering thousands of children and many Social Services Departments. The overall messages were strong and clear. The services, while generally satisfactory, generated major and significant problems for a minority of children in the care system, separating them from their family and failing to provide a better standard of care than they received at home. For the majority of children and their families, despite reasonable standards, there were difficulties over access to and communication with services (Fisher, Marsh, & Phillips, 1986) and the long standing aspiration to work in partnership (B.A.S.W., 1980; Pugh & De'Ath, 1989, pp. 15-17), recently reinforced by the *Children Act* 1989, was not often achieved. The research reviews recommended continuing attempts to develop partnership, and highlighted gains from such approaches. It drew attention to the need to tailor services to families' needs and the fact that there can be no unequivocal optimism that substitute care will necessarily be an improvement over family care.

The research has made it clear that families are the stable and enduring carers for the vast majority of children involved with the care system. Although it may be as much by default as by deliberate planning, around 90 percent of these children will end up with family members at various points during their substitute care or when this care ends. As a recent research report has commented:

> For the great majority of children in care, family members are the most important resources available to social workers, for it is parents, grandparents, siblings and wider family who are likely to provide continuing and unconditional support. It may be true that some children in care reluctantly go back to relatives because they have nobody else. Nevertheless, whether professionals like it or not, almost all children in care will eventually be restored to their family and our perspectives and interventions need to accommodate that fact (Bullock, Little, & Millham, 1993, p. 67).

This view has underpinned the introduction of family group conferences, but of equal relevance is the parallel research finding that developing a more partnership-oriented child welfare service, which generally maintains and supports children in their families, is a very difficult task for both practitioners and managers (Marsh & Fisher, 1992; Millham, Bullock, Hosie & Little, 1989). Without agency-wide initiatives, users' involvement, sound training, and consistent feedback, practitioners drift away from these developments or lose heart and revert to old styles of practice (Newton & Marsh, 1993). The *desire* to work in partnership is not always followed by relevant actions. Research indicates the need for approaches like family group conferences, but it also shows the difficulties of implementing them. The evaluation of conferences needs to take into account both the quality of the conference process and the outcome in terms of family links.

Users of Services

The voices of service users have become increasingly prominent in recent years. In part this has been through research studies, as mentioned above, which have made a powerful case for the relevance of users' views and the incorporation of these views into both policy and practice. In child welfare there has only been limited advocacy work by users' groups, but some have emerged to put the case for changes to services, usually along similar lines to but with a different emphasis from the reports from research. Young people in care have formed their own organisations and contributed directly to policies at national and local levels. The Who Cares Trust has published a quarterly magazine written for young people in care, and lobbying of government for care leavers has occurred. The overall cry from these voices has been for greater participation and, while the strong family orientation of family group conferences would not always be their aim, the conference's emphasis on high levels of involvement in decision-making is very much in line with their views. It is no coincidence that a voluntary support group for families dealing with the care system, the Family Rights Group, has played the leading role in establishing family group conferences in England and Wales. The research on family group conferences has been designed throughout to give a high profile to users' views of both process and outcome.

The Family Group Conference Programme

Work on family group conferences in England and Wales developed from links with New Zealand, including visits to England by practitioners, and other forms of exchange of people and literature (for example, Wilcox et al., 1991). This has been important and explicit (Marsh, 1994a; Marsh & Allen, 1993). With growing dissemination of the ideas there has been further developments in practice and there is a strong interest in family group conferences in a significant minority of Social Services Departments in England and Wales. From an early stage, these developments were supported by the Family Rights Group in London. Training events, literature and conferences have all played a role in creating interest and, in recent years, a substantial pilot programme has been coordinated in order to both test and take further the conference approach (Morris, 1994).

The current programme involves staff in specific teams in six key agencies (five Social Services Departments and one voluntary agency). They meet regularly and receive direct support from the Family Rights Group. Each of the agencies is conducting an evaluation of their work with a coordinating group led from the University of Sheffield, where a national review is also taking place (Marsh, 1994b). A second stage involving all of one Social Services Department's work in an area of 'children in need' began in the middle of 1995. Many professionals have needed to be involved, and concerns about leaving children unprotected and the loss of professionals' power have been much debated. In general, it has been professionals' unease and the need for policy and skill development, rather than lack of finance, which has caused the relatively slow start. At this stage, around 40 full scale family group conferences have been held as part of the programme. Work is continuing and the total should reach 60 or more in the relatively near future. The outline that follows represents the current state of development.

Starting Off

The projects were set up largely by two or three people in each district and usually they had been on training courses at the Family Rights Group, but one or two had direct experience of family group conferences in New Zealand. The typical 'developer' was a self-selected practitioner who was interested in the model and had obtained funding for his or her training. They came from a range of geographical and demographic areas. On returning from their training and keen to put the family group conference model into practice, 'developers' spoke to others they thought would be similarly interested and enthusiastic, and thus gathered a group together to take the idea forward within their area or district. This group most often became the steering group for the project. The future course of each project was to a large extent dictated by the membership of this group in terms of the amount of political, financial and social power it could wield. The extremes have ranged from a steering group which consisted of 11 people, including a nurse advisor, county solicitor, representatives from the police and social workers from different teams, to just four people, three of them social workers from one team.

Resources

The pilot projects participating in this study have been offered different amounts of support in terms of both time and money to get started; the scope of the projects was constrained by the resources available. In a number of projects 'creative accounting' was vital to their funding. In light of the very limited support that some project founders received, it is a tribute to their commitment to the idea of family group conferences that the development got off the ground at all. For many, the support of the national project group through the Family Rights Group was vital and continuing support at a local or national level is also very important.

The project steering groups spent time grappling with issues central to the family group conference model, such as power, empowerment and agencies' procedures. These debates, as befits a developmental programme, still continue though there is a danger that the debates will be too prolonged and thus avoid the need for action. All project initiators were surprised at the time it took to explore the implications of using the family group conference model, establish local agreements and put their project plans into action. The quickest took six months, while in another it was almost two years from first discussion to enactment.

Following the 'launch' of a project, it was a very common experience for there to be a lull in referrals and then for a much slower trickle of families to be recommended for a family group conference than had been expected. The research will explore this issue in some depth. The delay in referrals resulted in a frustrating wait for those keen to 'do' their first conference and often to a revision in the plans for evaluating the project. In addition, projects that had intended to run for a year were extended in order to complete a reasonable number of family group conferences. Many commented that at this stage they also benefited from being part of a wider, supportive project group that helped to carry them through these early frustrations.

The Conferences and Existing Agency Procedures

Most of the projects took the view that they would prefer to leave existing agencies' procedures intact. This decision seemed to be based on a number of factors. The pilot projects are quite small in scale and they probably do not warrant changing existing procedures. Even if they did, child protection procedures have a high profile and it might be unwise to suggest changes which could lead to prolonged debates and even jeopardise the whole project. As a further precaution, in the light of the high profile of child protection, most projects aimed to target cases where young people were being looked after by the Department or where requests for accommodation due to family breakdown were being made, rather than focus on child protection work.

Some projects did include child protection work but proposed that the family group conference be held as soon as possible after an initial (traditional) case conference, with the aim of the family making plans in the light of the case conference's decisions. In one project, the work grew from a concern that the Asian community was served badly by existing child protection approaches and the cases targeted were all child abuse cases. In the other projects, sexual abuse cases were specifically excluded. One project did seek to hold family group conferences in cases of child abuse before the first (traditional) case conference. The family plan was then presented to this initial case conference and it was proposed that it should be accepted and resourced as long as it did not place the child at risk of 'significant harm'. But, after much debate, it has been accepted that the family group conference will be held only after the formal child protection case conference. Debates with professionals both inside and outside of the Department of Social Services have often led to less radical change in the services than was hoped for at earlier stages in the projects. The research will provide some insights into these debates and examine the arguments of those who, in part or in whole, opposed the introduction of family group conferences.

The Family Group Conference

In all projects, cases falling within the referral criteria were to be discussed with the project manager or a project panel, together with the social work team manager. This group decides whether or not a family group conference should be offered to the family. Possible reasons for not offering a conference were thought to be: if plans had already been made and accepted; if the family had a long history of antagonistic involvement with the Social Services Department; and if it was already known that the family had no wider network to invite.

Coordinators

After agreement has been reached to offer the family a conference, a coordinator is identified who can take on the work; where possible she or he is matched to the needs and preferences of the family. In one project the coordinator's role is less clear cut; the social worker takes the main role in setting up the family group conference and the project initiator, who is employed by the Social Services Department but is not a social work practitioner, takes the role of chair. The projects all vary in the way they have recruited coordinators, the way they organise and support them, and how they are paid. This is not surprising in view of the fact that the projects were developing a new model, under different circumstances and with access to different resources. One area has only one coordinator and another has 12. Clearly, experience with the tasks will be traded for the ability to match coordinators to families. One area pays a fixed fee per conference and one uses seconded Social Services Department staff. Again, there may be a trade off between an element of independence and good knowledge of social services. Supervision of coordinators also varies greatly, some seeing a supervisor every two weeks, and some receiving ad-hoc supervision. Coordinators have been drawn from a wide variety of backgrounds. Some have social work qualifications; others have community work, education and other qualifications. A few have experience in relevant services such as foster care rather than formal qualifications.

The coordinator, sometimes assisted by the social worker for the child, generally:

- visits the family to explain the process of the family group conference and encourages them to participate;
- identifies members of the extended family and their whereabouts, and discusses with the young person and the family who else they might like to invite;

- arranges for the identified members of the family to be contacted (through visits, telephone or possibly letter), invites them and explains the reasons for the family group conference and the process to be followed;

- contacts other agencies involved with the case to discuss their attendance at the family group conference and explains the process and their role;

- continues discussing the family group conference with the family to make sure they are clear about the reasons and processes, answers their concerns and tries to maintain their commitment;

- finds out what plans the family are likely to make, anticipates difficulties and tries to negotiate them before the family group conference;

- discusses possible resource implications of the family's likely plans with the relevant budget holders and negotiates some provisional agreement to resource plans;

- agrees on a suitable time and place, arranges the chosen venue, informs family members and others of the time and place, arranges transport for family members and organises refreshments;

- ensures smooth running of the practical arrangements on the day of the family group conference, settles family in and chairs the first part of the meeting;

- makes sure that the concerns of the agencies involved are clearly identified and the family understands their task;

- withdraws with all other professionals and leaves the family by themselves for as long as they require;

- remains available to the family throughout their time alone to answer questions;

- receives the family's plan and, where necessary, initiates further negotiation or discussion around the plan, particularly if further details of the planned arrangements or resources are required;

- discusses ways in which the plan will be monitored and what part the family will play in this;

- confirms with the referring agency that the resources requested can be provided; and

- ensures that written copies of the plan are sent to the family members.

So far, these tasks have taken coordinators an average of 20 hours, although the range is wide – between 8 and 37 hours. At the end of this process, coordinators have completed their role. They are not expected to have any further contact with the family or the case workers unless a follow-up family group conference is arranged at a later date. Feedback from the coordinators suggests that the most difficult part of their job is in identifying members of the wider family and where they live (a potentially very time consuming task) and obtaining the agreement of the child's immediate carers/parents to invite them.

Coordinators are the linchpins of the conferences. Their work requires a high level of skill and often appears to move into the very difficult territory of negotiating 'what is right' and 'what is fair', an area that is perhaps at the core of social work (Jordan, 1987; 1990). As the projects progress, the research will focus on the work of coordinators to identify the characteristics of 'ideal' appointees and their training needs.

Examples of Conferences

So far, family group conferences have covered a wide range of family circumstances and resulted in a number of remarkably innovative plans. Innovation may well be the hallmark of the family group conference approach. Conferences have placed children temporarily with a football coach friend, they have had a young person welcoming conference members to 'my conference' as they arrive, they have revealed abuse when none had been known, and they have apparently stopped mischievous and untrue anonymous allegations of abuse. But there has also been one conference where family members cancelled their attendance at the last minute leaving the conference in disarray, one conference which caused a great deal of distress and ended without an agreement, and one conference where accusations were continually made that the professionals were lying and which again ended in no agreement.

Two brief examples are given here to show who has come to some of the conferences and what has happened as a result.

Family 1

This family consists of four adult children and two adolescent girls. The father is terminally ill with cancer. The elder of the two

162

adolescent girls was recently placed with her brother and his partner, but when that couple separated the partner applied for the child to live with her. The Social Services Department supported this application. The father was hospitalised but did not openly accept the severity of his condition and could not directly participate, emotionally or physically, in discussions about his daughter's future. Thus the family group conference was arranged for the siblings to formulate a plan for the care of the youngest child, aged 13.

The meeting took place in a family centre at 3:00 p.m. on a weekday. It lasted one and a half hours, and the social workers involved were asked to stay throughout, although the coordinator comments that they were largely silent. Attending were the young person, an adult sister, two adult brothers, and a partner of one of the brothers. The 15-year old sister did not attend, nor did another adult sister but both had made their views known to their attending siblings before the meeting.

The family plan was as follows:

- although the young person would prefer to remain living with the family, they were unable to realistically offer her more than short-term care;

- when the anticipated death of the father occurred, a local fostering placement should be offered;

- family members would be involved in pre-placement introductions and discussions, and would welcome continuing contact;

- the Social Services Department would pay for transport from the present placement to visit the hospital and get to school and continue payments to the relative who was caring for the girl in the short term; and

- the daughter closest to the father would tell him of the meeting and its decisions.

The coordinator commented: 'This meeting left workers (and I imagine, family members) feeling drained but satisfied with the process. The 13-year old had not really understood or accepted that her father was dying – not surprising as he had not understood or accepted it either. The adult siblings (who themselves have had rough times, several were in care as younger children and had mixed memories of social workers) were sensitive and gentle with her. Most had quite negative feelings about their father (the two younger girls have a different mother) but did not let their own feelings crowd hers, which were evidently very loving towards him'.

Family 2

The family consisted of mother, father and 3-year old girl. The child had been placed on the Child Protection Register and there had been social services' involvement since then, including two periods in care due to neglect. The child had been placed with an aunt who had been approved as a foster parent. The concerns all related to the parents' use of alcohol and the care that they provided to their child when they had been drinking; there were no concerns about the level of care at other times. The aim of offering a family group conference was to formulate the basis of a reunification plan.

The family group conference was held in the parents' home on a weekday afternoon. It lasted two hours with the family spending one hour alone. Attending were mother, father, and an aunt. The parents refused to disclose information about the grandparents as they did not wish to involve them. The family decision was: for the parents to tackle their continuing problem with alcoholism and to attend a rehabilitation centre with the child; for the aunt to continue to support and visit on a daily basis and have the child to stay whenever needed; and for the Social Services Department to help with the provision of a telephone and assistance with travelling arrangements to the rehabilitation house. These plans were agreed and the child returned home a week later. The rehabilitation programme, jointly funded by the Social Services Department and the Probation Service, was to continue for 10 weeks.

The Next Stages

The development of family group conferences is potentially far reaching. In a number of different areas they may contribute to the better implementation of the aims of the *Children Act* 1989 and may overcome the long-standing problems of the care system identified in research and criticised by users. By the end of 1996, when the research is complete, it is hoped to have a clearer idea of the particular benefits of this approach and a realistic view of the difficulties of implementing it. While the family group conference approach is not expected to provide perfect solutions to family problems, it is clearly going to be very important in the coming years.

Acknowledgments

This work would not be possible, nor worthwhile, without the families involved, and we would like to thank them for their willingness to take risks with new services and to be open with researchers. Our thanks also go to staff on the projects, who have shown remarkable dedication in the face of numerous obstacles, and to the Family Rights Group who have played a key role over many years in continuing support for partnership in child welfare. Finally, we are grateful to the Nuffield Foundation for providing the finance for the research.

References

British Association of Social Workers. (1980). *Clients are fellow citizens – Report of the working party on client participation in social work.* Birmingham: British Association of Social Workers.

Bullock, R., Little, M., & Millham, S. (1993). *Going home – The return of children separated from their families.* Aldershot: Dartmouth.

Coffin, G. (1993). *Changing child care-The Children Act 1989 and the management of change.* London: National Children's Bureau.

Cooper, D. (1993). *Child abuse revisited: Children, society and social work.* Milton Keynes: Open University Press.

Department of Health. (1989). *The care of children: Principles and practice in regulations and guidance.* London: H.M.S.O.

Department of Health. (1991). *Patterns and outcomes in child placements.* London: H.M.S.O.

Department of Health and Social Security. (1985). *Social work decisions in child care.* London: H.M.S.O.

Department of Health, Home Office, Department of Education and Science, Welsh Office. (1991). *Working together under the Children Act 1989.* London: H.M.S.O.

Fisher, M., Marsh, P., & Phillips, D. (1986). *In and out of care.* London: Batsford.

Hughes, R. (1995). Interview in *Children Act News 18.* London: Department of Health

Jordan, B. (1987). Counselling, advocacy and negotiation. *British Journal of Social Work, 17,* 135-146.

Jordan, B. (1990). *Social work in an unjust society.* Hemel Hempstead: Harvester Wheatsheaf.

Koren, P. E., DeChillo, N., & Friesen, B. J. (1992). Measuring empowerment in families whose children have emotional disabilities: A brief questionnaire. *Rehabilitation Psychology, 37*(4), 305-321.

Marsh, P. (1993). Family preservation and reunification-The need for partnership between professionals and users. In P. Marsh, & J. Triseliotis (Eds), *Prevention and reunification in child care* (pp. 39-53). London: Batsford.

Marsh, P. (1994a). Partnership, child protection and family group conferences-The New Zealand 'Children, Young Persons and their Families Act 1989'. *Tolley's Journal of Child Law, 6*(3), 109-114.

Marsh, P. (1994b). Family partners: An evaluation of family group conferences in child welfare. In K. Morris (Ed.), *Family group conferences-A report commissioned by the Department of Health* (pp. 17-24). London: Family Rights Group.

Marsh, P., & Allen, G. (1993). The law, prevention and reunification-The New Zealand development of family group conferences. In P. Marsh, & J. Triseliotis (Eds), *Prevention and reunification in child care* (pp. 69-84). London: Batsford.

Marsh, P., & Fisher, M. (1992). *Good intentions: Developing partnership in social services.* Community Care into Practice Series, York: Joseph Rowntree Foundation.

Millham, S., Bullock, R., Hosie, K., & Little, M. (1989). *Access disputes in child care.* Aldershot: Gower.

Morris, K. (Ed.). (1994). *Family group conferences-A report commissioned by the Department of Health.* London: Family Rights Group.

Newton, C., & Marsh, P. (1993). *Training in partnership-Translating intentions into practice in social services.* York: Joseph Rowntree Foundation.

Packman, J. (1993). From prevention to partnership: Child welfare services across three decades. *Children & Society, 7*(2), 183-195.

Packman, J., & Jordan, B. (1991). The Children Act: Looking forward, looking back. *British Journal of Social Work, 21*(4), 315-327.

Pugh, G., & De'Ath, E. (1989). *Working towards partnership in the early years.* London: National Children's Bureau.

Wilcox, R., Smith, D., Moore, J., Hewitt, A., Allan, G., Walker, H., Ropata, M., Monu, L., & Featherstone, T. (1991). *Family decision making: Family group conferences – Practitioners' views.* Lower Hutt, New Zealand/London, England: Practitioners' Publishing/Family Rights Group.

10

Family Group Conferences in Canada and the United States: An Overview

Russ Immarigeon

Canada and the United States currently have only a few formal programmes using principles or procedures associated with New Zealand's family group conferences. In Canada, family group conference programmes exist for child protection and family violence in Newfoundland and Labrador and for juvenile offending in Manitoba. In Oregon, the Family Unity Programme is the only fully developed programme in the United States that claims direct association with the family group conferences. While family group conferences have received expressions of support in other states and provinces in recent years, efforts to develop and implement them have either waned or stalled for a variety of reasons, including lack of adequate information about family group conferences, other child welfare policy priorities, and failure to attract sufficient financial or system support. Recently, though, Kansas, Michigan, and Vermont have taken specific actions to establish family group conference programmes.

This chapter describes the developments of family group conference in Canada and the United States, exclusive of the work being done in Newfoundland and Labrador, Manitoba and Oregon. Descriptions of work in these jurisdictions are covered in the following chapters. No actual pilots of family group conferences have yet begun at the sites to be examined; therefore, attention is given to the history of policy and programme development in each location.

Family Group Conferences in Canada

Family group conferences are being explored or used in major Canadian pilots. In Newfoundland and Labrador, family group conferences have been convened at three sites. In Manitoba, the family group conference has been used in Winnipeg with Aboriginal youths who are involved with the Canadian juvenile justice system, and, finally, the British Columbia government, as part of a major revision of child welfare policies and practices, is introducing legislation on family group conferences. Canadian interest in family group conferencing is broader than these initiatives suggest, however. Individuals in other provinces have attempted, so far with little success, to institute family group conferences. In Nova Scotia, for instance, at least one innovative practitioner who has been involved with the use of mediation in child protection cases is attempting to integrate the use of family group conferences into her private practice. But, at this time, no other known agencies or persons are directing or organising other legislative or programme initiatives. It is unclear whether or not the federal government is interested in this approach.

British Columbia

The reform of care and protection practices, including the introduction of family group conferences, emerged in British Columbia in the 1990s as a result of Aboriginal advocacy on adoption issues and governmental concerns that existing legislation gives insufficient attention to current knowledge about physical and sexual abuse against children and the needs and supports required by families where abuse occurs. In November 1991, the Minister of Social Services appointed a ten-member community panel to review provisions of the *Family and Child Service Act* enacted in 1980 which was guided solely by the principle of child safety. Provisions of the Act authorised state agents to apprehend at-risk children and to use force to counter parents resisting such action. The community panel consisted of representatives from advocacy groups, government and private agencies. Over a nine-month period, the panel visited more than 40 communities to hear and receive more than 1,200 submissions of oral and written testimony. In addition, Aboriginal members of the Panel visited 33 Aboriginal communities.

The purpose of the community panel was three-fold: 'To hear a broad range of opinion about child welfare issues and provide ample opportunity for people to comment and make recommendations for change, to participate in public meetings and other activities of the review, and to issue a public report that will provide the framework for new child protection legislation in British Columbia' (Child Protective Legislative Review, 1992, p.7). The Child Protection Legislative Review issued a booklet, *Community panel: We need your views*, that described the community panel, introduced members of the panel, outlined the Panel's role, general terms of reference, honour code, provided dates and sites of all Aboriginal and non-Aboriginal community meetings, and offered assistance on how to participate at these meetings.

In January 1992, before the public meetings to be held by the community panel, the Ministry of Social Services issued a consultation paper, *Protecting our Children/Supporting our Families*, to encourage discussion and debate on child protection issues. The 106-page report provided a descriptive, structural and statistical overview of the British Columbia child protection system, enumerated the rights of children and the rights and responsibilities of parents, discussed the role of the state in child protection matters, explored various aspects of Native child welfare issues, and compared different Canadian approaches to child protection work.

While less influential in terms of breaking new ground, the consultation paper started to open doors for compelling reform measures to receive careful and detailed attention. Concerning the apprehension of children, for instance, the consultation paper admitted that 'it is probably fair to say that the apprehension may sometimes appear to be simply the easiest and safest response from the child welfare system, but not necessarily for the child' (Ministry of Social Services, 1992a, p. 136). Further, the consultation paper started to address the feasibility of alternative Native approaches, including self-government legislation, Band by-law, transfer of provincial authority, government-operated Native child welfare agencies, protocol agreements, and partial transfer or delegation (Ministry of Social Services, 1992a, pp. 59-60).

In October 1992, two important reports were released. In the first report, *Making Changes: A Place to Start*, submitted by the general Community Panel, 'an integrated approach to change' (Ministry of Social Services, 1992a, p. iv) was offered:

> Having heard the voice of the people, we have concluded that new attitudes and directions are necessary. The problems identified and the recommendations proposed are a package. The needs of communities,

families and children cannot be carved into pieces. Neither can the family and child welfare system. To do so will lead to further confusion and heartache (Ministry of Social Services, 1992a, p. iv).

In the second report, *Liberating Our Children, Liberating Our Nations*, the Aboriginal Committee of the Community Panel reported the pain they heard in the stories told them in their visits of how the application of non-Native laws has devastated their Nation, their families, their people. The Aboriginal Committee was less interested in recommending specific programmes than in setting up principles that would be applied to the development, financing, and legitimacy of Native approaches. Children are our future, the Aboriginal Committee asserted, and non-Native treatment of Aboriginal children has created conflicts which must be mediated and healed:

> Your present laws empower your Superintendent of Children and Family Service and your family courts to remove our children from our Nations, and place them in the care and custody of others. The first step to righting the wrongs done to us is to limit the authority to interfere in the lives of our families, and to provide remedies other than the removal of our children from our Nations. This must be accompanied by the financial resources we require to heal the wounds inflicted upon us. At the same time, the responsibilities and jurisdictions vested in your Superintendent and the family courts must be vested in our Nations. Finally, as our Nations assert our own family laws to meet our contemporary needs, as we rebuild the authority usurped from our Nations, the laws of our Nations must have paramountcy over your laws as they apply to our people (Ministry of Social Services, 1992b, p. viii).

In cases of child abuse where children's safety is an important issue, the Community Panel argued that 'all alternatives to removal must be explored' (Ministry of Social Services, 1992b, p. 133). Possible use of the family group conference in British Columbia, first mentioned in the *Making Changes* report, started to have a clear focus:

> We must stress that the family conference is a planning process, not a professional 'case conference'. It is not a group of 'professionals' telling families what to do, but a group of family members and others deciding how they are able to help and support the child and family. We believe that a coordinator employed by government should be provided to organise and facilitate these conferences. This person must be independent from the day-to-day management of the case. Although we cannot prescribe all the procedures this would involve, we think it is important to clarify our reasons for proposing an independent coordinator. Organising a conference will take time and effort. Families, therefore, cannot be expected to accomplish this task on their own. Help in organising and facilitating the meeting should not come from the social worker, however, as the power imbalance that exists between family and social worker could undermine the conference. Also, the purpose of the conference is not to debate who is right or wrong, but to plan strategies that will address the issue of the

child's safety. This point must be made clear to all parties involved and doing so may not be an easy task. An independent coordinator would have the skills necessary to ensure that all participants understand the conference's purpose and the roles they will play. The coordinator must also be given the resources necessary to ensure that those people the child and the family consider significant are able to attend regardless of where they live (Ministry of Social Services, 1992a, pp. 133-134).

The Aboriginal Committee's failure to recommend a specific programme model does not invalidate the appropriateness of the family group conference. Instead, the Aboriginal Committee suggests that approaches that are culturally appropriate (controlled by indigenous communities) and mediative (healing) are vital principles that can probably be used in a number of programme structures, including but not limited to family group conferences. A recent review of Aboriginal self-determination and self-government, for example, found that different groups establish different approaches, partially dependent on the stage of their independent development (Durst, McDonald & Rich, 1995).

In July 1993, the provincial government released a White Paper in response to the recommendations of the community panel, suggesting that adversarial relationships characteristic of existing legislation be replaced with an approach that focuses on reaching agreement by consensus and that collaborative and cooperative approaches were preferred to confrontational approaches. The White Paper proposed to increase family decision-making control. 'If a child is in need of protection', the White Paper stated, 'the Director will offer the family an opportunity to develop a plan of care that will serve the best interests of the child. Family conferences will enable families to make decisions about the care and custody of the child' (Ministry of Social Services, 1993, p. 5). According to the White Paper, family conference participants would include the child, members of the child's extended family, a person who is familiar with the case and who is authorised to make an agreement, a person knowledgeable about the child's needs, and anyone else that participants agree should attend.

The *Child, Family and Community Service Act* was proposed in 1994 in the province. In New Zealand, legislation stipulates that all discussions in family group conferences are confidential. British Columbia addresses confidentiality concerns in its legislation in a different way. Specifically, the *Child, Family and Community Service Act* states that all persons involved with a family group meeting must not disclose or be forced to disclose information gained at a family group meeting. Several exceptions are noted: (a) when everyone at the family group meeting agrees that disclosure is in order; (b) when it is necessary to either make or implement agreement concerning the child; (c) when a family group meeting agrees that further investigation is necessary to determine if the child requires protection; and (d) when disclosure is needed to protect the child or is mandated when a person has reason to believe that a child is in danger and may require protection.

The provisions for family group conferences in the *Child, Family and Community Service Act* state that plans developed through family group conferences are intended to protect the child from harm, serve the best interests of the child, incorporate the wishes, needs and role of the family, and account for the child's community and culture. If a child is determined to require protection, the Director of Social Services must refer the parent or extended family to a family group conference coordinator. This must be done regardless of whether or not the child has been removed from his or her home. After talking with the parents or extended family, the coordinator may convene a family conference meeting. The plan which emerges from the conference must include provision for services that help the family to provide children with safe and secure environments. The initial plan of care is to last six months, and can be extended for up to 18 months.

Family Group Conferences in the United States

The use of family group conferences is rare in the United States, but the number of jurisdictions seriously investigating its use is slowly increasing. Very little published information on family group conferences is readily available and so this overview is based on articles in professional newsletters, correspondence, or foundation-sponsored forums.

Casandra Firman's 1993 article 'On Families, Foster Care, and the Prawning Industry', which appeared in the *Family Resource Coalition Report*, has been instrumental in giving practitioners and policy-makers their first glimpse of family group conferences. Firman, an Oregon child care worker who worked with the Family Unity programme, argued that state-regulated foster care was, in essence, bad practice; she offered the family group conference as a radical and realistic alternative. Firman's article, which has been cited by people in at least four states as the stimulus that got them interested in pursuing family group conferences, tells of her experience on a prawning trawler dragging chains across the ocean bottom to net small loads of prawns. The practice destroyed coral beds and sea creatures, even the prawns themselves. Firman then compares this experience with the practice of foster care:

> Traditional child welfare practice has focused on saving children from hurtful environments. The ultimate salvation occurs, perversely, when

parental rights are terminated in a court of law. After the painful establishment of a case which proves the parents' unsuitability, expert after expert publicly details the failings of the parents before a judge. Through this process, the child learns that his family is 'bad' — otherwise they'd be together. And might children not conclude that if their families are entirely too bad to care for them, then they must also have that badness within themselves, being of the same flesh and blood? In its attempt to harvest a good catch, to save a child's body and soul, the system drags its chains over families until all that was sound, strong, and life-sustaining is destroyed (1993, p. 11).

She promotes family group conferences as a way of avoiding these harmful consequences.

The W.K. Kellogg Foundation recently conducted a national assessment of adoption and foster care practices and policies. The study concluded that many children are waiting for permanent homes, their problems can be solved, cost savings can result, and barriers to adoption, including less access to the system by minorities, can be overcome through communication and collaboration (W.K. Kellogg Foundation, 1992). The Kellogg Foundation funds the *Families for Kids* initiative, a project designed to bring about system change through 'supporting families to solve their own problems, coordinating family services among professionals, providing families with a single casework team, providing children with a single foster care home in their own neighbourhood, and placing children in a permanent home within one year' (W.K. Kellogg Foundation, 1994). Recently, $21.7 million was awarded to nine sites to implement these objectives.

The Edna McConnell Clark Foundation, a strong financial and ideological supporter of family preservation programmes, is now further examining how to improve child protective services within its *Programme for Children*. As part of this effort, the Foundation has asked the American Humane Society and the American Bar Association's Center on *Children and the Law* to review family group conferences. In September 1993, Mark Hardin, an ABA attorney and nationally-known child welfare expert, visited New Zealand and interviewed 100 attorneys, judges and other officials associated with family group conferences. In a brief article, published in May 1994, Hardin observed that the United States tends to 'give much lip service to cultural competence and cultural relevance of social work practice. Under the New Zealand system, a worker is under far more pressure to obtain knowledge of other cultures within the country' (1994, p. 43). Hardin raised concerns about the stability of family group conference-determined placements, confidentiality, and whether or not children were protected from additional abuse, but he concluded that 'the

New Zealand approach is technically compatible with the level of court involvement which is required by Federal law' (1994, p. 46). The initiatives of these two Foundations provide a context for the various developments now described.

In Kansas, planning activities for the Kellogg Foundation *Families for Kids* initiative identified family group conferences as a potentially useful approach. Kansas has been awarded a three-year Kellogg Foundation grant to secure timely, safe and culturally appropriate placements for children who are stuck in the child welfare system without a permanent home and to reform the child welfare system so that children will not be lost in a bureaucratic web. Kansas *Families for Kids*, a private non-profit organisation, will coordinate programme development in three major population areas and in one rural setting. Later, successful efforts will be replicated statewide.

Project sites were initially selected because of local interest in participating. Accordingly, project planning committees consisting of local stakeholders have been organised to address legal, training, service delivery, health, safety, and financial issues related to the use of kinship care. A specific focus of this initiative is to divert the out-of-home placements of African-American children to caregivers who are relatives. Kansas initiatives on kinship care were assisted by a national workshop on kinship care convened by the Child Welfare League of America in October 1994.

Two approaches will be undertaken. One is 'concurrent case planning' which provides case assessment within 72 hours and alternative plans for the reunification and termination of parental rights for use where and when needed. Other principles of concurrent case planning include: identifying resourceful family members, informing the family of the negative consequences of substitute care, providing direct services to children while probing other permanent living arrangements, increased use of visitation to improve parent-child bonds, and full disclosure to family members of incidents and patterns of child abuse and neglect by one or both biological parents. The other approach is family group conferences.

Kansas *Families for Kids* aims to start family group conferences for approximately 80 children at two county locations. In 1994, adoption legislation was adapted to include the possibility of family group meetings. At the start of this initiative they had very little information on family group conferencing (except Casandra Firman's article). As of this writing, the project is looking for technical and training assistance on kinship care and family group conferences.

In Michigan, family group conferences were also raised in discussions associated with planning activities for the Kellogg Foundation's *Families for Kids* initiative. In Grand Rapids, an effort is being planned to use family group conferences to divert children from the child welfare system and to reduce the number of minority children in out-of-home placements.

In Vermont, state social service officials are actively working to establish demonstration or pilot initiatives in family group conferences in several of the state's 12 service districts. Last year, Bill Young, Commissioner of the Vermont Department of Social and Rehabilitative Services, read Casandra Firman's article, was intrigued and obtained copies of New Zealand's *Children, Young Persons and Their Families Act 1989* and other articles on family group conferences. The Department then contacted Gale Burford and Joan Pennell in Newfoundland. Commissioner Young reports that he especially liked the thoughtful way Newfoundland approached child safety concerns.

Simultaneously with receiving this information, the Commissioner was also building support for family group conferences. He sent information about them to all 12 social service districts and in November 1994 he went with two Vermont district supervisors, a University of Vermont training specialist, and a Family Court judge on a site visit to St John's, Newfoundland. In St John's, the team visited and spoke with as many people associated with family group conferences as it could in a week's time. The team talked with the local family group conference coordinator, judges, social service officials, community leaders and anyone else they could coax into conversation. The team reviewed everything from policy development and training guidelines to the forms used. Information from the trip was forwarded to all district supervisors and an attempt was made to foster discussion among case workers and others about the model.

This information dissemination campaign resulted in expressions of interest from several districts. Two districts were likely sites for a pilot project but the Department's budget experienced serious cutbacks. In April 1994, the Commissioner invited the Newfoundland co-directors and the St John's Coordinator to visit Vermont to speak with legislators, district supervisors, caseworkers and others. He expects that by the end of 1995 two pilot projects will be funded and underway. Some of this, of course, depends on legislative budget allocations. However, the Commissioner believes that the state already spends considerable sums on children (the average cost for a child in substitute care is $18,300) and that funds can be redirected.

Commissioner Young has several goals for the pilot projects: keeping kids safe, improving service delivery systems, saving scarce public funds, and generating greater state support for extended family care. Currently, only 8 percent of Vermont's foster care population is adopted; 80 percent are returned home and 12 percent come of age in care then go home. Commissioner Young does not see the need for any changes in child protection or child welfare law to enable pilot projects. Nor does he see family group conferences as a panacea but he is impressed by its principles of engaging families in making decisions.

Elsewhere in the United States, initial expressions of interest have stalled because of more immediate priorities or a lack of general direction in child welfare policy. In Maine, for example, a local social service district manager started to review the possibility of using family group conferences in a pilot project, but state-level managers imposed other projects on local managers that diverted them from looking into family group conferences further. However, Maine is preparing a five-year child welfare plan and has a new social services commissioner who is familiar with Oregon's innovations.

New York State, which made an application for a Kellogg Foundation grant, brought several speakers from Oregon, including Casandra Firman, to speak to state and local child welfare officials and practitioners about Family Unity Meetings. Later, an internal review sub-committee was established in the Department of Social Services to further examine family group conferences in the context of empowerment programmes. In November 1994, however, a new Governor was elected and, nearly a year into his first term of office, no clear direction has emerged regarding family group conferences. Nevertheless, in March 1995, Assemblyman Roger Green (D-Brooklyn), the African-American chair of the New York State Assembly's Committee on Children and Families, introduced legislation (A5495) on 'Family Group Conferences and Diversion' to preserve and prevent the breakup of families 'by removing unnecessary cases from the Family Court'. A memorandum in support of this legislation prepared by Assemblyman Green's staff describes the rationale for this Bill:

> Many of the cases filed [in Family Court] regarding child protection involve a problem of communication and coordination of services between the family and the caseworker. The services offered to at-risk children and their families are often fragmented, incomplete and difficult to access. The readiness with which children are removed from their homes, separated from their parents and siblings, and placed in foster care is often criticised as not being in the best interest of the child. These families are often in crisis and therefore amenable to change. Many of these could have been

avoided by providing needed services, often concrete in nature, and thereby keeping the family together. It is more cost-effective to keep a family together through the provision of services than for a child to enter foster care. Other states have successfully implemented such programmes. This legislation is modelled after New York's successful and cost-saving PINS diversion programme and New Zealand's successful Family Group Conference programme under their Child, Young Persons, and Their Families Act.

Assemblyman Green's staff also prepared a summary of the specific provisions of this proposed legislation:

> The Family Court in each county may appoint a local probation service, court-appointed special advocate (CASA), authorised agency or other group that is willing to serve to conduct family group conferences and arrange and coordinate services to avert the need for placement. The court may refer any child protective proceeding to the programme for up to 90 days. A child protective service or a parent may also file a petition requesting that the adjustment agency convene a family group conference. The adjustment agency will confer with the parties. It may notify the court if the local Department of Social Services has failed to provide necessary services, and the court, after a hearing, may also notify the court if adjustment attempts are not successful and request that the petition be restored to the court's calendar. At any time, the petitioner may petition to terminate the adjustment process and restore the original petition to the calendar. The petition to restore must allege the current problems of the family, their service needs, the efforts made to provide those services, and whether parents refuse to accept them or they failed to alleviate the conditions. The court must terminate the adjustment process if it finds no reasonable likelihood that the process will be successful. Statements made by a parent to the adjustment agency are not admissible at any fact-finding hearing. A referral to diversion or participation in the adjustment process shall not constitute a finding or admission of neglect.

However, this legislation, sponsored by only one legislator, is not expected to pass, no hearings are likely on the bill, public responses to the legislation are not being solicited, and professional opinions are not being sought.

In juvenile justice, no family group conference programmes have yet been implemented in the United States, although several initiatives are under way. For example, several state officials from Arizona travelled to New Zealand, became familiar with family group conferences and introduced legislation about them upon their return. And, in Minnesota, police officials are exploring the use of family group conferences and training sessions are being organised.

Conclusion

Family group conferences are not yet much used in either Canada or the United States. British Columbia is the only jurisdiction that is focusing heavily on legislative enactment to enable and guide their use. Kansas has altered its legislation so that family group conferences can be used, but the legislation is not specific to family group conferences. Most Canadian and United States jurisdictions exploring the use of family group conferences seem comfortable with fitting them into their current legislative and regulatory structures. No research is being conducted on the use of family group conferences and little attention is being given to connecting research and programme development.

In the United States, the use of kinship care has grown dramatically during the 1980s and 1990s (Child Welfare League of America, 1994). But this has occurred more because of the need for emergency placements and the impact of litigation than because of a family-centred approach to foster care practices that previously left kids adrift, subject to abuse or removed them from their extended family. Efforts to use kinship care more extensively have had double-edged consequences. On the one hand, extended family members are being brought into the foster care picture. On the other hand, they are not empowered to make decisions about children's placement. Thus, while the use of kinship care might naturally lead to the exploration of family group conferences, and in several places this has been the case, the use of kinship care has produced a backlash against funding relatives to care for their younger family members.

Practitioners and policy-makers, in the United States at least, commonly make several assumptions about family group conferences. First, they assume that only certain aspects of family group conferencing can be adapted to their procedures. Second, because New Zealand is a different country with different cultures and a different history, they assume that its practices cannot be transposed in a meaningful way. Third, they assume that family group conferences should be used as only one of a number of care and protection programmes operating in their States, rather than making them part of the statutory processes which they are in New Zealand. Finally, they often assume that their current practice is similar to family group conferences. Many of these assumption are open to doubt, as the chapters in this book show. Practitioners and policy-makers have not yet examined or explored the full implications of the range of changes achieved through family group conferences in New Zealand, including how professionals' roles have to change.

References

Child Protective Legislative Review, 1992, p.7

Child Welfare League of America. (1994). *Kinship care: A natural bridge.* Washington, DC: Child Welfare League of America.

Durst, D., McDonald, J., & Rich, C. (1995). Aboriginal government of child welfare services: Hobson's choice. In J. Hudson & B. Galaway (Eds), *Child welfare in Canada: Research and policy implications* (pp. 41-53). Toronto, ON: Thompson Educational Publishing, Inc.

Firman, C. (1993). On families, foster care, and the prawning industry. *Family Resource Coalition Report. No. 2*, 9- 11.

Hardin, M. (1994). Family group conferences in New Zealand. *ABA Juvenile and Child Welfare Law Reporter, 13*(3), 43-46.

W.K. Kellogg Foundation. (1992). *Families for kids: A grant program to change adoption systems.* Battle Creek, MI: W.K. Kellogg Foundation.

W.K. Kellogg Foundation. (1994). Families for kids: Program awards $21.7 million to support adoption, foster care reforms. *News Release*, December 28, 1994. Battle Creek, Michigan.

Ministry of Social Services. (1992a). *Making changes: A place to start.* Vancouver: Province of British Columbia.

Ministry of Social Services. (1992b). *Liberating our children/ Liberating our nations.* Vancouver: Province of British Columbia.

Ministry of Social Services. (1993). *Making changes: Next steps – A white paper for public review.* Vancouver: Province of British Columbia.

11

Family Group Decision-making in the United States: The Case of Oregon

Larry Graber, Ted Keys and Jim White

This chapter describes the development and use of family group decision-making in the state of Oregon's child welfare agency, particularly in child protective services. It covers background information on the use of family group decision-making in Oregon; the development of the 'family unity meeting model'; workers' attitudes and practices around this model; and a discussion of some other applications of family group decision-making in Oregon.

Breaking Ground for Family Group Decision-making

Family group decision-making has been used extensively in Oregon child welfare work with the State Office for Services to Children and Families for the past five to six years. The State Office is charged with protecting the safety of children and is a state-administered agency with branch offices in each of the state's 36 counties. Like most child welfare agencies in the country, State Office for Services to Children and Families is mandated by federal law to make 'reasonable efforts' to maintain children in their own homes and with their own families. State care is seen as a last resort to ensure the safety of a child. Oregon also has a tradition, since the early 1970s, of 'permanent planning' for children who have been placed in state custody. The focus of both 'reasonable efforts' and 'permanent planning' is to return children to their own homes as soon as possible if their safety can be assured. Because of these pressures to maintain children in their own homes, child welfare workers developed family-focused interventions to build and strengthen natural care-giving systems for children.

While Oregon does not have comprehensive legislation like New Zealand that requires the use of family group conferences in certain circumstances, various laws and administrative rules for State Office for Services to Children and Families require that families should be actively involved in care and custody decisions about their children. The use of the family decision-making process is one of several options to involve families in these decisions. Programme implementors within State Office for Services to Children and Families felt that freedom of choice was preferable to mandating the use of such meetings in the belief that plans were more likely to be carried out if choice about the method was available for both professionals and families. Courts, however, sometimes order the State Office and families to participate in a family group decision-making process such as the family unity meeting. These court ordered meetings are often viewed negatively by both the State Office and the families: families are usually more than eager to speak up for their children and to participate in meetings about their children voluntarily. In the family unity meeting families are given more status with respect to their children than they are in the court process where they and other relatives or friends have little opportunity to speak and where expert testimony is more highly valued.

The essence of family group decision-making in Oregon is establishing a collaborative relationship between the state and families to ensure the safety of children at risk of abuse. Two types of family group decision meetings have evolved. The family unity meeting was developed in 1989, around the same time as the development of family group conferences in New Zealand. There are similarities between the two types of meetings and Oregon child welfare workers and administrators became aware of them through the exchange of information. Eventually, in 1993, a training conference for many State Office staff occurred with trainers from New Zealand. Oregon workers who were already familiar with family unity meetings began incorporating aspects of family group conferences into their practice. The main difference is that in the former a facilitator is used throughout the meeting whereas in the latter the family more commonly deliberates for a time in private. This chapter focuses on family unity meetings.

The Oregon Family Unity Meeting Model

The Oregon family unity meeting model was developed in 1989 as a result of an audit of casework practice by the State Office for Services to Children and Families. Caseworkers were very angry with the use of an audit process which, like most audits, focused on reviewing case records for problems and mistakes and offering advice to 'improve practice'. The resistance of workers to this process was remarkably similar to the resistance workers encounter from a family when they enter a family's life uninvited. However, a departure from the audit process by one member of the audit team resulted in a dramatic change in attitude on the part of caseworkers. The audit shifted from looking for problems to asking workers for their best thinking on how to help families. Instead of resisting this, workers throughout the Western region of the State Office for Services to Children and Families lined up to participate and, in fact, a number of suggestions from caseworkers during this revised audit process formed the basis of the family unity meeting model. These suggestions can be summarised as follows.

- A family unity planning meeting should be held at the beginning of the case. The meeting should include the family and community and should focus on alleviating the crisis causing the possibility of a placement.

- The family's point of view should be strongly considered whenever possible.

- All procedures should be reviewed in terms of issues of respect. An atmosphere of trust should be established.

- The 'service agreement' should be replaced with a family unity plan.

- The focus should be on the positive intent of the agency to help the family re-unite or stay united.

- A tone of cooperation with families should be established from the beginning.

- The process should include milestone letters, celebration letters, letters of accomplishment, certificates, and awards of achievement.

- An attempt should be made to put money where the need is; protective service workers should be able to reduce stress in the family by helping with groceries, rent, electric bill, auto repair, diapers, bedding and the like.

- The process should include parent training programmes designed to help parents with the return of their children from foster care.

- Emphasis should be placed on strengths and aligning the strengths of the family, the agency, the extended family and the community toward finding solutions.

- There is power in simplicity. Start with the simplest way of resolving concerns, rather than with the most complicated way.

- Attribute best intent; very few people deliberately set out with the intent to be bad parents.

- Institute a quick response team that listens to families.

Another contributor to the new model was families. They were asked what seemed to be of most value to them. They mentioned workers who listened, cared about them, believed in them, respected them, noticed their strengths, trusted them and didn't give up on them. None mentioned the effectiveness of the investigation or the quality of the advice they received This fitted well with caseworkers' 'best thinking'. This new model was a clear departure from previous practice which focused on 'problems' and giving 'advice' through assessing 'risk' and developing 'service agreements'. Looking for problems and giving advice is a formula that weakens rather than strengthens families. It makes the assumption that the professional knows all the relevant factors in another person's life. Neither 'problems' nor 'advice' are part of the family unity meeting model.

Values and Beliefs Underlying the Family Unity Meeting Model

The family unity meeting model focuses on how we think about families. It is a tool that deals with attitude more than technique and rests on eight values and beliefs about families.

- Families have strengths and can change. They deserve respect. Families have wisdom and solutions. Families and communities are our best resource.

- Strengths are what ultimately resolve issues of concern. It is important to set up opportunities for families to show their strengths.

- Strengths are discovered through listening, noticing and paying attention to people.

- Strengths are enhanced when they are acknowledged and encouraged.

- People gain a sense of hope when they are listened to. People are more inclined to listen to others if they are listened to.

- Options are preferable to advice. They provide choices and thereby empower.

- Empowering people is preferable to controlling them.

- A consultant is more helpful to people than a dictator.

The Operation of Family Unity Meetings

The model was developed as an option for workers and families. If a child protective service worker visits a home and is convinced the child is not safe in that setting, the worker should be supported in any reasonable action taken to protect the child: for example, placement with a relative, in a shelter, or foster care. If, however, the worker does not see immediate danger to the child and sees strengths in the family, a family unity meeting is appropriate. If a worker would like a meeting and the family disagrees, there is no meeting. A more complex issue is when a family asks for a meeting and the worker disagrees. Even if a third party chairs the meeting, it is not likely to be successful. A worker who is not committed to the process can undermine the intent of the meeting as easily as a non-committed family.

The model is designed to be respectful to the family. It is not a meeting to bring in family, relatives and friends with the intention of telling them what they need to do. That is a family manipulation meeting; it is control in the guise of helping that will not be successful. The family is given a copy of the format for the meeting before they agree to attend. If they choose to attend, they are asked to bring anyone they would like with them.

Meetings have three basic parts (see Appendix A):

- listing the concerns of the agency and those of the family;

- asking the family and their friends for their best thinking on how to deal with the concerns which have been expressed; and

- outlining the final plan reached by the participants.

Listing the Concerns of the Agency and the Concerns of the Family

It is important here to be honest and deal with the toughest concerns, head-on. Surprisingly often, the family and their friends have concerns which are very similar to those of the agency. It is very important to talk about 'concerns' as opposed to 'problems'. The word 'problem' cripples the helping process because it carries with it implications of shame, blame and guilt. It leads to labelling and making negative assumptions about people who are hesitant to share their problems. The overall focus on problems is paralysing for both worker and family. It invites denial and defensiveness.

Asking the Family and their Friends for their Best Thinking on how to Deal with the Concerns which have been Expressed

'What is your best thinking on how could things be better here?' This question gives the family an opportunity to show their strengths. By asking the question you are affirming that you believe the families have ideas and that you are willing to listen to them.

In one family unity meeting, concern was expressed about a 14-year old boy who constantly ran away from home. When his father was asked for his best thinking on how to keep the boy at home, he responded by saying he would buy some lumber and nail the windows and doors shut, get some chain and tie the little 'snarf' to his bed. It would be very easy to reach the conclusion the father was crazy and to jump in and save the boy by placing him in foster care. Instead, the caseworker attributed best intent to his comments. 'You have lots of energy to put into this. You really want your boy to stay home'. Almost immediately the father began to talk about other workable options.

It is important throughout the meeting to pay attention to family strengths and acknowledge them whenever possible. People who have been severely hurt in their life might respond to questions about their views by saying 'I don't know'. The tendency is to jump in with advice. It is important to be patient through this part of the meeting and to ask and talk about the things going well in their lives, their successes, the occasions they were able to deal with their concerns and the skills they already have. It is important to treat *them* as experts in their own lives and to explore and discuss options with them. Options provide choices and choices empower people. The job of the facilitator is to assist in this process and evaluate the family's plan in terms of the extent to which it offers increased and adequate safety for their children. If the plan does not seem adequate, the family is asked to continue working on it. If a plan cannot be developed that offers safety for the child, alternative placement plans by the agency can then be explored with the family.

Outlining the Final Plan Reached by the Participants at a Family Unity Meeting

This is presented on a form that can be monitored by the agency or by a responsible person involved with the family. (See 'Touchpoints Partnership' in Appendix B.) The plan covers a three-month period. It charts who in the family, the community and the agency have agreed to specific tasks to help strengthen the family and on what days and times they will be involved. It is set up so that it can be monitored to ensure that all parties are involved to the extent that they have committed themselves. This is a critical part of this model, as it shares the responsibility for the safety of the child with family, relatives, friends and community.

Other Applications of Family Unity Meetings

Family Support Teams

The State Office has created special family support teams of social workers, drug and alcohol counsellors and public health nurses to provide intensive services to chemically dependent parents. A main component of their work is a family unity meeting to plan for the recovery of the parents and the safe resumption of their role as caretakers. These meetings often take on the flavour of an intervention where the addicted person is confronted by family friends and even co-workers who express concern about the effects of drugs or alcohol in their lives.

Touchstone- a school based drug and alcohol intervention project

The Touchstone project began in late 1991 as a joint effort between the Portland Public schools, the Multnomah County Alcohol and Drug Abuse Office, the Oregon Office of Alcohol and Drug Abuse programmes and the Oregon State Office for Services to Children and Families. The target schools for this project are inner city schools in Oregon's largest metropolitan community. These schools are adversely affected by high rates of poverty, drug / alcohol abuse and racism. As stated in the original community plan:

> Project Touchstone is specifically designed to serve families of students 4 to 14 years of age who are experiencing academic or behavioural problems which school personnel believe may be related to alcohol or other drug problems within the [child's] household.

Once a student has been identified, a project member is chosen to contact the family and share the school's concerns for the child. The Touchstone project is explained to the family emphasising the family unity meeting approach; the values and beliefs underlying this approach are stressed at this first meeting with the family. The family is then invited to participate in the meeting and to invite anyone they feel should be part of it. At the meeting everyone is invited to discuss the areas of concern and to create a 'Touchpoints' agreement. This agreement then becomes a part of the service plan for the family. An emphasis on recovery from alcohol and drug problems is emphasised. A family intervention specialist serves as the primary person to support and encourage the family as they carry out their agreed upon activities. Cooperative inter-agency agreements exist to coordinate community services and to coordinate specific services for each family.

Juvenile Corrections

In the Portland area, family unity meetings are used when young people and their families are referred for state juvenile corrections services. These referrals usually occur when all local resources have been exhausted and a young person is likely to need a more structured living environment than the family home provides. The meeting often occurs after the young person has been incarcerated for a serious offence or probation violation. The goal of the family unity meeting is to bring together all the interested parties to discuss the new charges and to plan for future solutions. Since inter-agency collaboration is often a problem in metropolitan areas the family unity meeting provides a forum for each agency to make specific commitments for services to the young person and their families. The young person is invited to the meeting as a full participant. Special emphasis is placed on noting any successes or exceptions to the problems that the young person or his or her family have been able to achieve.

The Use of Family Decision-making in Child Protective Services

The State Office for Services to Children and Families conducted a survey in Spring 1994 of caseworkers in the Western Region. This region has 12 Branch offices and comprises one-third of the State Office workload. The study's purpose was to gain a better understanding of current casework practice concerning the use of family unity meetings. Specifically, the survey focused on the use of these techniques for creating and implementing 'child protection plans'. With the recent implementation of a new direction in child welfare practice in Oregon emphasising the use of family group decision-making, it was seen as important to understand the philosophical and practice issues related to expanding the use of these techniques. Forms were sent to 212 social service specialists; 79 were returned: a response rate of 37 percent.

Results of the Study

General Use of Family Group Decision-making

Respondents were asked to indicate the frequency of their use of family group decision-making with families on their caseloads. Overall, 66 percent of the respondents indicated that they had used the technique during the prior year, one half (53 percent) during the prior six months, and one-quarter (25 percent) during the prior month. Staff were asked to indicate the range of situations in which they used family group decision-making. A summary of these results indicate:

- 42 percent had used family group decision-making to 'help families stay together';

- 53 percent had used family group decision-making to 'help reunite families';

- 20 percent had used family group decision-making 'with child and foster family to help stabilise a placement'; and

- 13 percent had used family group decision-making for other reasons. These 'other reasons' included: a) helping families decide on a permanent plan other than return home, b) exploring options for placement with relatives, and c) planning to deal with pregnancies among teenagers.

Specific Uses of Family Group Decision-making

Staff were asked to describe the specific situations in which they had used family group decision-making. They noted using family group decision-making 'sometimes' in the development of a service agreement with a family and 'rarely' in the assessment of a Child Protective Services referral. Staff were also asked how often various activities occurred when they used family group decision-making. 'The family and the caseworker choose the participants for the meeting' and 'the family and the caseworker have agreed in advance on the purpose for the meeting' were cited more frequently than the other three activities – providing a copy of the family unity meeting outline to the family before the meeting; developing a Touchpoints Partnership agreement (service agreement); and providing the family with some time by themselves.

Opinions Concerning Use of Family Group Decision-making

Staff were asked how useful they thought family group decision-making techniques were in various types and stages of a Child Protective Services case. They felt that these techniques were least useful in cases of sexual abuse and during the assessment or investigation process. The final three questions asked staff to respond to a statement by circling one of the following four response choices: (a) strongly agree, (b) agree, (c) disagree, and (d) strongly disagree. The first statement was: 'One of the major barriers to the acceptance and use of family group decision-making is its rigid adherence to a philosophy which on occasion compromises the safety of children'. The most common response was about halfway between 'agree' and 'disagree'. The second statement was: 'One of the results of family group decision-making is that it expands the circle of those who are responsible for the safety of the child beyond the sole realm of a single caseworker'. The most common response score of those responding (N=78) was between 'strongly agree' and 'agree'. The third statement was: 'One of the results of family group decision-making is that it increases the number of individuals and agencies participating in addressing the concerns which have been identified'. The most common response was about halfway between 'strongly agree' and 'agree'. Overall, this points to a favourable response by staff to the introduction of family group decision-making.

Summary and Conclusions

Family unity meetings are an option for both child welfare workers and the families they serve, and, in rare instances, can be court ordered. Oregon Child Protective Service workers remain cautious in some instances when using family group decision-making meetings as indicated by the 1994 survey. Another problematic area for Oregon workers is the use of family group decision-making meetings in family violence situations. The prevailing belief is that victims of family violence, like victims of sexual abuse, would be placed at further risk of retaliatory abuse for exposing their abusers and would be reluctant to tell the whole story in front of their or the abuser's family.

Collaboration is beginning to occur between major stakeholders such as the courts, child welfare, family violence programmes, the police and district attorney's offices to develop protocols for the use of family group decision-making meetings in family violence cases. Another effort is underway to train child protective service workers to use family group decision-making meetings to create better safety plans for abused children. These efforts seek to ensure victims' safety and support throughout the meeting process. Offenders, for instance, may be excluded from the meetings but allowed to submit letters. Workers in Oregon have recently been exposed to the Newfoundland project described in this book by Pennell and Burford. Their project's goal of creating greater family and community support for battered women and children corresponds with the direction that Oregon is beginning to take.

Oregon child welfare workers, like those in other communities, are faced with a difficult task: to protect children from harm and at the same time to preserve the family whenever possible. This dual role of protector and preserver requires new tools to intervene effectively in child abuse situations. The Oregon family unity meeting model was developed as a result of an audit which asked child welfare workers what worked best in helping families overcome the problems of child abuse. The resulting involvement of families in the decisions that affected them created a collaborative rather than adversarial relationship with child welfare authorities. The family's solutions were often unique and families were willing to carry them out.

APPENDIX A: Family Unity Meeting Facilitators' Guide

If you are thinking about having a family unity meeting, this guide might help with the process. What happens before the meeting is critical to a successful outcome. Please become familiar with the 'Family Unity Model' brochure.

To determine **the appropriateness** of a family unity meeting, the facilitator needs to know the following:

From the caseworker:

'Why do you want this meeting?'

> You should get one of the following two responses (purpose):
>
> - 'to see if there is some way this family can stay together' or
> - 'to see if we can reunite this family'.
>
> (Both of these purposes are major motivators for families.)
>
> If the purpose of the meeting is something other than the above, make sure the family is agreeable and supportive of the purpose. The purpose should provide the family and their friends with motivation (hope) to attend. Don't have this meeting if caseworker is intent on getting the family to see things their way.

'Does family know who caseworker is inviting?'

> The family should be encouraged to bring in anyone they want to help and should be told if there will be onlookers, videos or the like?

'Are you and the people you invite willing to put concerns (not problems) on the table honestly?'

> Most often concerns have to do with safety for children.

'Are you willing to look for and help build on family strengths?'

'Are you willing to listen to and give the family's ideas a chance?'

From the family:

'Do you agree with the purpose of the meeting and do you want to attend?'

'Have you been given a copy of the FUM prior to the meeting?'

'Have you been asked to invite anyone to the meeting you would like?'

For the meeting

Physical arrangements should enhance the meeting. The room should accommodate the family and their friends comfortably. There should be a chalk board or white board to record concerns. Treats (cookies, drinks, etc.) should be available at the meeting whenever possible

Possible introductory remarks for the person chairing the family unity meeting are:

> *'Thank you all for coming to this meeting. Special thanks to the family and their friends. This is an **unique meeting**. After we have all had a chance to meet one another, I would like to tell you why this is a unique meeting. Let's all get acquainted.'*

Unique features:

- *'We are going to try and accomplish a lot in a short period of time! The meeting will not go past ___a.m./p.m.'*

- *'We are here because we have hope for your family. We wouldn't be here today if we didn't think there were strengths in this family.'*

- *'We are going to talk about our concerns and your concerns, why we are involved in your lives. We are going to be honest. We want you to be honest.'*

- *'We are going to focus on strengths, not on problems. I'll tell you why. Problems don't fix anything. Too often our interaction with a family looks like this (table analogy, agency and family on opposing sides). Fighting over problems is like getting stuck in mud. Strengths are what resolve concerns.'*

- 'We are going to ask you and your friends, *for your best thinking on how to deal with the concerns.*' (The chair of the meeting does not have to have the solutions for the concerns.) Draw from the strengths that exist in this family.

- *Develop and monitor a Touchpoints Partnership.* We believe families deserve to be supported and children deserve to be safe.

  'So let's get to work. We have stated the purpose of this meeting is to _____. Is that something you want to do? Can we all agree on the purpose. If so, let's put all our energy into making it work.'

Follow family unity meeting format

1. Introduction of all persons present.

2. Purpose of meeting defined. Example: 'We are here to see if there are ways we can help. . .'

3. Family and agency concerns (What are we worried about?) State all concerns clearly, honestly, respectfully.

4. Strengths of the family assessed.

5. Options family has thought about to resolve issues of concern. 'What is your (family's best thinking on how things could be better here?' What ideas do they have to deal with this?

6. Any additional ideas or options for the family to consider from the participants. Co-create options with family.

7. Develop Touch Points Worksheet. Who will do what and when to help this family? Each participant gets a copy of the Touch Points Worksheet.

8. Make decision. Set date for implementation of the plan.

9. Meeting adjourned. Everyone leaves together.

APPENDIX B: Touchpoints

The Visual Creation of the Family Support Systems

- A way to offer support to the family, support to the worker and maximum protection to the child.

- A strength-oriented visual service agreement, a copy of which is given to each person agreeing to a specific part of helping the family.

- Works to extend the circle of people who care, aand create partnerships, of people who agree to help in specific ways.

- Helps to visually coordinate services to clearly see who is doing what, when and to plan the contacts with the family's input to insure the best possible support.

- A visual way of insuring the family is not bing over-loaded with services or obligations.

Touchpoints Partnership

A. Family agrees to:		Sun	Mon	Tues	Wed	Thurs	Fri	Sat
1.								
2.								
3.								
4.								
5.								

B. Community agrees to:		Sun	Mon	Tues	Wed	Thurs	Fri	Sat
1.								
2.								
3.								
4.								
5.								

C. Children's Services agrees to:		Sun	Mon	Tues	Wed	Thurs	Fri	Sat
1.								
2.								
3.								
4.								
5.								

12

Piloting Family Group Conferences for Young Aboriginal Offenders in Winnipeg, Canada

Lyle Longclaws, Burt Galaway and Lawrence Barkwell

This chapter reports on a pilot project using family group conferences for eight Aboriginal young offenders and their families in the city of Winnipeg. The cooperation of the probation service was secured to integrate family group conferences into the procedures for processing young offenders: the recommendations of the conferences were substituted for a predisposition report prepared by a probation officer and these were then presented to the court as the recommended disposition. The work was done from May through August 1993. The first eight young people referred for predisposition reports and who self-declared as Aboriginal were provided with the option of a family group conference. Young people who were on probation were excluded from consideration, but the project included young people who had previously been on probation as well as young people referred for a predisposition report for the first time. Participants were not limited to first offenders. The family group conference convenor was an Aboriginal graduate student who also consulted with families about incorporating culturally appropriate practices into the family group conference process.

Results

Families and Young People

A total of eight young people were referred to the project and six subsequently took part in a family group conference. One case (H) was withdrawn from the process by the prosecutor, who felt the charges were too serious and too numerous to proceed in this way. A second case (D) did not proceed to conference because the young person had run away from a Child and Family Service group home placement.

A description of each young person and their prior offence history is summarised in Table 12.1. Six were male and two were female. Their ages ranged from 13 to 17 years. Three offenders were charged with theft, one with house breaking, one with possessing a weapon, and three with offences of violence. Only three of the young people had no prior court record. All the young people had committed more than one offence and the number of charges ranged from 2 to 33.

Table 12.1: The Young People and Their Offence Histories

YOUTH (CASE)	SEX	AGE	PRIOR RECORD	MOST SERIOUS OFFENCE	NO. OF CHARGES PENDING
A	Indian Male	13	no	robbery	5
B	Metis Male	17	yes, 2 charges	possess weapon	4
C	Metis Female	6	yes, 2 charges	assault	4
D	Metis Male	15	yes, 1 charge	theft over $1000	2
E	Indian Female	15	no	theft over $1000	2
F	Metis Male	17	yes, 10 charges	assault	48
G	Indian Male	13	no	theft over $1000	2
H	Indian Male	17	yes, 1 charge	house break & enter	33

Initial Meetings and Planning for The Family Group Conference

Reports for young people held in custody were expected within two to three weeks of referral. Young people not in custody were given adjournments of four to six weeks for the preparation of a predisposition report. This is in contrast with the lengthy period of time, in some cases over one year, that elapsed from commission of the offence to a finding or plea of guilt. Nevertheless, it was necessary to spend an adequate amount of time preparing victims, offenders, and families for the conference: usually a minimum of three to four hours. An additional two hours was necessary to brief defence counsel and prosecutors.

The conference convenor met with the referred young person to discuss the delinquent behaviour and the subsequent court process and to determine whether or not the young person wanted to deal with the matter through a family group conference. The young person was allowed the opportunity to define who was considered to be family. These pre-meetings took place at the young person's home, the Manitoba Youth Centre, or a guardian's residence. After the young person chose to have a family group conference, pre-meetings were held with his or her family to discuss the process, the offence, and other disciplinary issues that had arisen either at home or in the school. At this time, the family decided whether or not they wanted to deal with the issue in a traditional Aboriginal or non-traditional manner. The family was at this stage given the opportunity to define who they considered to be family. They also determined whether or not victims would be invited to the conference. Most of these meetings were held in the parents' or guardian's home.

All of the families thought that the victims should be invited, although they wanted the convenor to contact the victims. Victims were all contacted and invited to attend the conference; they were briefed on the process and, if they were unable to participate, information for a victim impact statement was collected. Three victims were seen in their homes; the rest were contacted and interviewed by phone.

The young person and family took responsibility for inviting their immediate or extended family members. The family was also responsible for providing gifts if an elder was to be asked to participate. Four elders were asked to chair family group conferences and two agreed to do this. The convenor contacted additional family group conference members such as cultural advisors, school teachers, guidance counsellors, and ministers who had been approved by the young people and their parents or guardians to attend.

Family Group Conferences

Venue and Timing

The choice of venue was a decision made by the families. Most families, given a choice, preferred the conference to be held in their home or at a community location that was not a government office. Two conferences were held at the Indian Family Centre and two were held at the Manitoba Youth Centre, not by choice, but because the young people had been denied release on bail. One of these was held in the waiting room of the Youth Court housed in the institution and the other as held in a teepee located in the inner quadrangle of the institution. None of the families selected the probation office as a conference location. Each conference lasted from three to four hours. Most conferences were held during normal working hours to suit the professionals who were to attend. Only one meeting was held on a Sunday and another was held on-reserve on a weekend to facilitate the participation of a maternal grandmother. In practice, both the families and the victims had limited choice about the timing of the family group conference because social workers and other professionals would only attend during working hours.

Participants

Generally, the family of the young person took responsibility for arranging for the participation of immediate and extended family members. Families would also select and invite an elder or spiritual advisor. This initial process of locating and interviewing parents and the extended family was time consuming because of their complicated living situations and the low number of intact families. However, a total of 23 family members attended the six family group conferences. Eight family members were at the largest family group conference. In one instance, neither parent could be located and only a sister was present and, in another, only the mother was present. In only one case were both parents present. In at least six instances, relatives travelled from a distance at their own expense to attend the conference. The largest family group conference had 16 people present, the smallest had five. Table 12.2 presents information on attendance at family group conferences.

The convenor invited victims to attend the conferences. Sixteen victims were interviewed before the conferences, but only two chose to attend. Three of the victims could not be located due to the length of time between the occurrence of the offences and referrals from court. Two victims resided outside of Winnipeg and were not able to attend. One victim was not able to travel to the family group conference held on-reserve. The family group conference model was fully explained to all victims. Victims were prepared to share information for use at the conferences and many provided victim impact statements. No victim said that they did not want to attend because they did not want to meet with the offender and his or her family. A number said that they did not want to be involved beyond sharing information because they saw it as the judge's role to negotiate a resolution to the offending. All victims were interested

Table 12.2: Family Group Conference Participants

YOUTH	IMMEDIATE FAMILY	EXTENDED FAMILY	SOCIAL AGENCY	SCHOOL	VICTIM	OTHER	TOTAL	LOCATION OF FGC
A Yes	Mother, Father, Sister, Brother	Sister-in-law (2) Uncle, Aunt	MaMawi staff (3)	Teacher, Elder	Yes	Family friend	16	Manitoba Youth Centre (MYC)
B Yes	Mother	Grandfather	MaMawi Native Addiction Council	Teacher	Victim Impact Statement	Pastor (2) IFC	9	Indian Family Centre (IFC)
C Yes	Sister		MaMawi	No	Victim Impact Statement	Family friend	5	Youth's home
D No conference held - AWOL								
E Yes	Mother		Child & Family Services	Teacher	Yes		6	Child & Family Services (C & FS)
F Yes	Father	Grandmother, Uncles(2)	MaMawi C&FS Probation Officer	No	Victim Impact Statement	Cousin	9	MYC Teepee
G Yes	Father, Brother, Sister	Grandmother, Aunt, Uncle	No	No	Victim Impact Statement	Cousin	9	Grandmother's home
H No conference held - withdrawn by Crown							NA	Not held

in a reparative as opposed to a punitive sentence. Greater participation by victims could have been achieved by holding conferences outside of normal working hours.

The female victim (E) who attended a family group conference was very involved in helping the family reach consensus on a plan. It was an opportunity for her to resolve feelings associated with being a victim and enabled her to participate constructively. The other victim who attended (an older male victim (A)) was concerned that there was some assurance that the offence would not re-occur and that the family was taking responsibility for the young person and prepared to provide close supervision. In both cases, the victims had no concerns about meeting the offender and the offender's family.

In three cases, the young person's teacher was identified as a significant person and in all instances they attended. One of the teachers was Aboriginal and saw the process as quite appropriate. Teachers liked the idea of the family focus and the family's control over decision-making. All three teachers found it easy to participate. Ten social workers participated in different conferences. While it was evident that the three non-Aboriginal social workers (one of whom left a conference and all of whom raised the objection that the families could not make a decision that would be satisfactory to the court) seemed uncomfortable during the family group conferences. The Aboriginal agency social workers were helpful to the process and showed a willingness to bring all possible resources to the sharing circle. Social workers from the mainstream probation and child welfare agencies were not flexible in the times they would make themselves available to meet. Although all of the lawyers agreed to attend, none showed up. Lack of legal aid payments and high workloads were cited as reasons. Police took the position that they could not participate because 'charges were still before the court'. Aboriginal officers were frustrated with this departmental response.

Family Group Conference Process

The responsibility is on the family to invite mutually agreed upon family members to a culturally appropriate gathering – this might involve an on-reserve venue (where applicable), pipe ceremonies, the presence of elders, the use of Ojibway language, sharing circles, decisions by consensus and the involvement of extended family. It was up to the family to decide which of these components would be included. The convenor was responsible for inviting members who were not immediate or extended family and monitoring the outcomes. The family, having chosen the family group conference process and having been given an opportunity to determine its shape, were asked to commit themselves to this strategy from the outset.

The family group conferences were conducted in this manner.

- Participants assembled into a sharing circle. The convenor or an elder opened the sharing circle and explained the role of the young person and their family members.

- A feather, stone, talking stick, or other object was passed around the circle in a clockwise direction allowing an opportunity for all to participate.

- The convenor explained the purpose of the conference and outlined the expected outcomes of the process.

- The young person explained the circumstances surrounding the offences and the effects these had on different aspects of his or her life. Then, the other family group conference members shared ways in which the young person's behaviour had affected them.

- The victim, if present, described the offence and its impact on his or her life. This was followed by family members describing how the offender's behaviour had affected them. If no victim was present, the convenor gave the group the information obtained from the victim impact statement.

- The eagle feather or other object returned to the convenor or the elder, who summarised the general thoughts of all conference members and passed the object to the young person to respond to the expressed concerns.

- After the young person had completed responding to the concerns, family group conference members within the sharing circle discussed a series of recommendations or a plan that addressed the concerns and would satisfy the court.

- The family group then usually met separately with a social worker from an Aboriginal agency *(MaMawi)* who served as facilitator and decided by consensus on a plan of action that would alleviate the concerns. The family also had the option to meet privately to decide on a plan of action and recommendations. Roles and responsibilities jointly assigned by the elder and facilitators to each of the conference members were discussed.

Aboriginal young people were usually very reserved at the beginning of the family group conference. Therefore, it was not surprising to observe that they were unwilling to immediately share all the circumstances surrounding the offences. As the conference proceeded, however, they became more involved. Feedback from family members positively affected other participants and elicited involvement by the young person.

The typical family group conference was based on traditional Ojibway (*Anishinabe*) cultural procedure since all of the referred families were Indian or Metis with Ojibway *(Saulteaux)* as the common first language. In all cases, at least one pipe carrier was present. The convenor arranged for a pipe carrier to attend where families were not aware of a culturally appropriate person to do the opening ceremony. In two instances, the convenor was given tobacco by the family and asked to arrange the ceremony. The pipe was used in two cases. In all instances, sweetgrass was used and discussions took place in a sharing circle. Three families decided to proceed in a non-traditional format: in a sharing circle but without an elder and ceremonies. Families, relatives, friends, teachers, Native Child and Family Service staff and young people all participated in the sharing circles.

Plans Developed and Presented to Court

Plans for presentation to the court were developed by participating families and professionals. These reports were attached to the predisposition reports completed by the convenor along with victim impact statements and police reports. Since the family group conference's report was restricted to the predisposition report format, and since there is a limit to the amount of information that the court can process, only a very small portion of the information from the family group conference could be relayed to the court.

All family group conferences' plans included a cultural component, including culturally relevant educational programmes, probation supervision by an Aboriginal community agency, referrals to the Native Addictions Council, or attendance at traditional ceremonies. Probation supervision was recommended as an alternative to custody in all but one case and in four cases community service was also recommended. In four instances, the family requested a curfew, in three cases, non-association, in two cases, abstention from alcohol use and, in one case, prohibition of weapons. As none of the young people were employed, there were no recommendations for monetary restitution to the victims. The family group conferences' plans presented to the court are summarised in Table 12.3.

Table 12.3: Recommendations made to Court and Subsequent Court Dispositions 1993-1994

CASES	REST	CSO	CULTURAL PROGRAM	OTHER PROGRAM	OTHER CONDITION	PROB. SUP.	CURFEW	SCHOOL
A								
RECOMM.	No	200 Hrs	MaMawi Family Violence	Mamawi	Non-assoc.	Yes	Yes	Beedabun
COURT	No	No	No	No	Yes	Yes	Yes	Yes
B								
RECOMM.	No	150 Hrs	Mamawi Mamawi	NAC Int Supervision	No	Yes	No	Yes
COURT	No	No	No	No	Abstain	Yes	Yes	No
C								
RECOMM.	No	100 Hrs	No	MaMawi Intensive Supervision	Alateen	Yes	No	Children of the Earth
COURT	No	No	No	No	Abstain & Literacy Program	Yes	No	No
E								
RECOMM.	No	No	No	MaMawi Intensive Supervision, Private Therapist	Pritchard Huse	Yes	Yes	Children of the Earth
COURT	No	No	No	Yes	Yes	Yes	Yes	Yes
F								
RECOMM.	No	No	Ojibway traditional ceremonies & place with Grandmother	Diagnostic Learning Centre	NAC Non-assoc. No weapons	Yes	Yes	Children of the Earth
COURT	No	No	No	No	AFM	No Custody 2 Yrs	No	No
G								
RECOMM.	No	50 Hrs	No	MaMawi Intensive Supervision	Non-assoc	Yes	No	St Johns
COURT	No	No	No	Yes	Yes	Yes	No	Yes

Court Outcomes

In all cases, the family's plan was presented to the court as the recommended predisposition report. All the young people were represented in court by legal counsel and had at least one parent or guardian present at court with them. In each case, both the defence lawyer and the prosecutor spoke about the appropriate sentence. In no instance were the family members asked to make comments in court and in only one case did the judge ask the young person to comment. The convenor was never asked to comment although all the predisposition reports indicated that the convenor had prepared the report. The disposition hearings generally took no more than 30 minutes. The shortest hearing was about 15 minutes; the longest was over one hour as the judge adjourned the court in order to read the report.

A summary of the dispositions is presented in Table 12.3. Five of the six young people received alternatives to custody. One young person received a two-year custody order (one year in secure custody and one year in open custody), followed by one year probation supervision. In no case did the court order restitution for victims or make an order that the young person perform community service in lieu of restitution. The court made no conditions on probation orders with regard to the recommended cultural programmes with the exception of two of the Aboriginal education programmes and the one recommendation to attend a programme run by the Native Addictions Council. Case A, for example, involved a 13-year-old Indian male who had five charges pending, the most serious was a robbery. The family group conference made ten recommendations to the court, including community service, participation in a cultural programme, a family violence programme at MaMawi (an Aboriginal social agency), and other support programmes. The court, however, named only four conditions: probation supervision, school attendance, curfew, and no contact with named individuals.

Since judges do not give verbal or written reasons for dispositions, it is not known why the courts largely ignored the families' recommendations. Overall, neither defence lawyers nor prosecutors emphasised or advocated for the family group conferences' recommendations to be included in the courts' orders and the judges never strayed far from the lawyers' recommendations.

Conclusions

Several tentative conclusions can be reached from this pilot study. First, families were able to come to a consensus and develop reasonable plans for dealing with their young offender. This occurred in families which, to an outside observer, may have appeared 'disorganised'. The conferences themselves were conducted in a culturally appropriate way using a sharing circle with the appropriate opening ceremonies.

However, victims' involvement in the family group conferences was less frequent than expected. This is a matter of concern and careful consideration needs to be given to ways to effectively invite victims' participation in the process. Also, while families were able to develop recommendations for dealing with their young offenders, these recommendations were largely ignored by the judges. Attention, therefore, needs to be given to presenting the plans in a manner that ensures that they receive greater acceptance.

Nevertheless the fact that the families were able to meet and generate plans for these young offenders suggests that family group conferences are a viable approach. It may be timely to further pilot the concept and to include young offenders from reserve areas, from other ethnic and cultural groups, as well as young people from Canadian families of European descent.

13

Attending to Context: Family Group Decision-making in Canada

Joan Pennell and Gale Burford

Introduction

This chapter is based on preliminary findings from the Family Group Decision-Making Project, a trial implementation of family group conferencing in three culturally distinct regions of the Canadian province of Newfoundland and Labrador. The project sites are Nain, an Inuit community on the north coast of Labrador; the Port au Port Peninsula, a rural region in western Newfoundland with people of French, English, and Micmac ancestry; and St John's, the provincial capital primarily settled by the British and Irish.

This demonstration project focused on family violence and operated with a federal grant, which paid for salaries to staff the project and for the evaluation-research component. The provincial Department of Social Services paid for the costs of bringing families to the conferences and for the costs associated with carrying out the families' plans if those plans met the approval of the child welfare workers in terms of the safety of the children involved. The families referred by child welfare were those families where abuse against a child in the family had been confirmed through investigation. Later in the project, Correctional Services of Canada (Parole) entered into a similar agreement with the project managers to pay for the cost of travel and carrying out approved plans for the families of convicted offenders where abuse against adult members of the family was involved. The provincial probation department endorsed one referral after a request from a family was made directly to the project for help in settling a conflict between two sides of a family.

Two central principles were used to guide the project. First, family violence does not stop by itself; intervention is required by the mandated authorities (for example, parole or probation officers and child welfare workers) once the facts of the abuse have been established. Second, the best long-range solutions to family violence are those which give the affected parties the opportunities to come up with solutions that are appropriate for their family, their community and their culture. To participate in this way, it is understood that families and community members must be given protection so they can participate in the decision-making without fear of reprisal from the offender and that they must have the tools and supports available to them to work through the solutions they come up with. Hence, the project sought to bring the immediate family together with other kin who were expected to have a life-long concern with the safety of their family member(s) and to give them the opportunity to have a say in what should happen under conditions of support, safety and providing the resources needed to aid decision-making.

In addition to a range of measures being used in the research, the on-site coordinator and researcher provided extensive written descriptions and reflections on their involvement with families; and, whenever families gave their consent, the researcher observed the family's private deliberation time. These reflective notes have offered a rich source of information about the nature of family group conferences and the processes that families go through during the conference, including the unique adaptations that families made at each site. More detailed descriptions of the project, its philosophy and operation, and overall evaluation are available (Burford & Pennell, 1995; Burford, Pennell & Macleod, 1995; Pennell & Burford, 1994).

The purpose of this chapter is to show how family group conferences can challenge child welfare thinking that focuses on the individual failings of caregivers and, as a result, can promote a communal sense of responsibility for child and family well-being. Using a framework combining feminist caring labour theory (Baines, Evans, & Neysmith, 1991) with the criminological theory of reintegrative shaming (Braithwaite, 1989), a series of mechanisms is outlined by which the Family Group Decision-Making Project united family groups to work together to prevent further abuse and neglect. Examples of conferences illustrate how the process led from individual participant's experiences of shame at the beginning to an increased sense of accountability and pride in the family by the end. The examples also reveal how the families developed solutions to family violence suitable for their local conditions and way of life. Through these processes, families were able to comply with standards imposed by public authorities while attending to their particular contexts, reshaping interventions to their cultures, histories, and situations.

Standards on Family Violence

Regulatory standards are a way that governments respond to public outcries for correction of social problems. The difficulty is that communities feel imposed upon when these standards are implemented without consideration for local conditions and customs. This is evident in charges that family violence laws disrespect the integrity of families and communities by imposing the standards of the dominant culture onto other groups, particularly immigrants and First Nation peoples, whose cultures have been characterised as traditionally sanctioning child and women abuse. These arguments have been refuted by Aboriginal and immigrant women (Kuptana, 1991; LaRocque, 1994; 'When Racism', 1984) as ethnocentric/racist and misogynist myths, and national studies have documented the prevalence of child and women abuse across all societal sectors (Badgley, 1984; Statistics Canada, 1993). Caring labour theory offers an analysis of why women and children are at particular risk of abuse and why standards on family violence are required. Within this feminist analysis, reintegrative shaming theory offers a perspective on how standards on family violence can be enacted in ways that are culturally appropriate and empowering of all family members.

Caring labour theory is based on the premise that caring is labour but that this work is rendered invisible by the assumption of its being a natural function of women. Within modern society, women are expected to provide caring for which they are uncompensated in the family and undercompensated in the labour market. With their earning power limited by caregiving expectations, women become dependent on a male provider or state assistance, and as a result they are at risk of poverty and abuse and hamstrung in their efforts to nurture and safeguard their children and other dependents. Typically, abused children are doubly abused by witnessing violence against their mothers (Bowker, Arbitell, & McFerron, 1988; Stark & Flitcraft, 1988). Failures to provide for children's needs or to protect them from abuse, however, are blamed on individual mothers with fathers excused, rather than viewing these failures as a collective responsibility requiring collective action (Callahan, 1993; Swift, 1991). The model of individual maternal guilt directs attention to the 'best interests of the child' and leads to apprehensions and foster care (i.e., care by another woman) rather than to implementing standards that support and protect child and adult family members.

While caring labour theory provides insights into why children and women are so often the victims of violence in modern society and why women are held culpable for this victimisation, reintegrative shaming theory offers possibilities for the empowerment of victims, offenders, and their families and communities. Criminologist John Braithwaite (1989) hypothesises that mainstream justice responses which stigmatise offenders increase the likelihood of further recidivism while alternative responses which shame and then reincorporate offenders into the communal network reduce its likelihood. He explains that courts establish adversarial processes which sideline victims and families and degrade offenders, who then salvage their identities by rejecting the law. Conversely, programmes such as family group conferencing bring together offenders with victims as well as their support networks and offer the opportunity for shaming without fixing a permanent label of deviant on offenders (Braithwaite & Mugford, 1994). Empowerment is effected by bringing into the open the shame of all participants – the offender for the crime, the victim for being victimised, and the family and community for their responsibility to maintain personal and public safety – and then by giving the group the authority to make decisions for their individual and collective well-being.

Caring labour theory helps to clarify the structural context in which reintegrative shaming occurs and how this empowerment process spreads around the responsibility for caring. The family group conference makes it possible to listen to the voices of all participants and design culturally sound plans for meeting public standards.

Method of Analysis

Detailed and often verbatim notes were taken during the family group conferences to construct how family group conferencing was represented by different communities participating in the Family Group Decision-Making Project. These reflective notes on family group conferences were prepared by local coordinators and researchers at the three project sites. The notes covered 20 conferences held during the first phase of the project when the sole referring agency was the provincial Department of Social Services (Child Welfare and to a lesser extent Youth Corrections Divisions); in the second phase, referring agencies expanded to include adult correctional authorities – parole and probation. The first 20 conferences ranged in size from 6 to 22 family group members and from 1 to 6 non-family group members.

The coordinators' recordings gave their observations of those parts of the conferences at which they were present. These periods were typically at the beginning of the conference when the child protection worker laid out their areas of concern and other professionals/community members provided information of relevance to the family's situation; the breaks and lunch periods; and the end of the conference when the coordinator was invited back to finalise the plan for addressing the concerns. In all but one instance, the family group gave permission for the researchers to observe the entire conference, including their private deliberations to which the coordinators were not usually privy.

Besides the staff's reflective notes, the analysis in this chapter has drawn to a lesser extent upon written notes prepared by coordinators for presentations on the project (Pennell et al., 1994) and material from focus groups held at the three project sites around the mid-point of the first year of implementation. Focus group participants included family group conference attenders (e.g., family, friends, community members, and professionals), advisory committee members (who provided guidance on the local operation of the project), and community panellists (who provided guidance on organising conferences with specific families). They were asked to describe their experiences with the project and evaluate its effectiveness. Findings from the analysis are summarised under the following headings, each representing an important stage of integration during the process of the conference: openings; standards for caring; family shame; caring confrontation; supports for caring; and family pride.

Openings

All the conferences opened in ways that distinguished them from interventions of public authorities. The coordinators' introductory statements stressed that the conference belonged to the family, and this was reinforced by the presence of their extended families and social networks (e.g., friends, foster parents, support persons selected by abused family members and often perpetrators to give them emotional support and watch out for their welfare during the conference), the venue which was usually a community facility of the family's selection, the circular seating arrangement, and the research consent forms reaffirming confidentiality and voluntary participation. These similarities across the three project sites were, in part, a function of the training and manual provided by the project administrators with input from the local advisory committees (Burford et al., 1995).

The character of the openings in each setting reflected the local culture and set the tone for the entire conference. On the Port au Port Peninsula dotted by a string of small Roman Catholic communities along the roadways, conference participants were very sensitive to maintaining the family's privacy, that is keeping others out of their 'business', and found it reassuring to take part in a ceremony of swearing confidentiality around a large Bible placed in the centre of their circle; this Bible then remained the centrepiece of all of the subsequent discussions. In Nain, commonly the conferences began with the inclusion of an Inuktitut-English translator to cross the language gaps not only between family and professionals but also between family generations, and an opening prayer by an elder or the Moravian pastor. As the researcher observed in one session, after the prayer in which the elder asked for 'guidance and strength for the family', the family members 'all seemed relaxed and ready to go at it'. In St John's, the conferences might include a prayer depending on the family's religious affiliation, but generally the opening emphasised rules on how to work together. The St John's coordinator took the lead among the coordinators in drawing up hand-outs explaining safety measures and the roles of support persons and information providers. The proliferation of documents reflected higher levels of literacy than at either of the other project sites and also the community's expectations of more formalised procedures.

Standards for Caring

After the opening, each of the conferences was dominated by the referring agency's articulation of its standards for parental care. The child welfare workers, sometimes supported by youth corrections workers and the police, gave their reasons for referring the family to the project and stipulated the issues which the family's plan had to address before the workers could approve it. Their expression of concerns were shaped by the legislation mandating their intervention and, as a consequence, these concerns had a certain uniformity across the three project sites. The workers spoke mainly about single mothers neglecting their children; men and women abusing children; children witnessing the abuse of their mother and, in one instance, their father; adolescent boys and girls being out of parental control; and adolescent boys committing acts of violence against mothers, sisters, and younger brothers. Often accompanying these reports were presentations by information providers such as a counsellor on addictions, a doctor or nurse on a family member's health, or an Inuit elder on traditional ways.

As became evident in the families' responses, their concerns overlapped with those of the public authorities but were far more sensitive to the day-to-day struggles of the mothers in caring for their families. In St John's, the family group participants were often the most forthcoming in challenging the child protection workers; aunts pointed out that their niece could not meet her two young children's needs as long as she lacked sound housing, a washer and dryer, and another bed; and a foster mother rebuked the child protection worker for not allocating sufficient funds for the mother to cover the costs of her children's home visits. Families in the other two sites also brought out into the open the material needs of their relatives – these needs though assumed a somewhat different character in those northern or rural regions.

In Nain, family members were concerned that a young single mother would continue to mistreat her three small children as long as she lived in an unheated house without running water; and another family agreed with the child protection worker and the health professionals on the gravity of the infant's losing weight, but quietly explained that the baby's failure to thrive could not be alleviated until the power was reconnected and the mother provided with a stove on which to cook warm food. On the Port au Port Peninsula where stockpiling wood was seen as a man's responsibility, two lone mothers were left in impossible situations. In one family where the single mother was seen as neglectful and abusive by children's protection services, the woman explained that she and her son often entered into bitter fights over his not bringing in the wood; and a divorced woman, who was characterised by child welfare workers as too depressed to care for her daughter, broke down in tears because she feared the onset of winter with 'no wood' in the house and kept repeating that she felt like a 'charity case' having to depend upon the child welfare department financially.

Family Shame

Although the families' responses expanded understanding by placing the public authorities' concerns within actual living conditions, deep shame was evident. At all three sites, after listening to the presentations of the child welfare workers, immediate and extended family members appeared mortified, but it was more common for women and girls to turn inward in pain, and for men and boys to turn outward in anger. In Nain, the humiliation was expressed through the family becoming 'very quiet', with the men perhaps 'pacing' around or 'walking out' of the room. Mothers, in particular, became silent for protracted periods; and, in one case, the mother would not break her silence until the coordinator suggested that all of the other conference participants leave the room so that she could speak alone with her support person; on their return, this woman then was able to express her views. Another strategy used by families was to propose to adjourn the meeting to the next day so that they could reflect in private on the reports.

On the Port au Port Peninsula, family members were often more outspoken in their responses. One father began what the researcher described as a 'yelling match' with the female foster care worker after her report and, during the session, his outbreaks of 'swearing', 'butting in', 'pacing the floor', 'swinging his arms', and 'banging' were only somewhat contained by the male child welfare parent worker, who informally became his support person, and by the nun, who tended to have 'a calming effect on everyone' present. While the father expressed his feelings, his former wife and mother of the child in question fled the room in tears; his current partner attempted to sidestep taking any position; and his aunt, who was caring for the child, argued with her nephew, instructed him to 'sit because he was making her nervous', and finally became 'exhausted from crying'. The emotionality of the participants after the public authority's presentation at this conference was not an isolated example, as evident from another conference where a boy left the room crying and slamming the door and initially disregarded pleas to accept a ride on his long trek home. In other sessions, though, the reactions were more muted. For instance, at one conference, a mentally unstable mother cried briefly after listening to the child protection worker's report, and the family group treated her throughout the session with 'kid gloves', as she appeared 'very ashamed/guilty'.

Likewise, St John's participants were strongly affected by the social workers' reports as well as by many of the presentations of the information providers, who were asked to provide overviews of matters relevant to the families' deliberations. Typically, though, they were more guarded than the Port au Port residents in expressing their feelings and more talkative than the Nain participants. When a counsellor relayed the effects of exposure to abuse and alcoholism on children, the adolescent daughter 'effectively protected herself by huddling into the far corner of the couch, hiding behind her sister and refusing to make eye contact with anyone . . . [Some] family members misinterpreted many of the [counsellor's] comments on alcoholism to apply to the grandfather rather than to the men in the [mother's] life'. During this information-giving time the grandfather 'coughed', 'fidgeted', 'started looking for his medicine', and was soon afterwards taken home by a relative. In another conference, the extended family, which had a history of intergenerational abuse, 'listened very attentively' to a counsellor discussing the effects on children of witnessing abuse. Later in a focus group, this same counsellor, a well-experienced group worker, expressed her discomfort in making the presentation. She explained:

> I was working with clients [in the conference] but I wasn't talking *with* them, I was talking *to* them, there was no dialogue and that was actually disconcerting. I was more nervous there than I have ever felt. I sort of looked at this group of twenty-five people and thought . . . Oh God, I'm not prepared, what do I say here? . . . I think I rely on the interaction to know what's appropriate to say and how to say it!

She had sensed throughout that her words were applying to more than the couple referred to the project.

Caring Confrontation

Because in most cases the family group took on a collective sense of shame, relatives and friends were able to reach out to the referred family in caring confrontation. In their feedback on the conference, some participants wished that there could have been even more challenging, but overall family members were pleased with how the conferences went. The gentle challenging helped family members express their feelings and firm their resolution to take part in change. Although women – aunts, grandmothers, foster mothers – often took the lead, men also took part in offering support. In Nain, the elders were commonly the catalyst in moving families out of shame into problem solving by giving younger family members' permission to speak. In one family where a child had died from neglect, a community elder at the start of the session 'talked about the importance of family and that it is good to have family support. He said that it is sometimes very hard to talk about personal things in front of other family members especially when they are a large crowd. [He] encouraged everybody to speak as this is the only way of knowing what each person is thinking', and 'offered the family the option of consulting with the community elders as a source of information and guidance in the future'. When the elder was preparing to leave the family to their private deliberations, the family requested him to stay 'because he was a trusted leader and understood what the family has been going through'. He agreed, and then 'the grandmother . . . took charge of the meeting, she not only encouraged family members to speak openly about matters and reminded everybody that "we are not against anybody when we speak, it's just that we care and want to help even though we might bring up very touchy matters"'. With the grandmother's kindly push, the son-in-law 'began to speak' and 'told family members that he always thought it was other people who had the problems of drinking . . . that he didn't ever see anything wrong with getting drunk even though sometimes he never knew what he was doing. That father said that it took the life of his daughter to make him realise that he did have a very serious problem'. His wife remained silent despite the encouragement of the grandmother (her mother) and her support person to speak, but in the next session after the opening prayer, she was 'the first to speak, she said that she had thought about what she has been doing and was feeling ashamed of herself. . . She explained that she wanted to try and get help. . . The whole atmosphere seemed to change and all of a sudden family members began making suggestions and offering support, it was obvious that they were pleased. Everybody took part in making the plan'.

At a St John's conference, safety issues were foremost in the Coordinator's mind, given the father's 'particularly notorious history of violence, alcohol and drug abuse, and criminal behaviour', the lack at the present time of 'social controls (parole or probation) monitoring his behaviour', and his 'overprotective' posture toward one daughter. Not alone in her worries, the mother and children spoke of fearing to raise sensitive issues because of his potential to explode. In response, before the conference the coordinator strategised with the father and his relatives as well as his wife and children on ways of safeguarding against his volatility. Tactics developed were to prepare in advance personal statements to be read at the conference and arrange for support persons to be present for all family members, including the father as 'he identified this as a way he could feel more in control of his emotions and a way that would ensure he would not blow up or leave during the [conference]'. For his support persons the father selected two uncles for whom he 'had respect' and from whom 'he wanted their approval'. At the conference, 'it was they who made him feel shame about what he had done, not the officials present' and from whom he received deep caring. 'The uncle (mom's brother), who was his support person, cried when reading the dad's statement as did most family members; however, they did not let him off the hook at all, and the statement was sincere rather than an attempt to glean sympathy and minimise the behaviours'.

A conference on the Port au Port Peninsula demonstrated how the participants could rally around a family long stigmatised in the community as 'that family' and given up as a 'lost cause'. Again, the coordinator's 'first priority' in organising the conference was the 'safety of the immediate family' because of the father's alcoholism and violence toward his wife, the son's aggressiveness toward his mother and sister, and the mother's quick temper and verbal outbursts. The father never consented to attend the conference but sent along a pot of soup for lunch; the mother and son, after much preparation by the coordinator, agreed to attend. During the conference, they both required and received constant support from their designated support persons as well as their relatives. When the mother quickly exited the room during the presentation on violence against women and children, her support person accompanied her and stayed with her while she cried. During the child protection worker's report, her support person was sensitive to how this would affect her, 'had his arm around her the whole time', and, over the breaks, the mother stayed with her support person, who in response to her agitation 'put his arm around her and patted her back'. Likewise, when the son broke down in tears as he listened to the police officer's report on his offences, his foster father, serving as support person, 'put his arm around him and said "it's OK"'. After the police officer finished speaking, the mother retreated with her support person to a separate room for a while, but the crying boy stayed with the relatives who all offered him support. The 'mom's sister comforted him and put her arms around him. Two remaining aunts went to check on him and joked around with him, tried to make him laugh . . . his grandmother went and gave him a hug of support. The family group also reached out to the mother and recognised her love and care for her children; and nearly all gave a little true-life story exemplifying that every family at some point has problems. . . They all were open and honest and tried to eliminate any/all barriers to open up mom and child. They also reclaimed the identity of the absent father as a '"good man" but when he drinks, things get really bad in the home'. The researcher observing the conference characterised them as a 'very funny group', who knew how to use laughter and joking to put everyone at ease. Over the one-day meeting, the family group moved their relatives a long way from the image of 'that family'.

Supports for Caring

The supportive interventions of the family group led to the formulation of plans to meet the standards set by the public authorities as well as their own concerns for their relatives' well-being. These plans showed consideration for the emotional and material supports that mothers and fathers required for taking care of their families in their particular locales. In addition, they showed that families saw the need for further public and community aid and for both male and female extended family members to assist their relatives. In the case of a St John's family where parents of limited mental capacity were resisting taking their children to their many medical appointments across town, a less costly and more effective alternative was proposed to the current one of relying on taxis authorised by the Department of Social Services. It was agreed that the Department would provide funds to purchase a used car for which the two uncles, both mechanics, would take responsibility for maintenance and that a female relative would accompany the family on the trips to the hospital to alleviate the parents' fears that their children would be detained if any injuries were detected.

For a Nain single mother with numerous children, it was decided that public funds would pay for the woman to receive help for her addictions problem, that a female friend would take care of the children while the mother was receiving treatment, and that the brother would follow 'the traditional way . . . that when a family member kills fresh meat like seals, caribou, ptarmigan, or catches fish, this is first shared with family members' without their having to ask. Out on the Port au Port Peninsula, the family group made very concrete plans around returning the children from their grandmother, who was currently caring for them, to their single mother. These plans included the Department covering costs for transporting children on home visits and paying rent for the mother's new apartment, the brother arranging for a driver and assisting with babysitting, and friends and a sister helping with the move and with child care.

Family Pride

At all of the conferences, child welfare workers approved the plan on the spot or asked for some revisions, checked with supervisors on some expense items, and then granted approval. Having their plans approved generated a sense of family pride and heightened family members' sense of control over their lives. This approval was particularly satisfying for a St John's adolescent girl who had taken responsibility for writing down her family's plan. When the coordinator asked 'her at the end of the [conference] if she was satisfied with the plan, she grinned and said "I wrote it, didn't I?"'. After finishing its plan, a Nain family, who had been uncertain as to whether or not members would even be willing to take part in the deliberations, left 'very pleased with themselves'. On a follow-up visit, the Port au Port researcher found a single mother looking like 'a whole new person' – 'glowing', 'smiling', and 'laughing' – as she stood next to 'two loads of wood' and 'stocked up on her necessities'.

Conclusions

An analysis of 20 family group decision-making conferences found that family members considered the conference a success when they were able to use the process to move from a sense of personal shame and helplessness to family pride and efficacy. Family members typically entered the conference ashamed: for failing to protect and nurture, for having committed violence, for suffering victimisation, or for witnessing violation. Mothers and wives, in particular, held themselves and were held as culpable for not creating a family setting of caring and safety. The structure of the conferences made it possible not only to confront individual shame but also for other members of the family group to accept some of the responsibility. By staying within the customs of the family rather than the practices of the public authorities, the opening of the conferences highlighted that the family owned this meeting and could take charge of its affairs. At centre stage, the family group could hear the reports of the child welfare workers and other professionals and their assertions of public standards for child and family well-being without experiencing a sidelining of the family's responsibility for its members. This context generated a sense of shame across the extended family for not having acted in the past to safeguard its relatives as well as a sense of shared identity because often the problems which their relatives experienced were common in their own lives. With the links across the family group affirmed, the participants could reach out to each other in caring confrontation, neither excusing nor rejecting, but instead encouraging growth for change. In such a climate, the family groups were able to make plans which emphasised supports for caring to come from the family, community, and government. The approval of the plans by the public authorities concluded the conferences in a manner that heightened family pride and responsibility.

Public standards against family violence are necessary to advance the voices of those who are victimised but they also stand as impositions which label families as dysfunctional unless they are translated into the culture of the families and their communities. The intent of conventional child welfare approaches is to promote the best interests of the child, but in practice this is carried out by assessing the inadequacies of parental caregivers, usually mothers, to protect and nurture their children. Thus, attention is focused upon failings of individual women and diverted away from collective responsibility. By introducing the family group conference as a joint family-community-government planning strategy, responsibilities for communal care are reaffirmed in a way that attends with sensitivity to the families' cultures, histories, and situations.

Acknowledgments

This chapter is based on a demonstration project Family Group Decision Making, which has received funding from the federal departments of Health (Family Violence Prevention Division), Human Resources Development (National Welfare Grants Division and Correctional Services Canada), and Secretary of State (with provincial Public Service Commission). Seed moneys for developing the project came from the Department of Social Services, Child Welfare Division, with on-going funding provided by this department. In Nain, the project is co-sponsored by the Labrador Inuit Health Commission. In addition, other groups such as the provincial Department of Justice, Royal Newfoundland Constabulary, Royal Canadian Mounted Police, Women's Policy Office, and the Provincial Association Against Family Violence have assisted in the development of province-wide protocols for the project.

References

Badgley, R. (1984). *Sexual offences against children* (Report of the Committee on Sexual Offences Against Children and Youth). Ottawa: Minister of Supply and Services.

Baines, C. T., Evans, P. M., & Neysmith, S. M. (Eds). (1991). *Women's caring: Feminist perspectives on social welfare*. Toronto: McClelland & Stewart.

Bowker, L. H., Arbitell, M., & McFerron, J. R. (1988). On the relationship between wife beating and child abuse. In K. Yllö & M. Bograd (Eds), *Feminist perspectives on wife abuse* (pp. 158-174). Newbury Park: Sage.

Braithwaite, J. (1989). *Crime, stigma and reintegration*. Cambridge: Cambridge University Press.

Braithwaite, J., & Mugford, S. (1994). Conditions of successful reintegration ceremonies: Dealing with juvenile offenders. *British Journal of Criminology, 34*, 139-171.

Burford, G., & Pennell, J. (1995). Family group decision making: An innovation in child and family welfare. In J. Hudson & B. Galaway (Eds), *Child welfare in Canada: Research and policy implications* (pp. 140-153). Toronto, ON: Thompson Educational Publications.

Burford, G., Pennell, J., & MacLeod, S. (1995, May). *Manual for coordinators and communities: The organisation and practice of family group decision making* (revised). St John's, NF: Memorial University of Newfoundland, School of Social Work.

Callahan, M. (1993). Feminist approaches: Women recreate child welfare. In B. Wharf (Ed.), *Rethinking child welfare in Canada* (pp. 172-209). Toronto: McClelland & Stewart.

Kuptana, R. (1991). *No more secrets: Acknowledging the problem of child sexual abuse in Inuit communities: The first step towards healing*. Ottawa: Pauktuutit (Inuit Women's Association).

LaRocque, E. D. (1994). *Violence in Aboriginal communities*. Ottawa: Royal Commission on Aboriginal Peoples. (Reprinted from *The path to healing*.)

Parker, I. (1992). *Discourse dynamics: Critical analysis for social and individual psychology*. London: Routledge.

Pennell, J., & Burford, G. (1994). Widening the circle: The family group decision making project. *Journal of Child & Youth Care, 9*(1), 1-12.

Pennell, J., Burford, G., Peckford, B., Crawford, E., Campbell, S., Lyall, G., MacLeod, S., & Tuck, K. (1994, June). Developing a family empowerment model in partnership with community and government. Panel presented at *Protection through empowerment: Caring for children and families*, first annual symposium of the Chair in Child Protection, School of Social Work, Memorial University of Newfoundland, St John's, Newfoundland. (In press as Conference Proceedings).

Stark, E., & Flitcraft, A. (1988). Women and children at risk: A feminist perspective on child abuse. *International Journal of Health services, 18*(1), 97-118.

Statistics Canada. (1993). 'The Violence against Women' survey: Highlights. *The Daily*, Cat. No. 11-001E.

Swift, K. (1991). Contradictions in child welfare: Neglect and responsibility. In C. T. Baines, P. M. Evans, & S. M. Neysmith (Eds), *Women's caring: Feminist perspectives on social welfare* (pp. 234-271). Toronto: McClelland & Stewart.

When racism meets sexism: Violence against immigrant and visible minority women. (1994, Summer). *Vis-'-Vis, 12*(1).

14

Concluding Thoughts

Allison Morris, Gabrielle Maxwell, Joe Hudson and Burt Galaway

Introduction

The first formulation of a family decision-making model was given statutory effect in New Zealand in 1989, but participatory processes and principles evolved around the same time in parts of England and Oregon. As this book shows, family group conferences are now found in many countries. South Australia and New Zealand have incorporated family group conferences as statutory processes; England is experimenting with family group conferences as a way of giving meaning to the philosophy underlying the *Children Act* 1989 and Immarigeon in his chapter in this book describes the evolutionary development of family group conferences in various states and provinces in Canada and the United States. Interest in their practice has also been expressed in countries as diverse as South Africa, Israel, Singapore and the Philippines. They are being adopted as a preferred decision-making forum for young offenders and young people in need of care and protection and some jurisdictions are now carrying out or are contemplating experiments in other areas - for example, family violence, arrangements for the care of the children of parents in prison, decisions about custody and access, offending by young adults, and managing the affairs of those unable to manage them themselves. Truly the ideas underlying family group conferences have now reached maturity.

Family group conferences reflect, in their philosophy, an emphasis on the participation of families, young offenders and victims, cultural sensitivity and consensus decision-making and, in their practice, a capacity to be translated into diverse social contexts and jurisdictions. Despite these central emphases, the chapters in this book demonstrate that the detail of the philosophy guiding and shaping family group conferences has been somewhat differently stated and construed in different jurisdictions. For example, an emphasis on accountability through 'sanctions which are sufficiently severe to provide an element of deterrence' (the South Australian *Young Offenders Act* 1993 s. 3), cited by Wundersitz & Hetzel), is a clearly stated element in youth justice in South Australia in contrast to New Zealand, and the roles which professionals exercise in controlling referrals and determining process and outcomes differed in many of the jurisdictions discussed. 'Family responsibility' has also been given meanings both between and within countries - for example, the emphasis on extended family support is a key component in New Zealand as opposed to an emphasis on the provision of care by the local authority in England. On the other hand, in New Zealand, financial responsibility for children has been relocated onto families in contrast to the continued provision of support services in England.

In this final chapter, we draw out the themes which transcend jurisdictional differences, discuss the potential of family group conferences and address issues not yet resolved. In doing so, we have drawn largely but not exclusively on material discussed within the chapters.

Resolved Questions

Crossing Cultural Boundaries

Perhaps the first important conclusion that we can draw is that the family group conference process has been successfully implemented in a variety of different countries, by a number of different cultural groups and for a range of different purposes. The chapters in this book are witness to that. A process which was created in New Zealand and which was importantly influenced by New Zealand Maori (Hassall gives a detailed account of how this occurred) has found a place within societies and cultures which are very different. Examples of family group conferences that have incorporated the traditional processes of other cultures are found within the chapters by Fraser & Norton for a Pacific Island family, by Pennell & Burford for Inuit, by Wundersitz & Hetzel for the Aboriginal communities of South Australia and by Longclaws et al. for the Ojibway of central Canada. These examples are an effective and moving testament to the radical transformations possible within a family group conference framework.

Unfounded Fears

Second, many of the critical questions raised initially in all jurisdictions which have adopted family group conferences appear to a large extent to have been resolved by experience and with practice. For example, concerns about not being able to locate extended family or family supporters, to engage families or to effectively involve so-called 'dysfunctional' families, about families forming a coalition to conceal abuse and about families' failing to honour agreements do not prove to have been well-founded in any of the jurisdictions reported in this book.

A repeated finding is that family group conferences are able to bring together a number of people who have an interest in resolving a crisis which is real and immediate for them and for those about whom they care and who show a willingness to participate in taking and implementing decisions. This casts a new light on families that have been previously dismissed as 'incapable', 'disinterested' and 'dysfunctional'. The research reviewed fails to identify inadequate family functioning as associated with poor family group conference outcomes and none of the chapters reported this as a central problem. On the contrary, those working in jurisdictions with family group conferences appear to have reconstrued the problem as one of finding appropriate supports and services to strengthen families. When parents find it difficult to cope, aunts and uncles can share responsibility; extended families can come together and new social bonds may be forged. That is not to say that questions of whether or not families can cope adequately and whether or not children should be removed from their families are not everpresent. But a shift in focus has occurred from parent blaming to family support and recognition of family strengths.

Some jurisdictions were initially cautious about providing private time for families to consider outcome options, fearing what families may decide in the absence of professionals to guide them and that families may reproduce past patterns of conflict. However, there is again no evidence from these chapters that this has proved problematic despite the fact that private time sometimes involves vigorous debate and considerable emotional tension. Indeed, Wundersitz & Hetzel report that, in South Australia, it was not originally intended to give the young person and family members 'time out' to deliberate options but that coordinators are now experimenting with providing private time to them. The essence of moving towards resolutions in which family members take responsibility for their actions and for the future of their child crucially depends on their feeling responsible for the decisions that are made. This is not likely to occur unless it can develop and emerge without the heavy and present hand of professionals determining the process.

In care and protection, concerns are repeatedly raised about family group conferences putting children at risk by allowing families who may wish to protect their own interests to make the decisions. There is no evidence for this. Robertson and Pennell & Burford promote an alternative view: that the family group conference process can increase children's safety by sharing knowledge of the abuse or neglect and by enlisting family and their supporters in the community as protectors.

Another early concern was that families would not honour the agreements made. Though this was not always explored in the chapters, the research presented by Maxwell & Morris and by Wundersitz & Hetzel suggests that, where the family group conference process itself has been successful, families are likely to implement what has been decided regardless of monitoring by professionals. The research and experience presented collectively challenge the fears and concerns which have been often expressed and circulated about family group conferences.

Effective Involvement

Attendance at a family group conference is not a guarantee of effective involvement. Traditional decision-making processes gave little opportunity for the voices of women and children to be heard; power was located within patriarchal structures. Inevitably questions were raised about the extent to which family group conferences would simply replicate this. However, fears raised by commentators about the disempowerment of women have not been supported by observers and researchers who note their active participation in the process in contrast with their non-participation in judicial processes. The case studies cited by Pennell & Burford in particular illustrate this point. Cynics might argue that women's participation in family group conferences merely reflects women's responsibilities for caring for children rather than a process of empowerment. Alternatively, it can equally be interpreted as a recognition and positive endorsement of the value of women's role as carers.

Questions have been raised about the reality of participation by children and different social expectations can affect this. However, the research cited in these chapters shows that abused children and young offenders can play a role in family group conferences especially when supported by their peers and encouraged to do so by the adults and professionals who are present. The chapter by Wundersitz & Hetzel describes in detail how this is achieved in South Australia. This stands in contrast to previous research on the passive role played by young people in courts.

Victims also have no or little voice in Western criminal justice systems and doubts were expressed about their willingness to attend and play a constructive part in family group conferences. Doubts were also raised about the appropriateness of victims' participating in family group conferences for serious offences. Again the research in these chapters puts these doubts to rest and show that many victims express a willingness to participate, do participate constructively, and can contribute effectively (personally or through their representatives) even when the offence is serious. The family group conference process can be healing, can allay victims' fears and can provide reparation.

Overall, then, family group conferences emerge from this review as more likely than more formal dispute resolution fora to give effective voice to those traditionally disadvantaged. Despite this evidence, that many of the early concerns about family group conferences were unfounded, other concerns remain unresolved and new concerns have emerged.

Unresolved Issues

Locating the Management of Family Group Conferences

One of the issues that remains unresolved is where best to locate the management of family group conferences: in a government department of welfare, with the police, with courts or in independent organisations. Each of these options are reflected in the jurisdictions covered in this book and each option has both advantages and disadvantages. Locating family group conferences in agencies independent of statutory authorities (the jurisdictions described by Ban, Marsh & Crow and Pennell & Burford) can reduce state control over people's lives but runs the risk of marginalisation because of a dependence on state referrals. Location within the police allows speedy resolution of cases but may give too great a gatekeeping role to a prosecutory agency (for instance, as in the 'Wagga Wagga model' cited in the chapter by Wundersitz & Hetzel). Location in courts, as in South Australia and described by Wundersitz & Hetzel, has an apparent neutrality and focuses on the protection of children's rights but has created another type of gatekeeping through courts and appears to be associated with an emphasis on deterrent sanctions. Location within social welfare departments endorses a focus on children's interests but two main difficulties have been raised with this. First, family group conferences have responsibilities towards victims' and families' interests as well as children's and this can lead to confusion over the family group conference's aims (see the chapters on the New Zealand and English experiences). Second, both Wundersitz & Hetzel and Graber et al. refer to the existence of 'cultures of control' within welfare departments in which bureaucratisation occurred and professionals 'took over'. The chapters do not provide a resolution to this dilemma but offer a basis for debate.

Criteria for Referral

There is a larger issue here. Location is only one of the factors determining the criteria for referral for family group conferences and the gatekeeping agency. For care and protection, the gatekeepers in all the examples presented in the book are the statutory welfare authorities but criteria for referral are very different. In New Zealand, those cases likely to be referred to family group conferences are those where it is difficult for the social worker to obtain the agreement of the immediate family to a suggested plan and where there are serious concerns about the safety of the child. In England, the approach adopted seems diametrically different; family group conferences are not likely to be offered to a family that has 'had a history of antagonistic involvement with social services' or 'had no wider network to invite'. In contrast in Newfoundland, preparedness to fund family group conference decisions seems to be a precursor for referral from the welfare system to the pilot project. In Victoria, Ban indicates that a critical condition for referral is that families are seen as possessing the necessary decision-making skills. And in Oregon, cases involving family violence are excluded and the use of family group decision-making meetings appears to depend primarily on the family's and the professional's preferences.

In the youth justice context, the police invariably have a role in determining who enters the system and in Wagga Wagga, South Australia and New Zealand it is they who choose whether or not to refer young people for a family group conference. However, in New Zealand, the police are required to consult with the coordinator who may be able to negotiate a lesser form of intervention. The criteria for referral to a family group conference used in these three jurisdictions are also different and this has two principal consequences. First, many of the young offenders dealt with by family group conferences in Wagga Wagga as it operated in its early days would probably have been dealt with through less formal police diversionary processes in both New Zealand and South Australia. This has led to criticisms of net-widening. Some commentators see netwidening as potentially positive because it makes services accessible to those at risk. The position is arguable. We have adopted the standpoint that processes that make services voluntarily available must be distinguished from the use of statutory coercive power to ensure that children and families opt for what society considers to be in their best interests. It is the widening of nets of coercion that it is desirable to limit.

Second, in both South Australia and Wagga Wagga, most of the more serious offenders are dealt with solely through the courts in contrast to the use of family group conferences for such offenders in New Zealand. This affects the formality of intervention.

Criteria for referral can fundamentally change the meaning and purpose of the family group conference. The chapters in this book tend to deal with either young offenders or children who are in need of care and protection. Research and experience both indicate that this distinction is problematic. Those who offend may be in need of care and vice versa. How best to respond to the multiple needs of young people has not been dealt with here but is likely to become important as the number of uses for family group conferences grows.

Power and Control

While the voices of women, children, victims and culture are heard more in family group conferences than in alternative conflict resolution fora, there are clearly conditions which can work for or against this. Central here is the role of the professionals in their management of the process and the way in which the state makes real its commitment to accommodating cultural differences.

Professional Versus Family Decision-making

Family group conferences demand that professionals change their orientation and role to develop partnerships with families; this is underlined in many of the chapters. On the other hand, the chapters by Wundersitz & Hetzel, Robertson and Maxwell & Morris show that this does not always occur. Professionals continue to feel responsible for the decisions and outcomes and their behaviour in family group conferences can signal this to other participants, for example, by the use of jargon and statements about 'bottom lines'. Furthermore, as pointed out by Fraser & Norton, the reality of statutory authority and responsibility does not sit well with the philosophies of empowerment and the devolution of responsibility. This conflict is at its most acute in the crisis intervention role of care and protection social workers with respect to children in dangerous situations. A similar issue arises in youth justice when children are seen as potential dangers if they abscond from open placements. Responding to public concerns about safety and protection may be at odds with finding ways to give meaning to values and philosophies that are participatory and it may be difficult for the same person to move from these 'policing' roles to one of facilitation.

Regardless of its central philosophy, a family group conference can assume a very different face in practice. Instances of professionals assuming responsibility for decision-making, different emphases on professionals' powers to veto families' decisions, the reluctance to give families time to deliberate in private, the number of professionals attending the family group conference and the extent to which outcomes must be ratified by a court all point to questions about who is really deciding. Family group conferences can, therefore, be a mechanism for coercing families and controlling them. But equally they can be a mechanism for enabling and supporting families. Arguments about the balance between these two positions will probably be active and ongoing in all jurisdictions which introduce family group conferences.

Effective participation of those traditionally powerless requires effective preparation and appropriate information; this is stressed in a number of chapters. Two points can be made here. First, it is important to provide the time needed for and the costs of participatory decision-making which are inevitably greater than those associated with traditional methods (this emerges from the chapters by Wundersitz & Hertzel and Pennell & Burford). Second, participants may unduly rely on professional's advice (this emerges from the chapters by Robertson, Marsh & Crow and Graber et al.). Skill is required to find a balance between informing participants and influencing them.

Venue and timing are factors that can affect the perceptions of participants about the locus of control of family group conferences and can impact differently on victims and offenders. The chapters show that considerable variety exists within various jurisdictions with respect to venue. The greatest contrast is offered by Longclaws et al. when some family group conferences were held in a traditional tepee within a secure youth detention centre. Commentators variously emphasise the importance of 'neutrality', a place where both victim and offender feel 'safe and secure', venues that are 'familiar' and 'comfortable' for participants, and holding conferences at a time that will enable all to attend. However, to meet the needs of the professionals, family group conferences are sometimes held in offices and often, understandably, inside working hours. This undermines attempts to give power to the non-professionals.

Practice varies within and across jurisdictions in the degree to which professionals monitor the plans and recommendations of conferences. Debate has centred on whether professionals or families should fulfil this role. The research presented by Maxwell & Morris shows that professionals' monitoring may not be essential for effective outcomes: if the family group conference process itself has been successful, families are likely to implement what has been decided regardless of monitoring by professionals. Where the safety of a child within a family is a primary concern, the most usual approach is for the state to monitor the situation. However, the literature abounds with examples of instances where this has proved to be inadequate and it could be suggested that children's safety is more likely to be ensured by also enlisting as monitors the families' supporters in the community and the extended family. The chapters show that giving meaning to partnerships between families and the state is a difficult task, bring into focus the many factors which subtly influence success and provide a starting point for the development of practice guidelines.

Accommodating Cultural Differences

Adapting family group conference processes to different cultural practice *is* possible as a number of case studies show. But it is not necessarily simple and has not always been effectively implemented because of the different power structures, perceptions, values and practices reflected within Western and indigenous systems. Wundersitz & Hetzel describe the considerable organisational problems court staff are experiencing in developing a process that is comfortable for Aboriginal clients in traditional communities because of the remoteness of the communities and the different meaning given to appointment arrangements. In contrast, urban family group conferences in South Australia are little different for Aboriginals compared to white Australians. The New Zealand papers indicate that family group conferences for Maori have, on occasion, been similarly criticised, despite the high proportion of Maori staff managing the process and that modifying procedures by including Maori greetings and blessings is little more than tokenism.

A more serious undermining of family group conference processes seems to have occurred in the pilot project using family group conferences for young offenders reported on by Longclaws et al. where police refused to attend conferences and judges failed to endorse families' recommendations and did not invite the families' participation in the court hearing. It is ironic that this occurred in the family group conferences which perhaps most faithfully replicated traditional cultural practices and seems to highlight the difficulty which Western legal systems have in accommodating indigenous practices.

The experience in all the indigenous communities discussed in this book is that more time and resources are inevitably required if family group conferences are to be held using traditional protocols and in traditional time-frames. These are not readily accepted by managers responsible for funding. There is also the matter of the cultural appropriateness of services which are available. But there is more at issue here; inevitably systems belong to those with whom the locus of power resides. Some redistribution of both resources and power is required for cultural difference to be validated. These issues are part of wider debate about sovereignty and self-determination for indigenous peoples within the Western world.

Restorative Versus Criminal Justice Values

Family group conferences in youth justice have been criticised on three main grounds: young people are not provided with legal representation before them making admissions; penalties do not conform to standards of proportionality and consistency; and family group conferencing is a system of social control in disguise.

These criticisms can be addressed at a number of different levels. First, they are accusations that can be levelled at *any* informal process and would rule out any form of diversion. There can surely be no support for such a retrogressive step. Second, these are criticisms which traditional criminal justice systems have not been successful in solving. For instance with respect to standards of proportionality and consistency, Maxwell & Morris demonstrate that, in reality, much the same offence factors which influence the severity of sanctions imposed by courts influence decisions in family group conferences. Third, it is possible in some degree to develop strategies for overcoming these failings, if failings they are, by using similar strategies to those developed within the traditional system: for example, children could be provided with legal advice before a family group conference; rules could be developed to ensure that sanctions are not unduly harsh; and criteria for referral could be developed which would limit net-widening. Fourth, at perhaps a more fundamental level, the values underlying these criticisms stem from a traditional criminal justice process and are at variance with those underlying a restorative justice model. Systems of formal legal representation impede the ability of victims and offenders to talk directly to one another. Consistency and proportionality of outcomes are constructs which serve abstract notions of justice that stand in place of agreements that restore the social balance between victims and offenders within their communities. And while social control remains an integral part of restorative justice (and family group conferences), it must assume a new meaning as power and control are relocated within the social group.

Providing Services

Family group conferences are not only a decision-making fora; they are also a route to services within families, communities and institutions. The chapters in this book focus principally on the family group conference process rather than on service provision yet it is this latter factor which may be critical in determining successful outcomes for families. Families can only make good decisions if there are appropriate and realistic options for them to choose from. The families involved in care and protection family group conferences are often families who have been unsuccessful in providing unaided for the needs of their children. If their children are to remain with them, support may be required over months and even years. Other families will not be able to continue to care for their children. This means that there must be quality foster placements and, for some children, institutional and residential programmes to provide for their rehabilitation or the community's protection. In some jurisdictions, notably New Zealand, the introduction of family group conferences has not been accompanied by an appropriate development of the services. In part, at least, this is linked to the cuts in spending on welfare services which are occurring throughout English speaking countries.

Ensuring Funding

To some extent, the motivation for the expansion of family group conferences came from both the left and the right, from both humanitarians and market reformers. A focus on family decision-making has often been accompanied by a shift in philosophy toward family and community placement of children rather than foster-care and institutional placement. As countries move towards pruning welfare budgets, so too there is a readiness to prune the cost of the care of children. Family group conferences that can arrange for community placement emerge as an attractive option which shifts the burden of funding from the state to families and communities. Cost-cutting can also affect the organisation and management of the family group conference process itself. These actions can be criticised as short sighted: to short cut investments in services will, in the end, invalidate the family group conference process and leave children and families in situations in which there is a risk of future offending, future abuse, mental health problems, substance abuse and incarceration. Despite agreement within this book about the importance of providing sufficient funding to meet the requirements of good practice and effective intervention, political debate about appropriate levels of funding is likely to take place in the wider context of welfare reforms. In the meantime, the existence and development of family group conferences remains fragile in some jurisdictions.

Lasting Tensions

Tensions arise in a number of ways in family group conferences. Many of these have already been alluded to in this chapter: the tension between acknowledging professionals' statutory duties and encouraging family decision-making; between valuing the input of families and adequately protecting abused or neglected children; between providing continuity of care and respecting children's interests, wishes or needs; between protecting rights and maintaining the informality of the process. Others have been identified in earlier chapters. For example, Robertson refers to decisions about whether a child should remain with a family which has been abusive or neglectful or be placed in alternative care; Maxwell & Morris raise the question of whose culture should determine procedure when people come from different backgrounds and Wundersitz & Hetzel raise the issue of ensuring equity and proportionality in youth justice outcomes while giving autonomy to families and victims in such matters. Various chapters also point to the tension between ensuring accountability and providing for children's welfare and between meeting the interests of victims and the needs of offenders.

While there is no easy blueprint for resolving these tensions, in individual cases decisions are possible and recognition that competing factors have to be balanced is part of an effective family group conference.

Guidelines for Good Practice

Each chapter has described how family group conferences operate in their individual jurisdictions. Despite some differences in emphasis, there seems to be considerable agreement about many of the characteristics essential for good practice. These include:

- ensuring that the professionals involved in conferences are committed to the goals and philosophy;
- ensuring that professionals are trained and skilled in ways appropriate to the culture of the participants;
- ensuring the attendance of those who are important in the child's life and who can contribute to the child's future;
- briefing participants about what will occur and their role and involvement in the process and providing appropriate information on which they can base decisions;

- providing an environment in which those present feel comfortable;

- allowing participants to have a real say in the process, to participate fully, to understand what is happening at all times, and to have some control over their participation;

- ensuring participants have help and encouragement to say what is important for them;

- ensuring the presence of those with resources and abilities to aid both the process and outcomes;

- providing support for participants before, during and after the family group conference;

- allowing families to have private time together;

- ensuring outcomes are adequately reviewed and monitored;

- resourcing the agreed plans.

Other questions about practice warrant debate both within and across jurisdictions:

- what should be the criteria for referral?

- who should agree on and decide about the composition of the conference and its venue?

- when co-offenders or a number of victims are involved, how should conferences be arranged?

- how best can the participation of children, women and victims be encouraged?

- should peer group support play a greater part in the process?

- how can indigenous practices and protocols best be protected within systems where professionals' experiences and views have been shaped by Western thinking?

- whose culture should determine issues of venue and process?

- what rules should there be about the confidentiality of family group conference proceedings?

Some of these questions may require further research before they can be resolved.

Conclusions

This book has described the development and evolution of family group conferences in a number of jurisdictions. Consensus has emerged about the aspects of practice that are important for success. Satisfaction for participants appears to result when they are involved in the decision and agree with the outcomes, even where major interventions occur for the child or when sanctions are severe for young offenders. Similarly victims can be satisfied even when reparation is not available.

Nevertheless, many questions about the impact of practice remain unanswered. More information is needed about the conditions that will enhance or decrease the success of family group conferences. These are likely to revolve around the social context in which family group conferences are actioned and understood as well as around the rhetoric in which they are embedded. When expectations do not include the participation of women and children, miraculous changes are unlikely to occur at a time of crisis resolution, however potentially supportive the process might be. The behaviour of victims is likely to be shaped, not only by individual differences, but also by the climate of opinion within society. And the philosophy that informs the expectations of professionals who manage and work within the justice and welfare systems will have an impact on the way in which family group conferences are managed. An important challenge for the future is how to ensure the effective participation of all.

This book reviews the research that is available and describes a variety of pilot projects. To date, the focus has been on translating family group conferences into new contexts and examining process concerns. As yet, there are no long-term studies that follow developments over time and there is only limited information on the experiences of participants. It is important to continue to evaluate processes, test theories, determine the factors critical for success, assess the achievement of objectives and measure outcomes for children, victims and families.

Family group conferences are a new and radical way of making decisions based on partnership between families and the state, particularly for children who are abused, neglected or committing offences. They reflect a paradigm shift: in the youth justice context, they represent a shift from criminal justice to restorative values and, more generally, they represent an understanding of what harms children, how families and children can be assisted to change and the importance of culture for identity. The chapters in this book show that family group conferences are a practical and realistic option which families accept and use. They can be an effective vehicle for enabling participation, strengthening families, acknowledging cultural diversity and respecting the interests of victims. Family group conferences have established their place as viable alternatives to decision-making by professionals.

Index

235